IMAGES
of America

OTSEGO

On the cover: A snapshot in time, this traditional farm was home to Willard and Lizzie (Parker) Holt and the three rambunctious boys raised there: Ralph, Clifton, and Erwin. Willard, sometimes called William, but most often simply Will, was born in Otsego to William Henry and Julia Francis (Ingersoll) Holt on January 26, 1860. Willard purchased land adjacent to William's farm and built this beautiful home for his family. Willard died in 1937, but his memories live on through the pages of the *Holt Diary*, which captures daily events from May 1878 through December 1890. The *Holt Diary* was donated to the Otsego Heritage Preservation Commission by Robert Leroy Holt, the grandson of Willard's brother, Sydney. (Courtesy of Arne Engstrom.)

IMAGES
of America

OTSEGO

Paulie Skaja-Bell and Chris Wilson

ARCADIA
PUBLISHING

ISBN 978-0-7385-5071-8

Published by Arcadia Publishing
Charleston, South Carolina

Printed in the United States of America

Library of Congress Catalog Card Number: 2007924209

For all general information contact Arcadia Publishing at:
Telephone 843-853-2070
Fax 843-853-0044
E-mail sales@arcadiapublishing.com
For customer service and orders:
Toll-Free 1-888-313-2665

Visit us on the Internet at www.arcadiapublishing.com

*To all who believe that knowing our history
helps us to appreciate today.*

Contents

ACKNOWLEDGMENTS

This book about Otsego was written because the *Elk River Star News* ran an article on Paulie Skaja-Bell and the book she created for Rogers, Hassan Township, and Fletcher. When I went to her home to purchase a copy she shared the evolution of the book and a glimpse at the computer programs she used to create the contents for that book. When I asked her if she would help me assemble a similar book for Otsego, she generously agreed.

We were blessed to have access to the great quantity of material gathered by previous members of the Otsego Heritage Preservation Commission, most notably Elaine Norin, Joyce Swenson, and Arlene Holen. There are also many members of the community that have recently shared their time, stories, and photographs. Thank you to everyone that provided information to fill the pages of this book: the staff at Wright County History Center; Bev at Elk River Star News; Ed at the Drummer, located in Buffalo; Loretta Moos; Arne Engstrom; Adeline Weber; Marie Corbin; Mary Anne and Tim McNeil; Richard, Patty, Stella, Gordy, and Eddie Lefebvre; Mae, Bob, and Sally Spencer; Don and Sally Ebner; Joan Vasseur; Pamella Collins; Bob Saxon; John and Della Anderson; Wayne Lahn; Elma Pouliot; Chuck and Dave Christian; Michelle Matchie; Harvey Hauan; Mary Ann and Merle Eden; Lloyd and Marie Ann Cyr; Diane DeMars; and everyone who provided tidbits to enhance the book along the process. We greatly appreciate your support and hope you enjoy the outcome.

—Chris Wilson

Introduction

Through great dedication from the Otsego Heritage Preservation Commission, events and highlights since the community's beginning have been captured as a form of appreciation and gratitude to the pioneers that settled the area. It is through the efforts of that organization that made this book, *Otsego*, possible. One of the purposes of the commission is to "foster civic pride in the beauty and notable accomplishments of the past." One of the duties is "to work for the continuing education of the citizens of Otsego with respect to the historic and architectural heritage of the city." *Otsego* will be used to help fulfill the commission's purpose and duties by raising awareness of the community's rich heritage.

The content of *Otsego* was compiled using several resources. Books, such as *Otsego in the Beginning, Otsego the Family Farm Years, Otsego Life at the Brick House, Otsego View on the Great River Road Historical Highlights, St. John the Baptist Historical Cookbook, Anna: Letters from the Attic*, and the *Holt Diary* were filled with nuggets of information used to help populate the pages of this book. In addition, many lifelong members of the area were interviewed to reveal a more personal perspective on building the town. Local newspapers and historical museums offered even more insight.

On September 21, 1990, the Minnesota State Municipal Board proclaimed that Otsego would be Minnesota's 885th city, making it the youngest city in the state. Although this monumental occasion deserved great hoopla, it seemed to be merely a formality to some. The community of Otsego welcomed its first permanent settlers in 1852. Currently the city has almost 12,000 residents with no stall of growth in sight. Pioneers traveled from Maine, New York, Canada, and other locations looking for opportunities and families are still drawn to the beautiful city surrounded by agriculture.

Prior to the first Caucasian settlers, this land was inhabited by Native Americans. The years 1772 and 1773 mark when two of the deadliest battles fought between the Ojibwa and Dakota tribes took place on the banks of the Crow, Elk, and Mississippi Rivers in Otsego. Evidence of these dwellers was confirmed when relics, such as arrowheads, were found by settlers. Mounds believed to contain members of the warring tribes have also been located.

The boundaries of Otsego lie within the "Big Woods" region, an area of Minnesota that was thick with deciduous trees and bushes. It took a lot of work to clear the land and make it suitable for homes and farming, but the early settlers were ambitious. In the beginning, many Englishmen entered the area with the intentions of claiming land to be sold later to those interested in making Otsego their home. Frenchmen were attracted to the area, viewing it as a haven for lumberjacks. German families entered the territory seeking newly created farming opportunities with the clearing of the forest. Families from many other walks of life also helped settle Otsego, making the community a literal melting pot of rich heritage.

Otsego became a desirable destination in the early years because the community is located at the crossroads of three major waterways, the Mississippi, Crow, and Elk Rivers. Water was a primary mode of transportation in the mid-1800s, making Otsego an attainable destination. The concept of creating the Great River Road was approved on July 2, 1855. It was recommended that this road run from Waterville (also named Aydt's Town), through the town of Otsego to Monticello. It is still a primary route traveled between communities today. In addition to easy access, early settlers were also looking for farmland and were attracted to logging opportunities.

When the first permanent settlers arrived at Otsego, Minnesota had not yet become a state; this occurred May 11, 1858. Otsego was the first community formed in Wright County. In the early years, the area was known as Pleasant Grove precincts; however, some reference materials refer to the area as Pheasant Grove. Upon achieving statehood, the board of county commissioners was directed to create boundaries for townships within their area. John McDonald, first permanent settler in the county and Otsego, was one of the commissioners. The boundaries for Pleasant Grove were adjusted, and the community was renamed Otsego. The town was named from Otsego in the state of New York because the majority of settlers were from New York at that time. Otsego is a Mohawk word. One translation of the word is "rock place," another is "place of rendezvous," and still another is "welcome water."

McDonald has the distinct honor of facilitating some firsts for the community. McDonald was the first permanent settler, arriving with his family in July 31, 1852. He served on the first board of county commissioners and was the first postmaster in Otsego. The first school in Wright County was in Otsego. Margaret Cooley taught classes from her home until a school was built in 1855. Norman McPherson was the first child born in Wright County on April 18, 1853. The first marriages were between Charles Lambert and Matilda Cooley on November 26, 1856, and Lewis McDonald and Climena Spencer on December 25, 1856. The first church services were held in 1854 by Reverend White in McDonald's home. The first ferry was established opposite the village of Elk River in 1854 by Samuel Carrick.

A notable fact is that several other town sites were established with the township during 1856 and 1857. Northwood was located on the Mississippi River about one mile north of the mouth of the Crow River. Waterville, also known as Aydt's Town, and Portland were both formed just south of Northwood. Lily Pond, also referred to as Bedford, was located near the present intersection of County Road 39 and Kadler Avenue. The town of Otsego was formed on the bank of the Mississippi and is the only town site that survived the storm of financial crisis, grasshopper plagues, and personal disputes. These challenges caused many businesses to fail, stores to close, and towns to cease functioning. In 1857, Otsego consisted of a school, town hall, post office, general store, ferry, sawmill, blacksmith, church, parsonage, tabernacle, campgrounds, and hotel in addition to many family homes.

As with many nearby communities, several of the families that settled the land in Otsego still have family in the area. It is not uncommon to meet a fourth or fifth generation family member helping out in the community. The foundation of Otsego was based on church, school, family, and friends. These fundamental ideas are still the foundation for the quickly growing community today. *Otsego* illustrates the warmth and friendship within the community as people work together to weather the challenges of the time.

One

IN THE BEGINNING

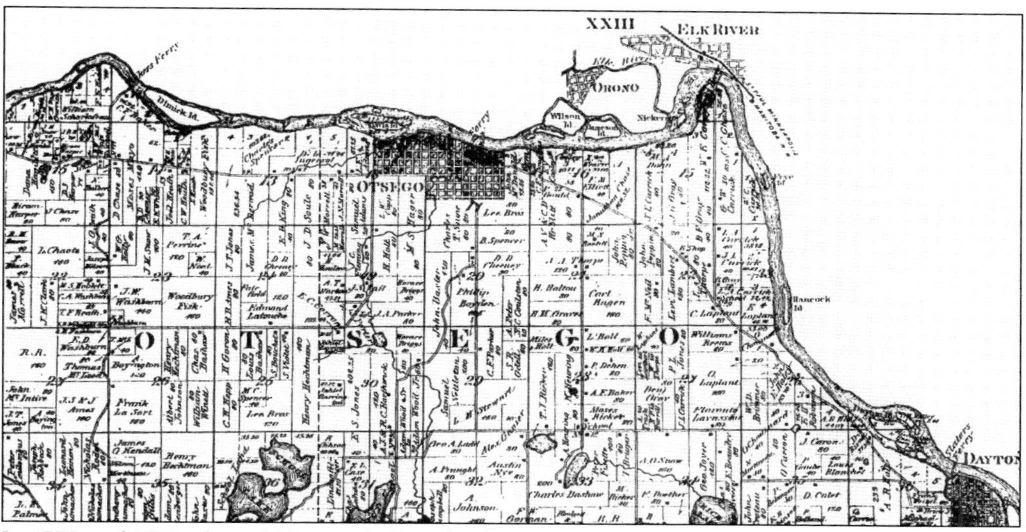

In 1772 and 1773, about 100 years before the first European settlers entered the area now known as Otsego, the banks of the Crow, Elk, and Mississippi Rivers served as a battleground for two of the bloodiest conflicts fought between the Ojibwa and Dakota tribes. John McDonald was the first permanent settler in Wright County, arriving in 1852. The area was platted as Pleasant Grove precinct (also referred to as Pheasant Grove in some records). Township boundaries were adjusted in 1858. McDonald held the first town meeting to vote on a name. New Yorkers were a majority, and Otsego was the winning name. One translation of the Mohawk word Otsego is "place of rendezvous." The 1879 Wright County plat map is pictured here. (Courtesy of Joan Vasseur.)

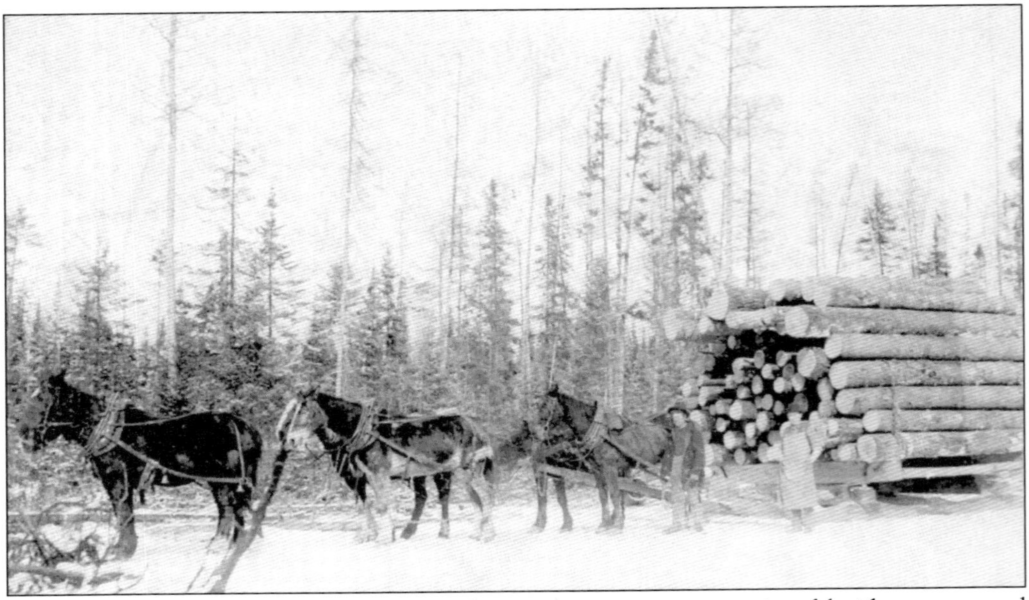

Otsego was part of the "Big Woods," an area known for its massive quantity of deciduous trees and undergrowth of bushes. Pictured here are loggers retrieving trees from the Mississippi River for delivery to John McDonald's sawmill at Otsego creek. According to Lloyd Cyr, the Frenchmen came to log, and the Germans settled in the area to farm. Petit (pronounced petesee) Martin was a lumberjack and a good fighter. Joseph Plude, Marie Ann Cyr's grandfather, became Martin's good friend and bet a pocket watch that Martin would win a particular fight. Martin won, and Plude received the watch, which still works 110 years later. Otsego was settled under the Preemption Law of 1841, which allowed squatters to claim and improve up to 160 acres of land for 14 months before paying the government $1.25 an acre. (Above, courtesy of Otsego Heritage Preservation Commission; below, courtesy of John and Della [Bell] Anderson.)

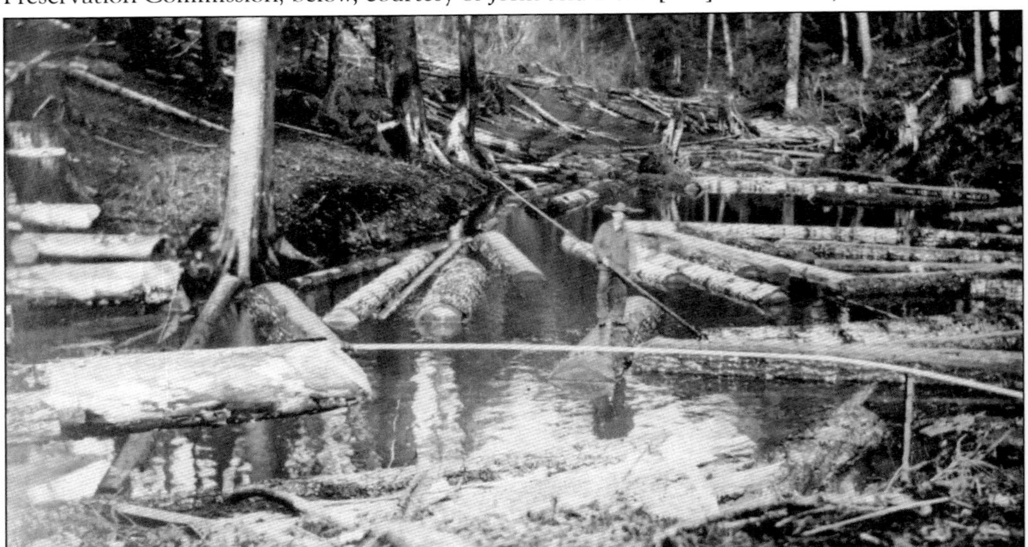

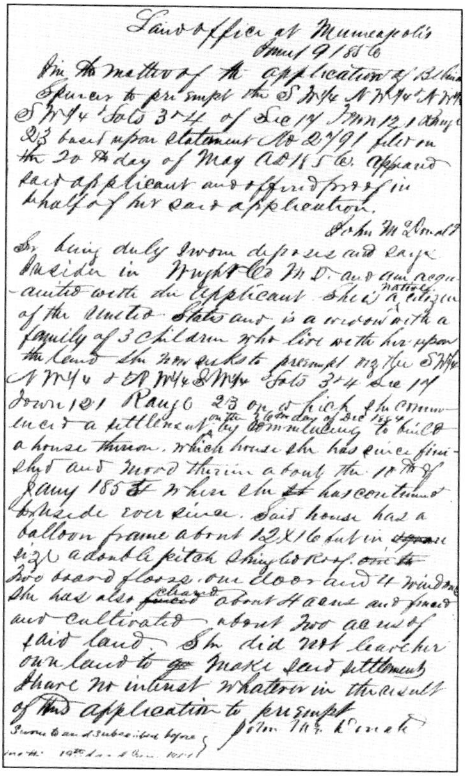
Land Office at Minneapolis
June 9 1856

In the matter of the application of Belinda Spencer to pre-empt the S W 1/4 N W 1/4 & N W 1/4 S W 1/4 Lots 3 & 4 of Sec 17 Town 121 Range 23 based upon statement No 2791 filed on the 20th day of May AD 1856. Appeared said applicant and offered proof in behalf of her said application.

John McDonald

Sr being duly sworn deposes and says I reside in Wright Co M T. and am acquainted with the applicant. She is a native citizen of the United States and is a widow with a family of 3 children who live with her upon the land she now seeks to preempt viz the S W 1/4 N W 1/4 & N W 1/4 S W 1/4 Lots 3 & 4 Sec 17 Town 121 Range 23 on which she commenced a settlement on the 26th day of Dec 1854 by commencing to build a house thereon. which house she has since finished and moved therein about the 10th of Jany 1855 where she has continued to reside ever since. Said house has a balloon frame about 12 X 16 feet in size a double pitch shingled roof. two board floors. one door and 4 windows She has also cleared about 4 acres and fenced and cultivated about two acres of said land. She did not leave her own land to make said settlement. I have no interest whatever in the result of this application to preempt

John McDonald

Sworn to and subscribed before me this 19th day of June 1856

The oldest census record of Otsego is dated 1855, three years after the first settlers arrived. There were 212 residents—139 males and 73 females. At that time, only the "heads of families" names were listed on the census, followed by the number of males, females, and total in the family. The only female listed as the head of the family was Belinda Spencer. Belinda (Marsh) Spencer was born in Maine and married Ephraim Spencer in 1834. They were the parents of Emeline, Charles, Climena, and Ephraim M. (later known as Martin E.). Belinda's husband died between 1847 and 1850. Belinda's sister Zilpah Marsh married John McDonald in 1841. McDonald wrote this letter of support on behalf of Belinda. Belinda's name is the first to appear on the abstract of the John and Della (Bell) Anderson farm, shown below. (Right, courtesy of Pamella Collins; below, courtesy of John and Della [Bell] Anderson.)

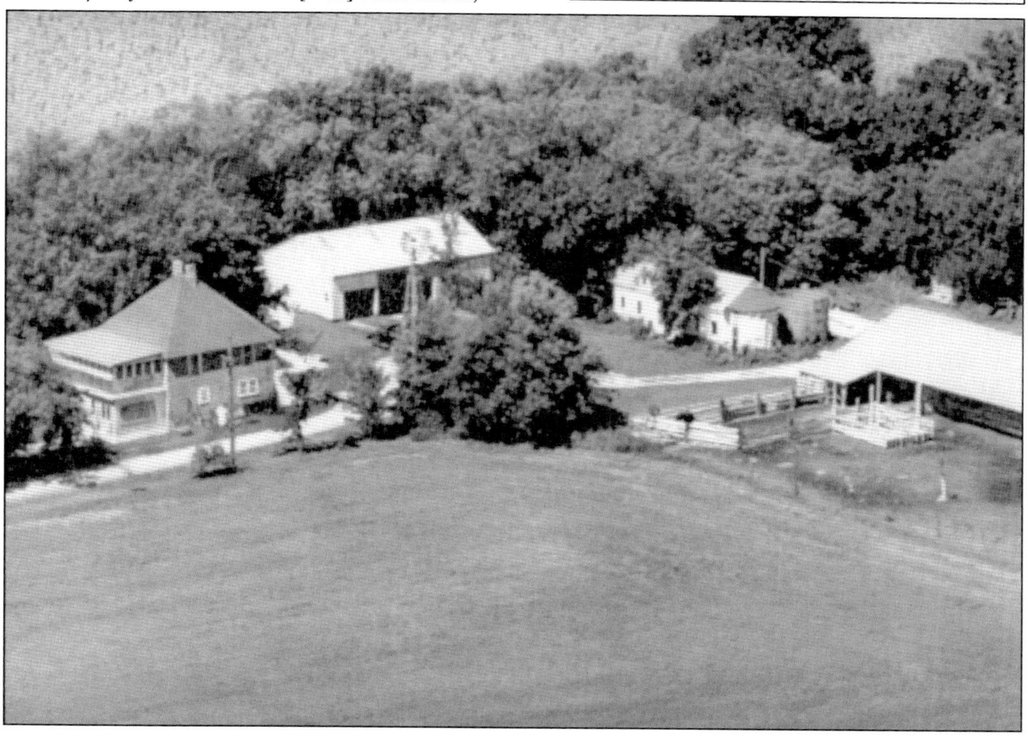

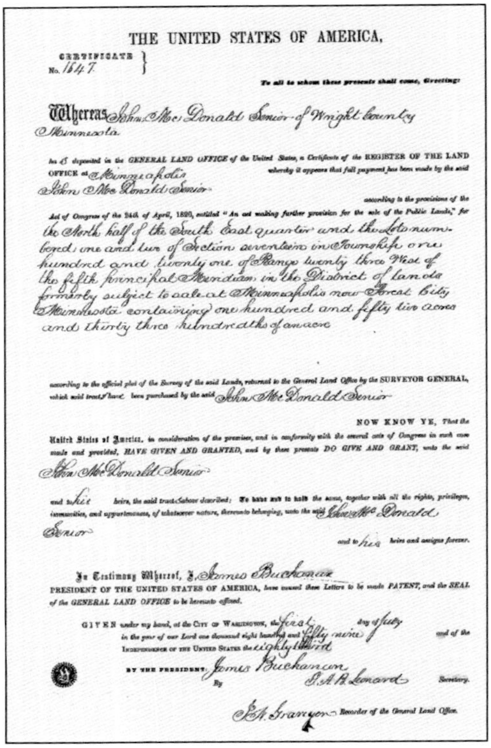

THE UNITED STATES OF AMERICA,

CERTIFICATE No. 1647

To all to whom these presents shall come, Greeting:

Whereas John Mc Donald Senior of Wright County Minnesota has deposited in the GENERAL LAND OFFICE of the United States, a Certificate of the REGISTER OF THE LAND OFFICE at Minneapolis whereby it appears that full payment has been made by the said John Mc Donald Senior according to the provisions of the Act of Congress of the 24th of April, 1820, entitled "An act making further provision for the sale of the Public Lands," for the North half of the South East quarter and the Lots numbered one and two of Section seventeen in Township one hundred and twenty one of Range twenty three West of the fifth principal Meridian in the District of lands formerly subject to sale at Minneapolis now Forest City Minnesota containing one hundred and fifty two acres and thirty three hundredths of an acre

according to the official plat of the Survey of the said Lands, returned to the General Land Office by the SURVEYOR GENERAL, which said tract has been purchased by the said John Mc Donald Senior

NOW KNOW YE, That the United States of America, in consideration of the premises, and in conformity with the several acts of Congress in such case made and provided, HAVE GIVEN AND GRANTED, and by these presents DO GIVE AND GRANT, unto the said John Mc Donald Senior and to his heirs, the said tract above described: To have and to hold the same, together with all the rights, privileges, immunities, and appurtenances, of whatsoever nature, thereunto belonging, unto the said John Mc Donald Senior and to his heirs and assigns forever.

In Testimony Whereof, I, James Buchanan PRESIDENT OF THE UNITED STATES OF AMERICA, have caused these Letters to be made PATENT, and the SEAL of the GENERAL LAND OFFICE to be hereunto affixed.

GIVEN under my hand, at the CITY OF WASHINGTON, the first day of July in the year of our Lord one thousand eight hundred and fifty nine and of the INDEPENDENCE OF THE UNITED STATES the eighty third

BY THE PRESIDENT: James Buchanan
By J. A. B. Leonard Secretary.
J. N. Granger Recorder of the General Land Office.

John McDonald has been identified as the first permanent settler in Wright County. The McDonald family of four males and one female arrived in Otsego on July 31, 1852. It is believed that the widow Belinda Spencer followed her sister and brother-in-law to Otsego. McDonald and Spencer filed for adjacent land on June 19, 1856, and received the deeds on July 1, 1859, as reflected in the documents shown here. McDonald and David McPherson arrived in Otsego about the same time; however, McPherson continued his journey west after a couple of short years. The next settlers were John B. Pepin, Charles LaPlant, Samuel Carrick, Caleb Chase, Alvah Cooley, D. L. Ingersoll, Archie Downie, Otis T. True, Dudley P. Chase, Ezra Tubbs, and Josiah B. Locke, making Otsego the oldest town in the county. (Courtesy of Pamella Collins.)

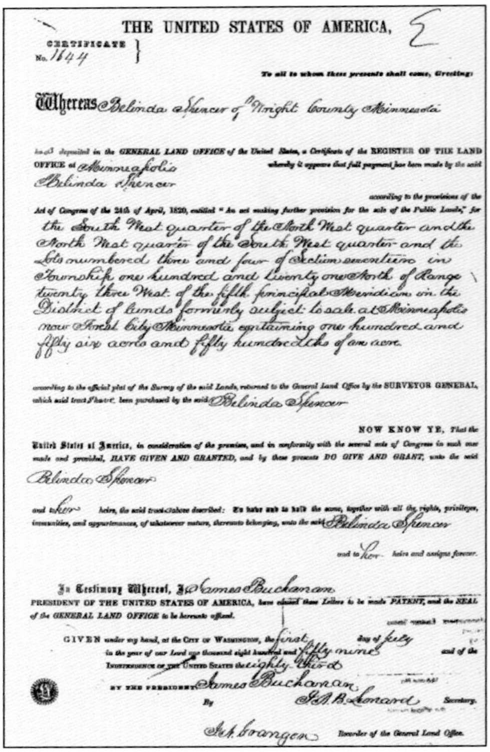

THE UNITED STATES OF AMERICA,

CERTIFICATE No. 1644

To all to whom these presents shall come, Greeting:

Whereas Belinda Spencer of Wright County Minnesota has deposited in the GENERAL LAND OFFICE of the United States, a Certificate of the REGISTER OF THE LAND OFFICE at Minneapolis whereby it appears that full payment has been made by the said Belinda Spencer according to the provisions of the Act of Congress of the 24th of April, 1820, entitled "An act making further provision for the sale of the Public Lands," for the South West quarter of the North West quarter and the North West quarter of the South West quarter and the Lots numbered three and four of Section seventeen in Township one hundred and twenty one North of Range twenty three West of the fifth principal Meridian in the District of lands formerly subject to sale at Minneapolis now Forest City Minnesota containing one hundred and fifty six acres and fifty hundredths of an acre

according to the official plat of the Survey of the said Lands, returned to the General Land Office by the SURVEYOR GENERAL, which said tract has been purchased by the said Belinda Spencer

NOW KNOW YE, That the United States of America, in consideration of the premises, and in conformity with the several acts of Congress in such case made and provided, HAVE GIVEN AND GRANTED, and by these presents DO GIVE AND GRANT, unto the said Belinda Spencer and to her heirs, the said tract above described: To have and to hold the same, together with all the rights, privileges, immunities, and appurtenances, of whatsoever nature, thereunto belonging, unto the said Belinda Spencer and to her heirs and assigns forever.

In Testimony Whereof, I, James Buchanan PRESIDENT OF THE UNITED STATES OF AMERICA, have caused these Letters to be made PATENT, and the SEAL of the GENERAL LAND OFFICE to be hereunto affixed.

GIVEN under my hand, at the CITY OF WASHINGTON, the first day of July in the year of our Lord one thousand eight hundred and fifty nine and of the INDEPENDENCE OF THE UNITED STATES the eighty third

BY THE PRESIDENT: James Buchanan
By J. A. B. Leonard Secretary.
J. N. Granger Recorder of the General Land Office.

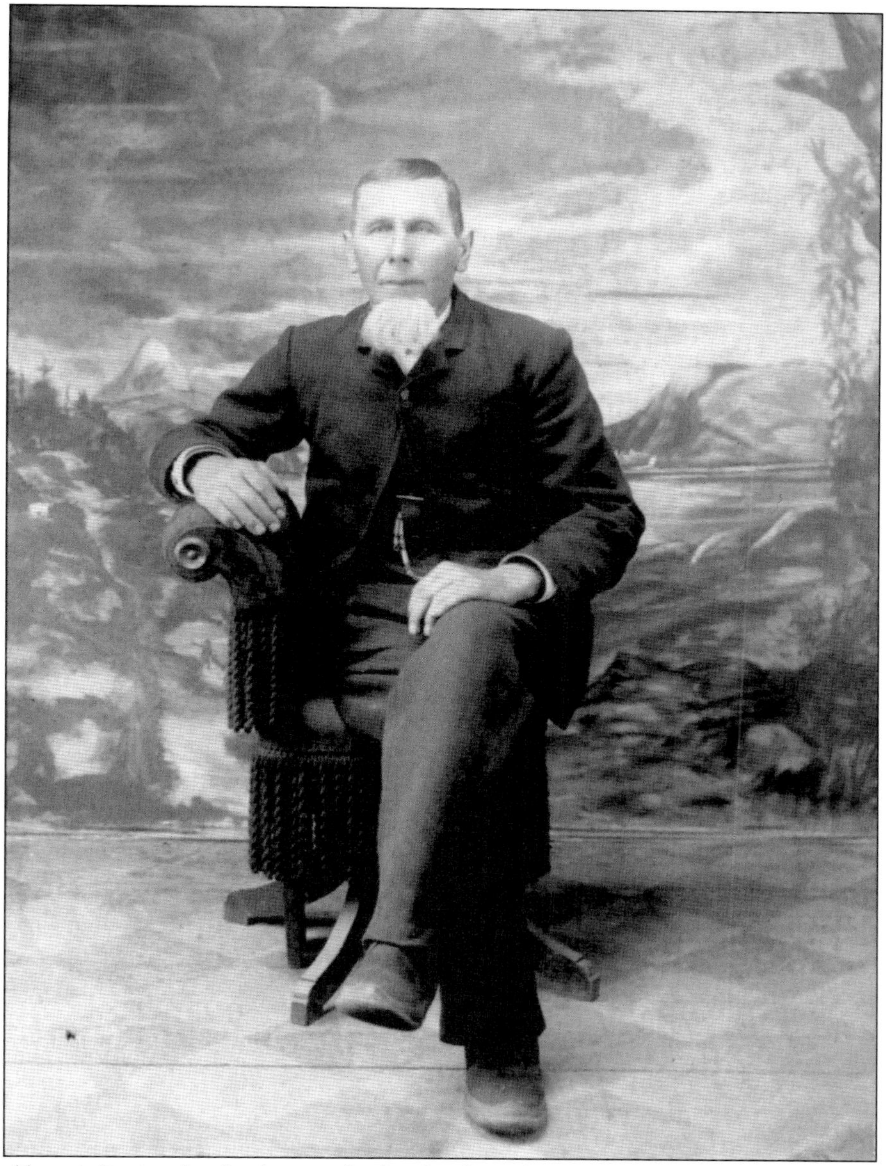

Pictured here is Pepin, the third signer for free land northwest of where the Crow and Mississippi Rivers join. It is interesting to note that over the course of seven censuses, John's last name was spelled five different ways: 1855, Pipin; 1857, Pippin; 1860, Papa; 1870, Pepin; and 1880, Peppin. Pepin was Charles LaPlant's brother-in-law. LaPlant and his family came to Otsego in 1854, only one year after the Native Americans sold their land to the United States government. LaPlant was an experienced lumberman, hunter, and trapper who used his skills to support his family. A folktale passed through the years tells of a time when LaPlant was not satisfied with a price offered at the nearby trading post in Dayton. The next day he walked to St. Paul, where he found the prices below those in Dayton, so he returned to Dayton and circled the town entering from the direction of his home as though he just came from there. LaPlant sold the pelts for the original price after covering almost 80 miles on foot in one day. (Courtesy of Wright County Historical Society.)

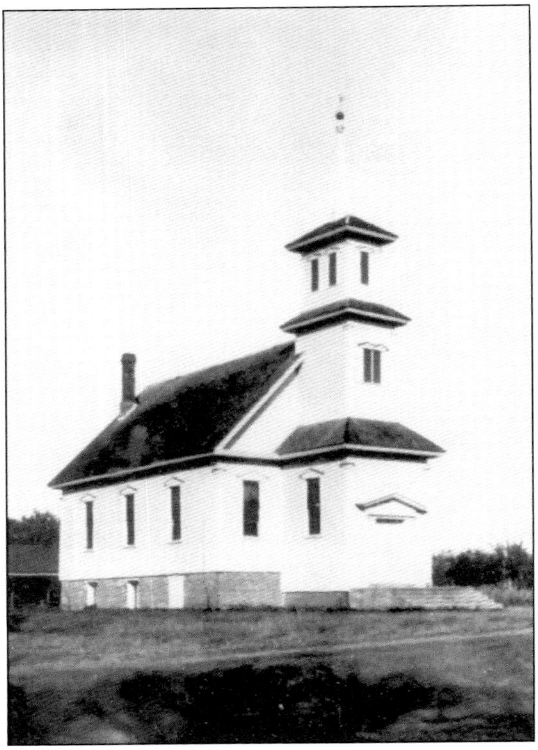

In 1854, the first religious services were conducted by Reverend White, a Methodist. The Methodist Episcopal Church was organized in 1857, holding services in John McDonald's new barn until a log meeting place was built. The Methodist Episcopal Church, pictured on the left, was built in 1871, across the street from McDonald's home and was considered a credit to the society and an ornament to the town. In 1870, a Baptist church was organized, but did not have a strong following. The Advent Christian Church was organized in 1872 and attracted quite a large membership that met in a local school. This picture below of Carrie McDonald was taken in 1855. Carrie was the wife of Joseph McDonald. Joseph was the grandson of John McDonald and the son of Lewis and Climena (Spencer) McDonald. (Left, courtesy of Wright County Historical Society; below, courtesy of Otsego Heritage Preservation Commission.)

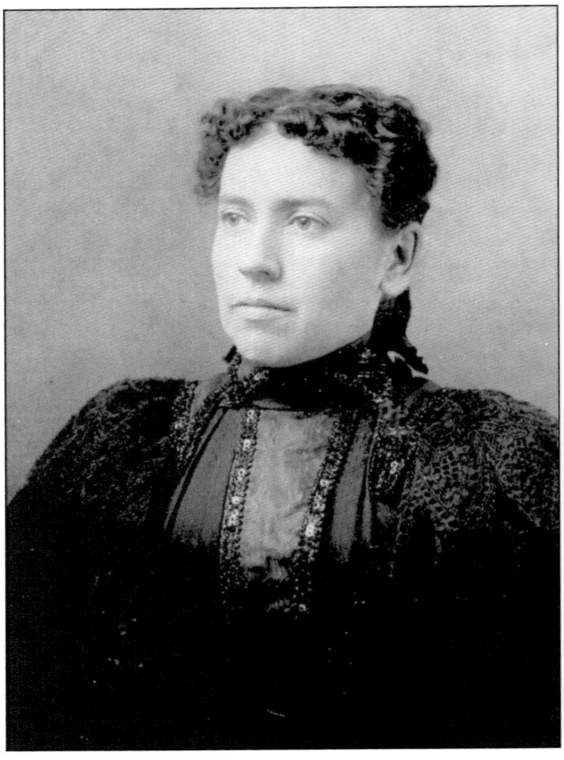

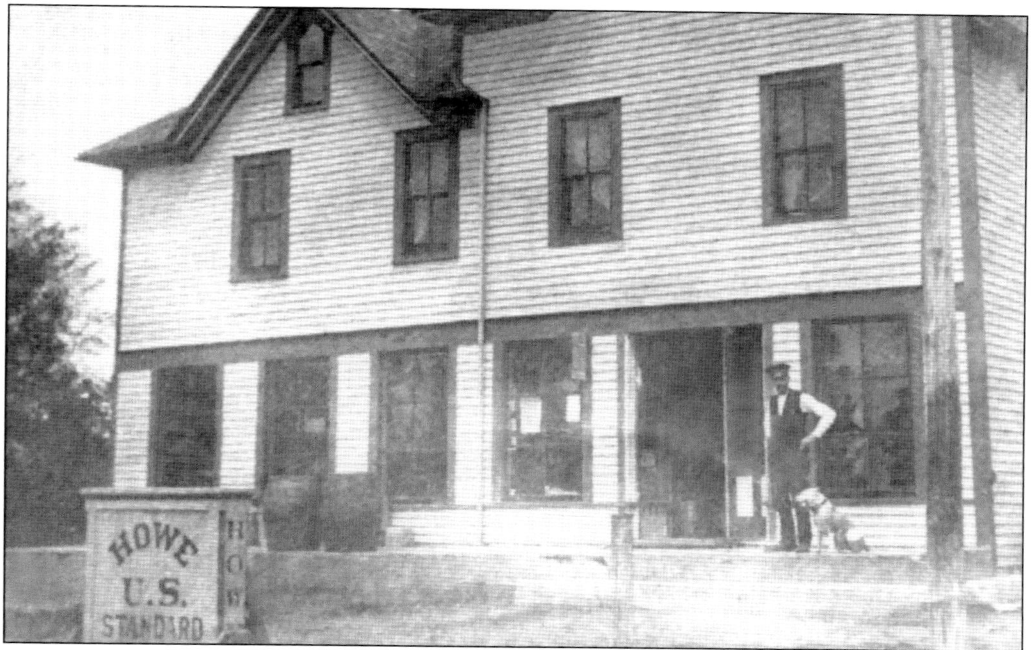

The first county road was approved on July 2, 1855, to run from Waterville (also named Aydt's Town), through the town of Otsego to Monticello. Otsego included a school, town hall, post office, ferry, sawmill, store, blacksmith shop, church, camp grounds, and hotel along with several homes. On May 11, 1858, the town officers were elected: chairman, Thomas Ham; recorder, Phillip Boyden; town clerk, Charles Lambert; assessor, John McDonald; treasurer, William Barnard; justices of the peace, Israel Record and C. B. Jordan; and constables, Luther Tubbs and Phillip Boyden. Other town sites formed within the Otsego township included Northwood on the Mississippi River one mile north of the mouth of the Crow River; Lily Pond (also called Bedford); and Portland. The financial crisis of 1857 halted development and caused many businesses to close. Pictured here are the general store (above) and blacksmith shop. (Courtesy of Wright County Historical Society.)

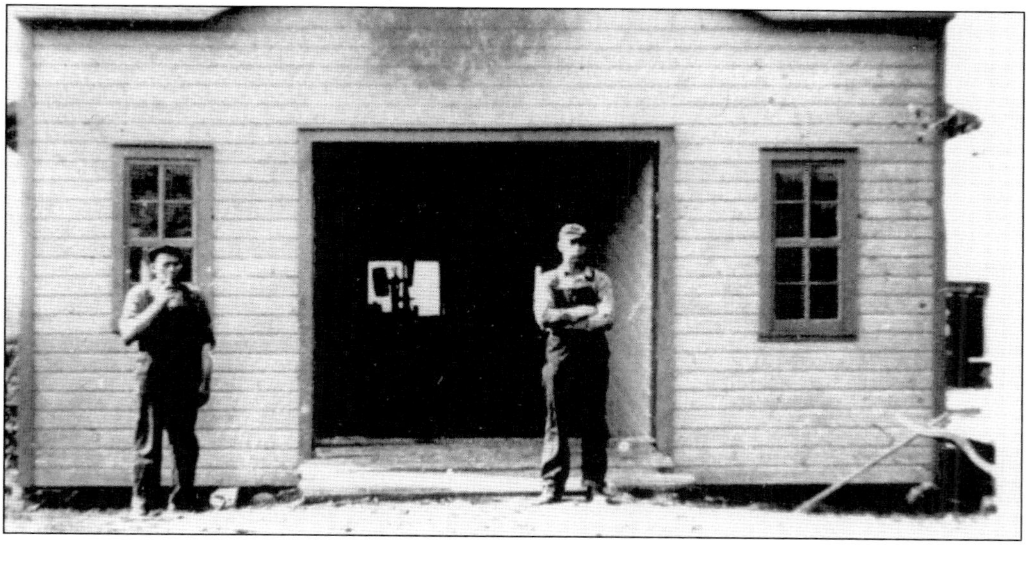

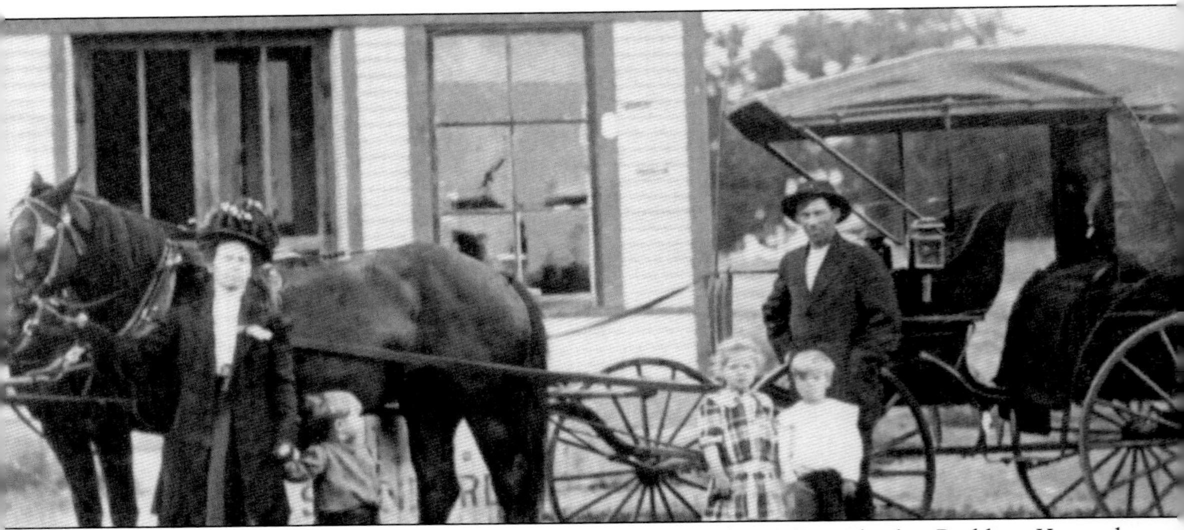

Standing in front of the Otsego store are, from left to right, Nellie, Charles, Buddice, Kenneth, and Frank Spencer. Seated in the buggy is Frank's mother, Mary Elizabeth "Libbie" (Slater Richardson) Spencer, daughter-in-law of Belinda Spencer. The general store was built near the original town site at County Road 39 and Nashua Avenue, and was operated by John McDonald. McDonald opened the first post office in the store in 1856. C. B. Jordan ran the store in 1857 and 1858. The store was also operated by Rollin Thorp, who kept the store and post office for several years, providing a trading post for local families. Martin E. Spencer ran the store and post office until his death, when his wife, Josephine, served as the postmistress. Joseph McDonald (a grandson of John McDonald), Leon Snow, B. L. Hall, and D. B. Edwards also operated the store. (Courtesy of Sally Spencer.)

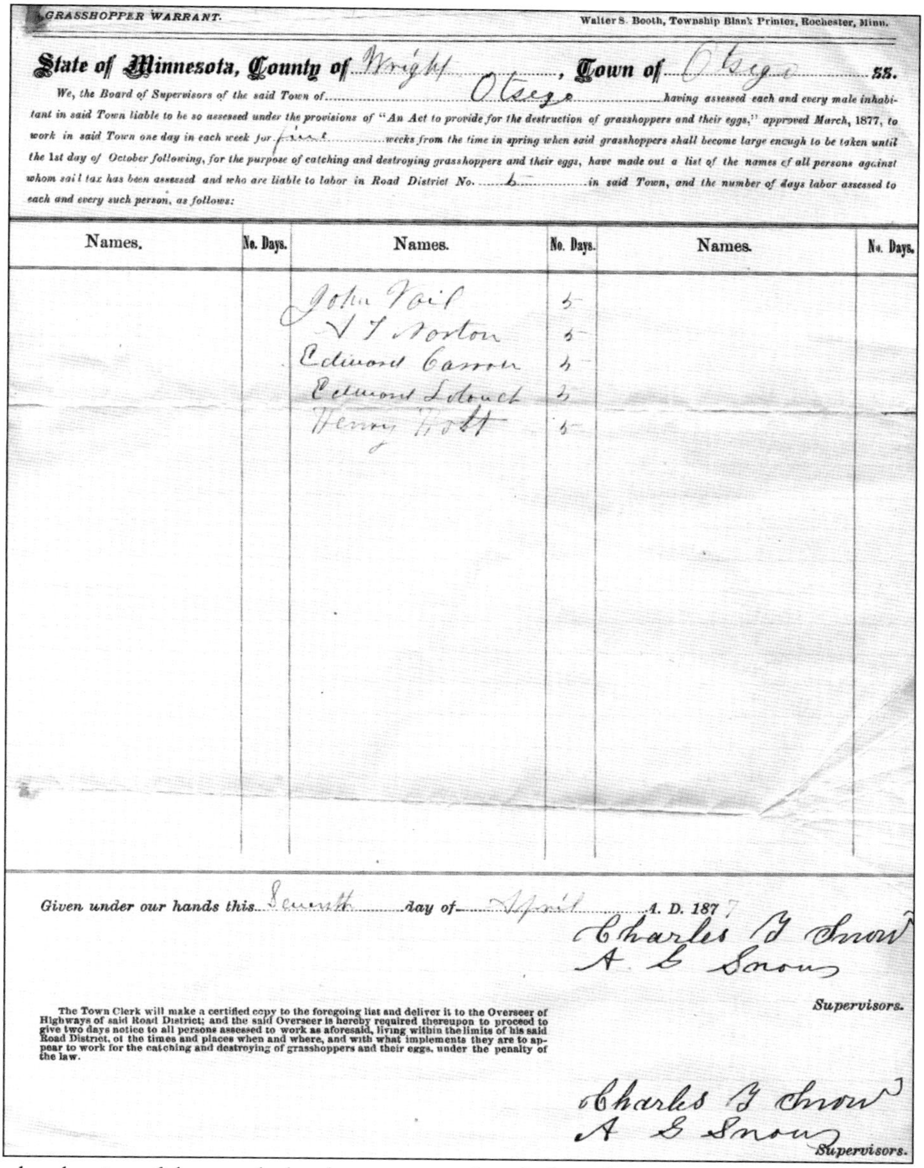

GRASSHOPPER WARRANT. Walter S. Booth, Township Blank Printer, Rochester, Minn.

State of Minnesota, County of Wright**, Town of** Otsego **ss.**

We, the Board of Supervisors of the said Town of Otsego *having assessed each and every male inhabitant in said Town liable to be so assessed under the provisions of "An Act to provide for the destruction of grasshoppers and their eggs," approved March, 1877, to work in said Town one day in each week for* five *weeks from the time in spring when said grasshoppers shall become large enough to be taken until the 1st day of October following, for the purpose of catching and destroying grasshoppers and their eggs, have made out a list of the names of all persons against whom said tax has been assessed and who are liable to labor in Road District No.* 6 *in said Town, and the number of days labor assessed to each and every such person, as follows:*

Names.	No. Days.	Names.	No. Days.	Names.	No. Days.
		John Vail	5		
		N T Norton	5		
		Edward Carron	5		
		Edmond Lalouch	5		
		Henry Holt	5		

Given under our hands this Seventh *day of* April *A. D. 187*7

Charles G Snow
A G Snow
Supervisors.

The Town Clerk will make a certified copy to the foregoing list and deliver it to the Overseer of Highways of said Road District; and the said Overseer is hereby required thereupon to proceed to give two days notice to all persons assessed to work as aforesaid, living within the limits of his said Road District, of the times and places when and where, and with what implements they are to appear to work for the catching and destroying of grasshoppers and their eggs, under the penalty of the law.

Charles G Snow
A G Snow
Supervisors.

With the clearing of the woods, land was open and ready for cultivation in 1856. Wheat, rye, oats, barley, and corn were grown in great quantities. These grains attracted swarms of grasshoppers on August 20, 1856. The wheat, corn, and garden vegetables were almost destroyed; however, the oats, rye, and barley stocks were nearly ripe, allowing much of these crops to be saved. In the spring of 1857, young grasshoppers devoured crops planted early; about half of the late planted corn, potatoes, and other vegetables were raised that year. The plague discouraged many farmers, who subsequently either sold or abandoned their farms. This created a serious loss in general wealth and prosperity and retarded the settlement of the town for several years. A grasshopper warrant was filed on April 7, 1877, to help guard against the grasshoppers. The supervisors of Otsego signed the warrant, stating they had assessed each and every male inhabitant in Otsego under the provisions of "An act to provide for the destruction of grasshoppers and their eggs," which was approved March 1877. (Courtesy of Otsego Heritage Preservation Commission.)

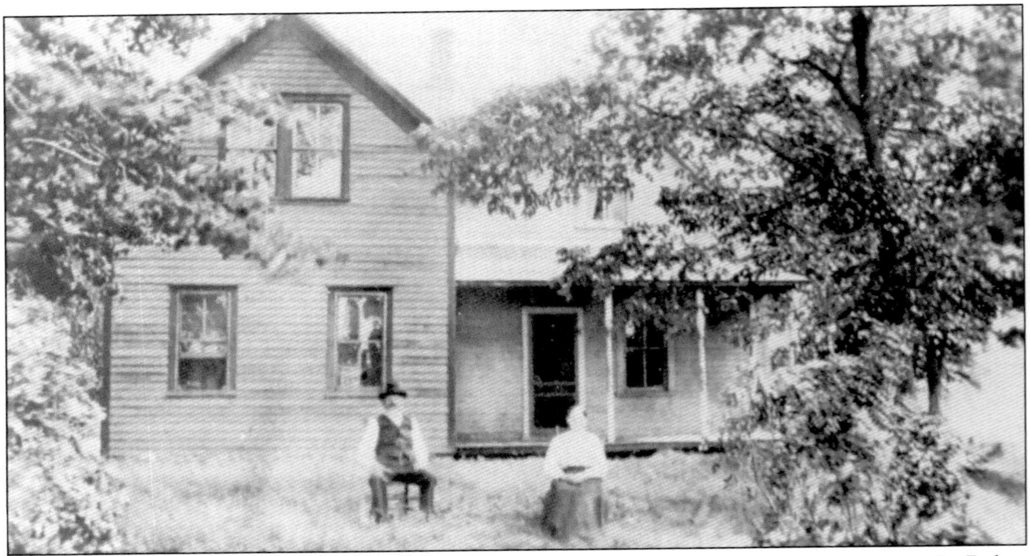

Caleb and Emeline (Stevens) Baker moved to Otsego with their children in 1867. Baker established the "Baker Ferry Crossing" near their farm in the Lily Pond community. This picture of Caleb and Emeline was taken in 1900. The first ferry was established even earlier than that by Samuel Carrick in 1854. John McDonald established a ferry at the Otsego town site in 1855. Charles Aydt also ran a ferry at Waterville near the mouth of the Crow River from 1854 until 1856. The ferry later became known as Slater's Ferry, run by George Slauyter. Oliver Perrault ran the ferry until 1902, when he sold it to Adolph "Duffy" Martin. Martin discontinued service in 1937. Pictured below in 1921 is Edward Michael Kiichli, by the big elm tree at the Ingersoll farm near the river where steamboats were tied. (Above, courtesy of Wright County Historical Society; below, courtesy of Otsego Heritage Preservation Commission.)

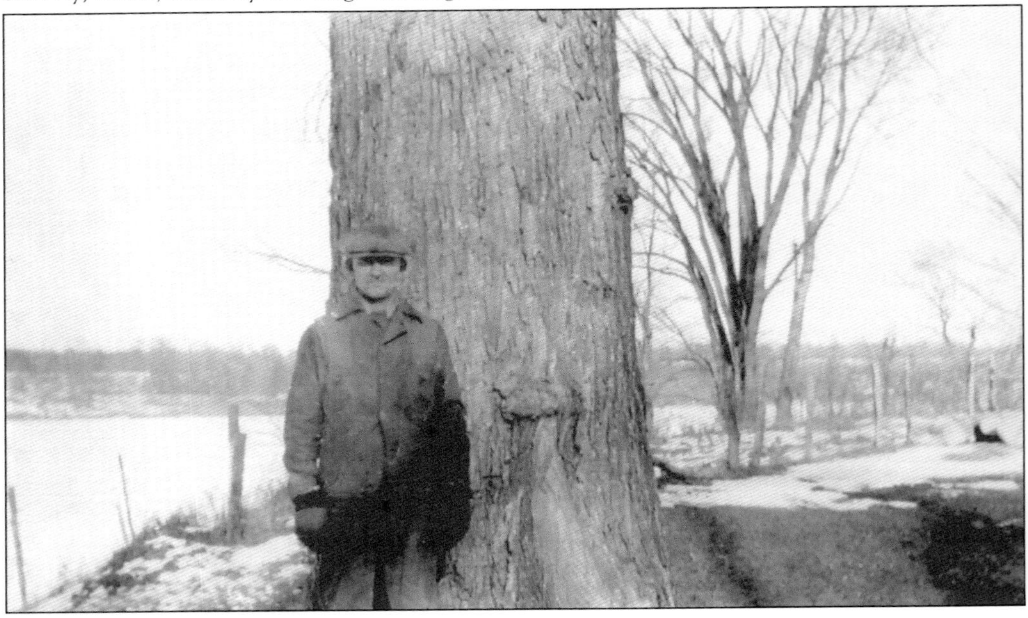

Two

A Way of Life

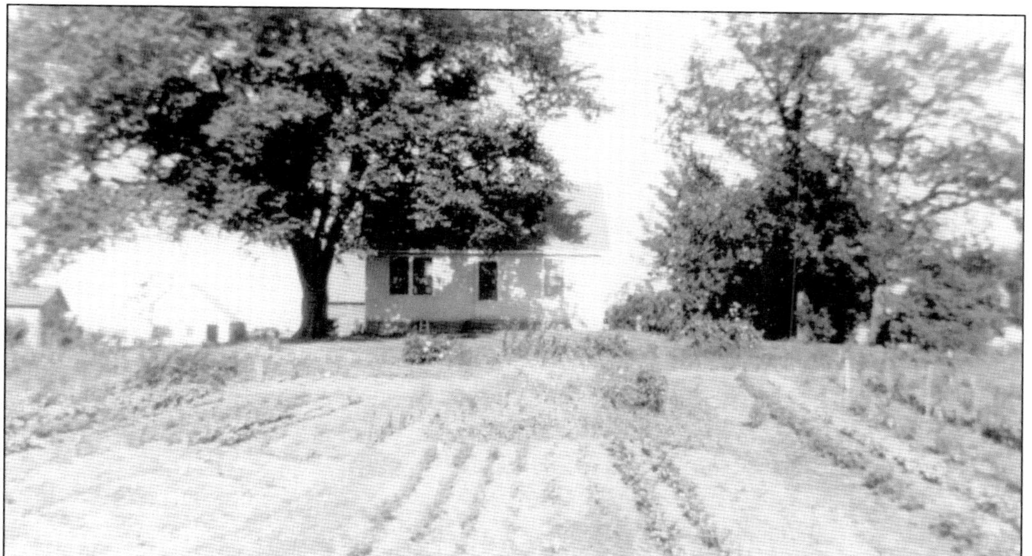

This picture, taken of the Pouliot farm during the summer of 1939, is an excellent example of how Otsego families made a living. Farmland was relatively easy to secure in the mid-1800s. The Homestead Act was instated on May 20, 1862, by Pres. Abraham Lincoln and provided freehold title to 160 acres of undeveloped land with a house built on the section and lived in for five years. In the early years, crop prices were poor. In 1858, ginseng root, a thick-rooted herb used as medicine, was found in the area, harvested, and sold for cash to ginseng traders from Virginia. This enabled families to pay off debt and enjoy relative prosperity rather than abandoning their land. (Courtesy of Elma [Hagel] Pouliot.)

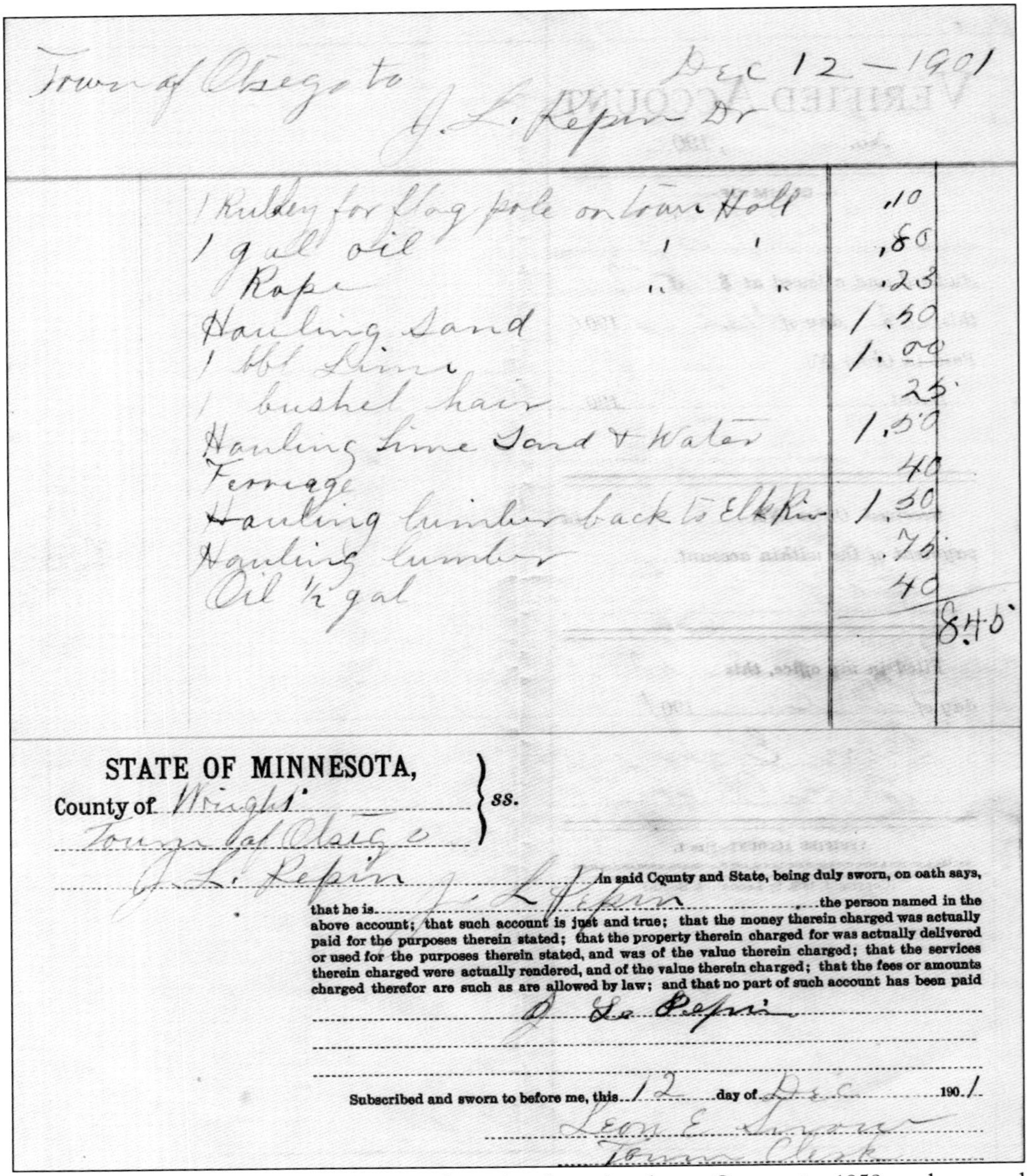

Town of Otsego to J. L. Pepin Dr — Dec 12 — 1901

1 Rubber for flag pole on town Hall	.10
1 gal oil	.80
Rope	.23
Hauling sand	1.50
1 bbl Lime	1.00
1 bushel hair	.25
Hauling lime sand & water	1.50
Ferriage	.40
Hauling lumber back to Elk Riv	1.50
Hauling lumber	.75
Oil ½ gal	.40
	8.45

STATE OF MINNESOTA,
County of Wright } ss.
Town of Otsego
J. L. Pepin in said County and State, being duly sworn, on oath says, that he is J. L. Pepin the person named in the above account; that such account is just and true; that the money therein charged was actually paid for the purposes therein stated; that the property therein charged for was actually delivered or used for the purposes therein stated, and was of the value therein charged; that the services therein charged were actually rendered, and of the value therein charged; that the fees or amounts charged therefor are such as are allowed by law; and that no part of such account has been paid

J. L. Pepin

Subscribed and sworn to before me, this 12 day of Dec 190 1

Leon E. Swan
Town Clerk

John Baptiste and Julia (Ozier) Pepin brought their family to Otsego in 1858 and secured section 22 as the Pepin farm where their children were raised. Their children included John L. who married Nellie Parker; Mary Priscilla who married Finley McNeil; Harriet "Hattie" who married Charles Wood; Julia who first married Edwin Parker and then Sidney Holt; George Alfred "Fred" who married Gertrude Holt; William who married Eva Cooley; and Charles L. The 80-acre farm had dairy cattle, pigs, and chickens. The Pepin's primary cash crop was potatoes. Loretta Moos shared that potatoes were hauled to Elk River in horse-drawn wagons. Moos's father, Fred Jacobs, was the only farmer with a horse-drawn potato digger; others harvested the potatoes by hand. Moos commented the potatoes had to be perfect or they could not be sold. Pictured here is a copy of John L. Pepin's account with Otsego; notice the cost of goods and services in 1901. (Courtesy of Otsego Heritage Preservation Commission.)

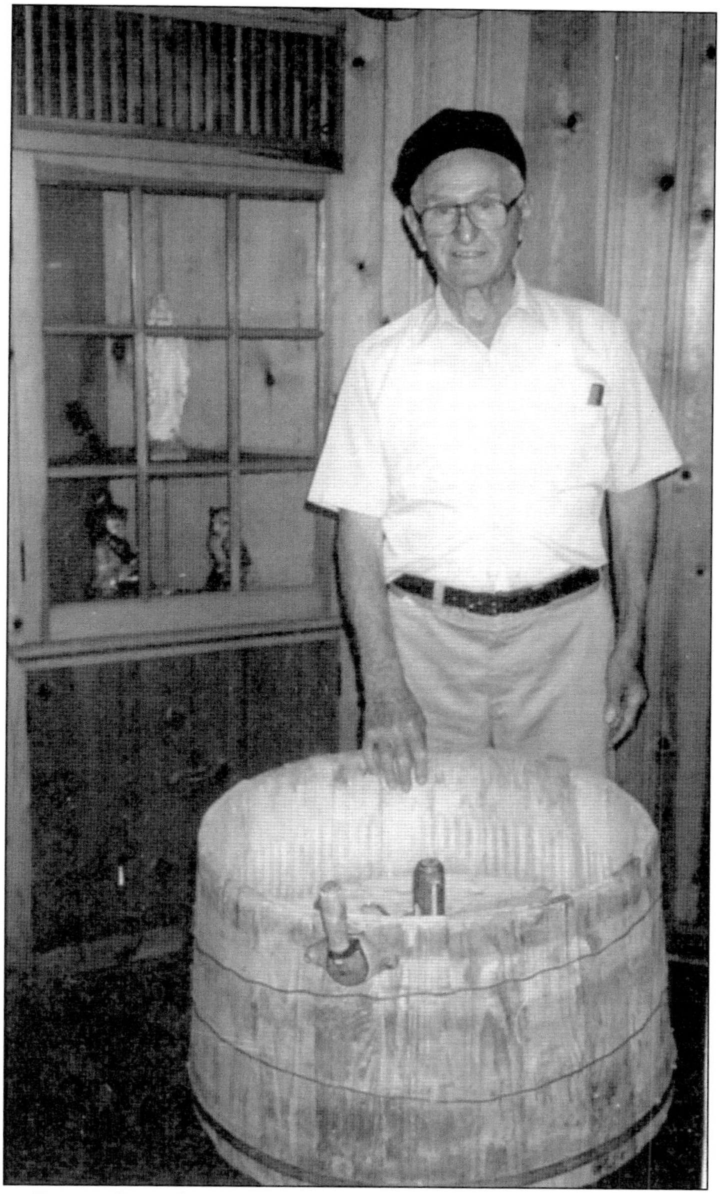

At a young age, George Joyer became an orphan when his parents died of the plague as the family immigrated to Canada from Ireland. In Canada, Joyer was adopted by the Croteau family, who gave him the last name of Joyer because he brought the family so much happiness; some believe, however, he was not given the Croteau family name to prevent bringing shame to the family if Joyer turned out to be a bad seed. Joyer was well educated and very religious. Joyer lived and farmed with John Croteau prior to marrying Justine Chouinard on May 22, 1877. Joyer homesteaded 80 acres and purchased an additional 40 acres about a half-mile up the road. Based on tax receipts from 1889 through 1906, it was revealed that Joyer was a good farmer. Pictured here is Melvin Joyer with the original washing machine given to Justine (Chouinard) Joyer by her daughter Josephine Elliott. The machine was used from the time Justine received it in 1914 until 1925. (Courtesy of Michelle [Christian] Matchie.)

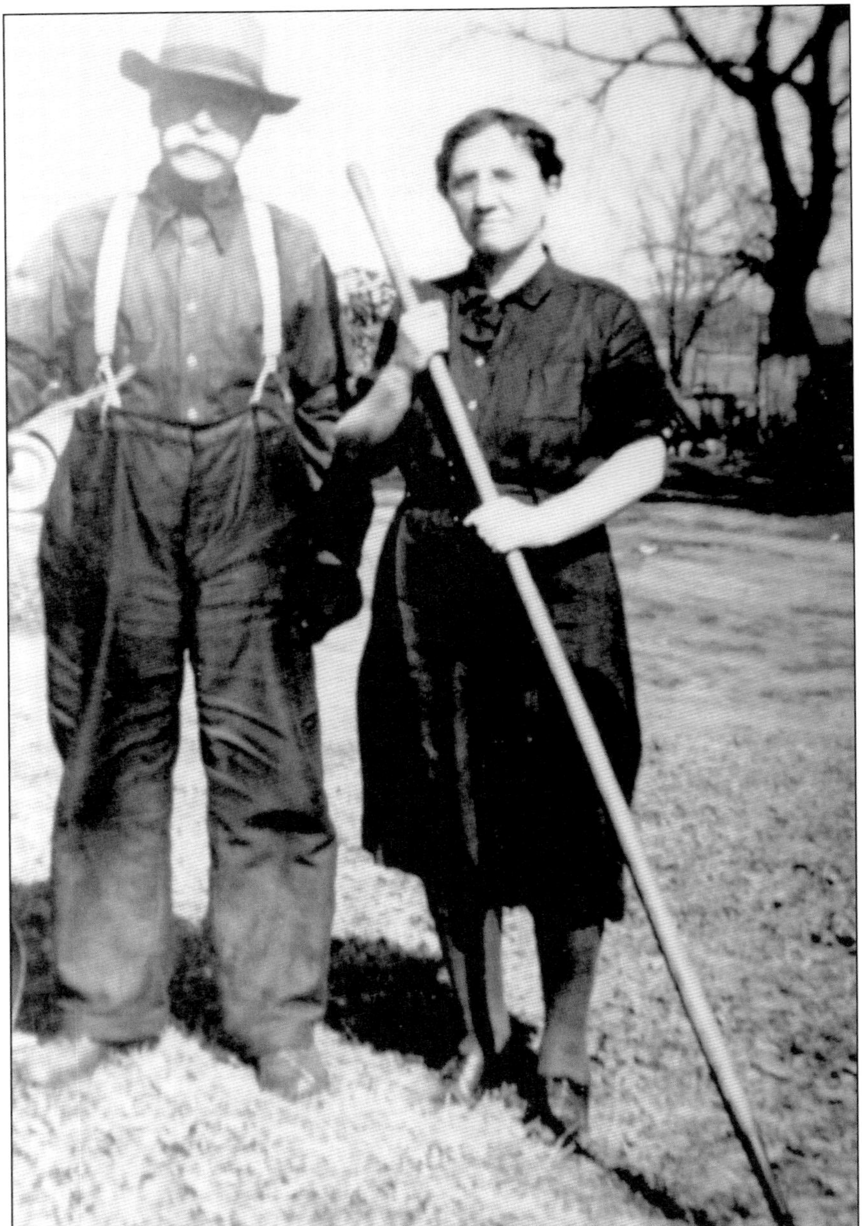

Orion Davis, pictured here, was referenced on November 12, 1879, in the *Holt Diary* as being a good husker. One day the group husked 179 bushels. Davis is the son of Joseph and Emeline (Spencer) Davis, who came to Otsego in 1864. Willard Holt kept the *Holt Diary* during his farming years from May 1878 until December 1890. A realistic idea of the times can be gleaned from the *Holt Diary*. The diary included historical records of births, deaths, and marriages along with information about farming conditions and prices and even a few jokes, such as these: "Why is a colt like an egg? Because it will have to be broken before it is used. Why is a ladies belt like a scavenger? Because it goes around and gathers up the waist/waste." (Courtesy of Otsego Heritage Preservation Commission.)

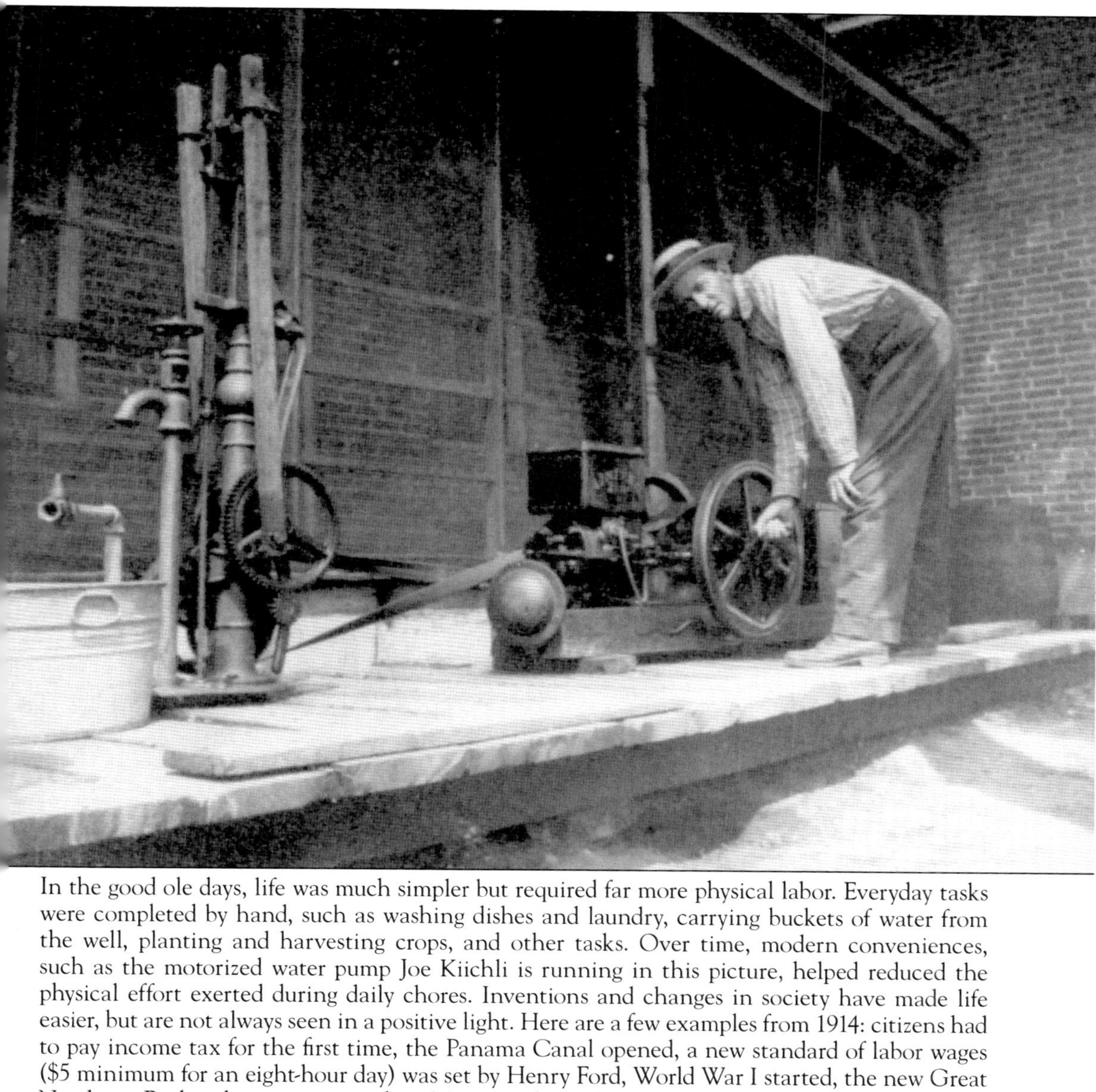

In the good ole days, life was much simpler but required far more physical labor. Everyday tasks were completed by hand, such as washing dishes and laundry, carrying buckets of water from the well, planting and harvesting crops, and other tasks. Over time, modern conveniences, such as the motorized water pump Joe Kiichli is running in this picture, helped reduced the physical effort exerted during daily chores. Inventions and changes in society have made life easier, but are not always seen in a positive light. Here are a few examples from 1914: citizens had to pay income tax for the first time, the Panama Canal opened, a new standard of labor wages ($5 minimum for an eight-hour day) was set by Henry Ford, World War I started, the new Great Northern Railroad station opened in Minneapolis, sirloin steak was 32¢ a pound, milk was 8¢ a quart, the Ebner Box Factory had one of its biggest productions to date creating 80,000 crates of berry boxes, and state land was sold for $5 to $14 per acre. (Courtesy of Otsego Heritage Preservation Commission.)

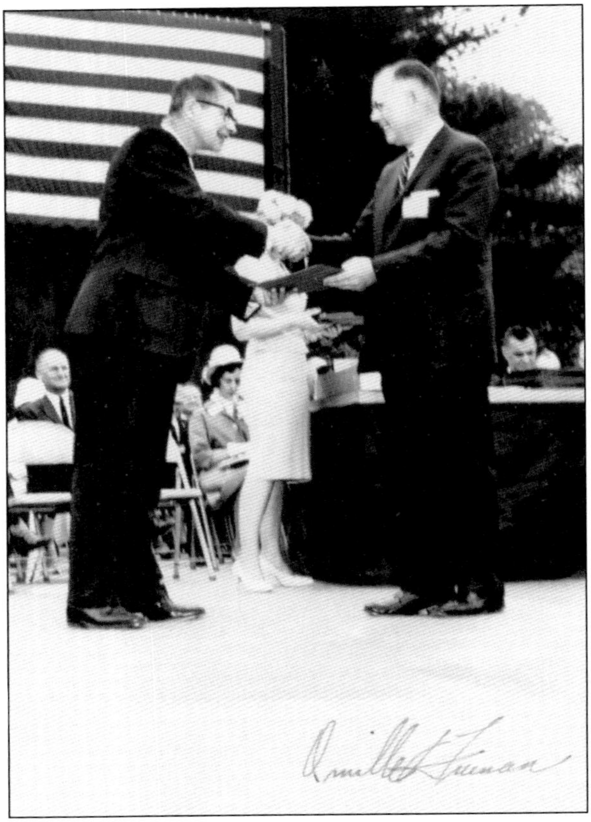

Pictured at left is Camille Lefebvre shaking the hand of Orville Freeman, who was an ex–Minnesota governor and then the secretary of agriculture. Lefebvre worked diligently on the Barberry Eradication Project in 1922 and was recognized for his contributions to the effort. (Left, courtesy of Wanda Lefebvre; below, courtesy of Mary Anne McNeil.)

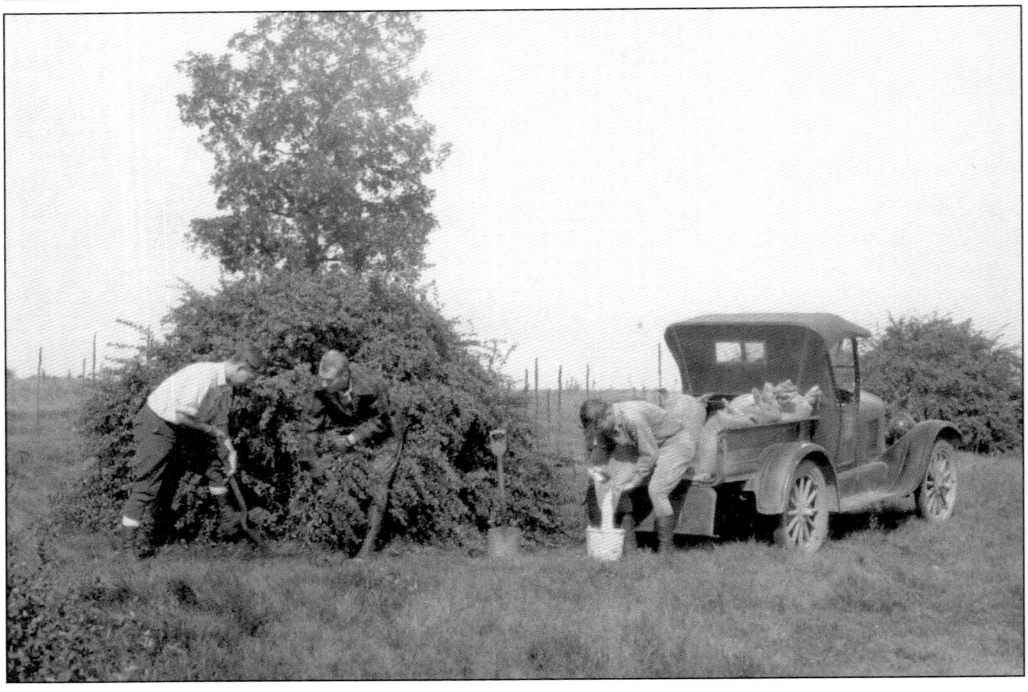

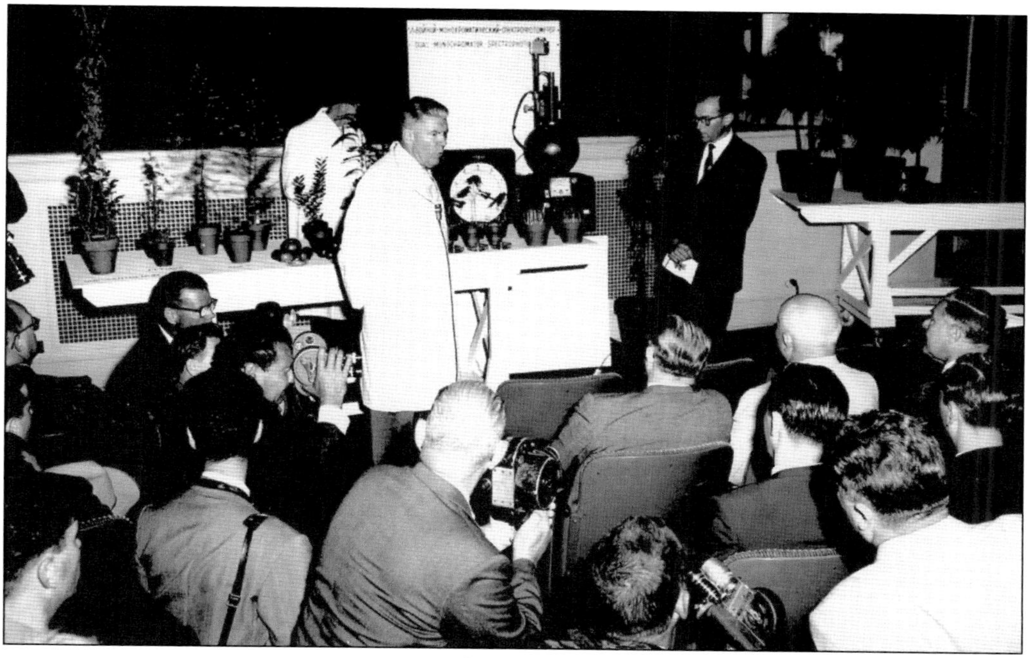

Harry Alfred Borthwick was born on January 7, 1898, to Alfred and Frances Estella (Humphrey) Borthwick. Frances was the aunt of Hubert Humphrey, who became vice president of the United States, and the sister of Harry B. Humphrey, a leading phytopathologist. Harry Humphrey influenced Harry Borthwick to enter the School of Agriculture of the University of Minnesota in 1917. Borthwick transferred to Stanford University in 1919, where he majored in botany. Borthwick became a member of the *World Who's Who in Science* for his research on the effect light has on the biological response of plants. Borthwick's work earned him a seat in the ARS Science Hall of Fame on November 28, 1995, and the Nessim Habif World Prize from the University of Geneva, Switzerland, for contributions to plant science. Pictured above is Dr. Harry Borthwick (standing, left) speaking in Beltsville, Maryland, with Soviet premier Nikita Khrushchev seated in the front row, and seen at right is Borthwick working in his lab. (Courtesy of Otsego Heritage Preservation Commission.)

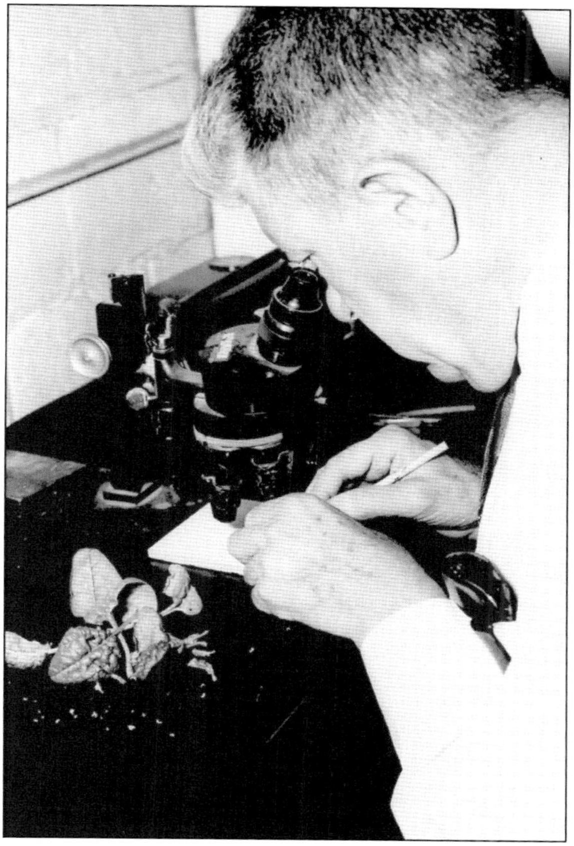

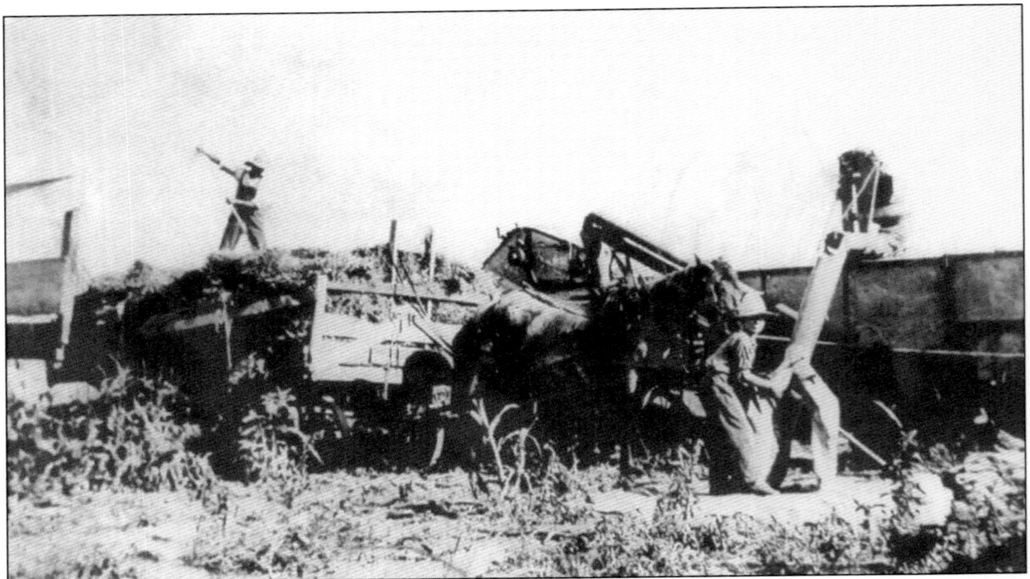

Mary Ann (Hauan) Eden remembered when her grandfather Arthur Joyer would help with the community threshing bee. Eden shared that farmers would go from farm-to-farm threshing. The women would prepare a big meal and make the event a lot of fun rather than seem like work. The picture above was taken on August 15, 1932, during a threshing bee. Lester Beaudry is on the wagon, and Ray Carron is standing on the ground sacking in front of Alrick Martin's threshing machine. The picture below is of Joyer with his five sons: from left to right, Earl (on the load of hay), Clement, Arthur, Melvin (on tractor), George, and Harvey. The picture was taken in 1943 when they were making hay. (Above, courtesy of Diane DeMars; below, courtesy of Michelle [Christian] Matchie.)

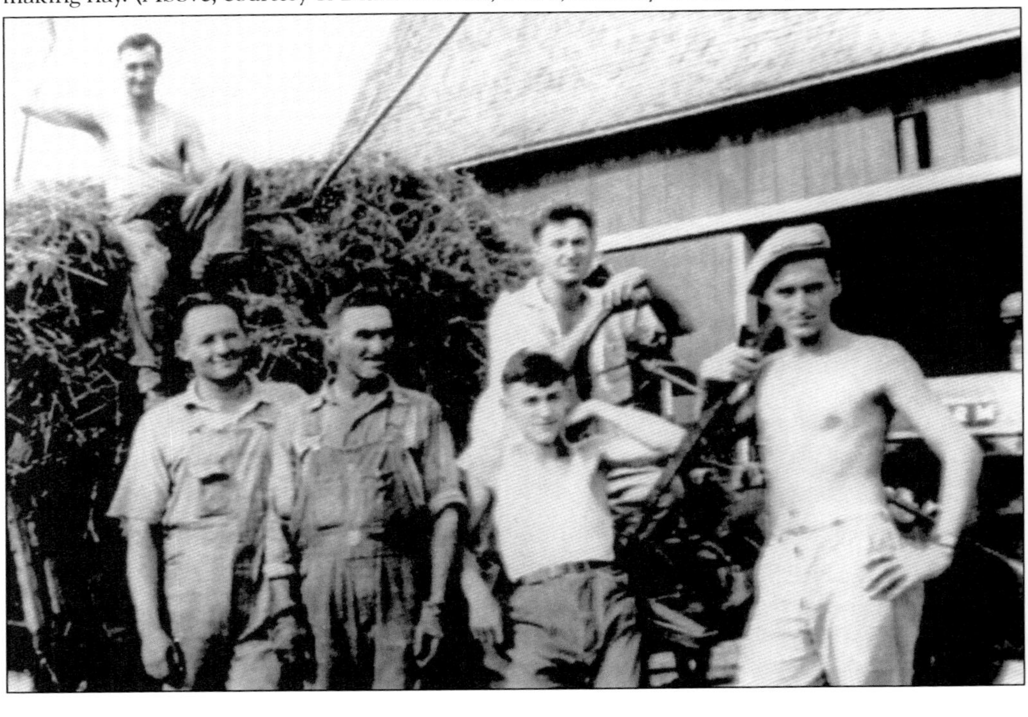

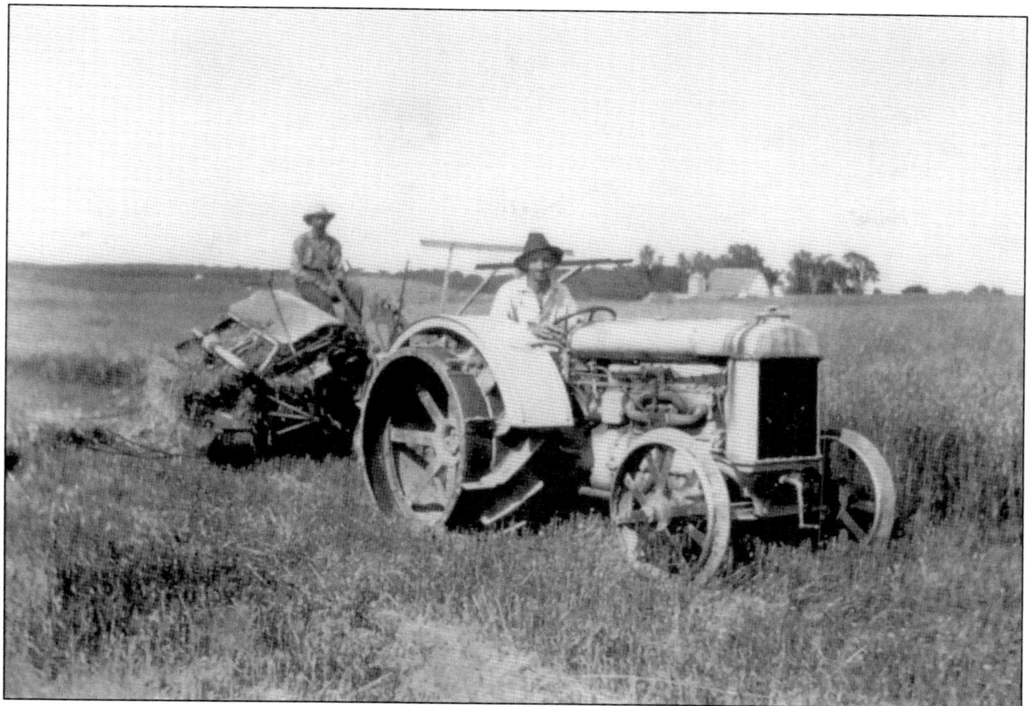

Families worked together to get the fieldwork done in a timely manner. This land was once the Tebo farm, which later became the Carron farm. In the background is the Joe DeMars farm, which is currently the Jim DeMars farm. (Courtesy of Diane DeMars.)

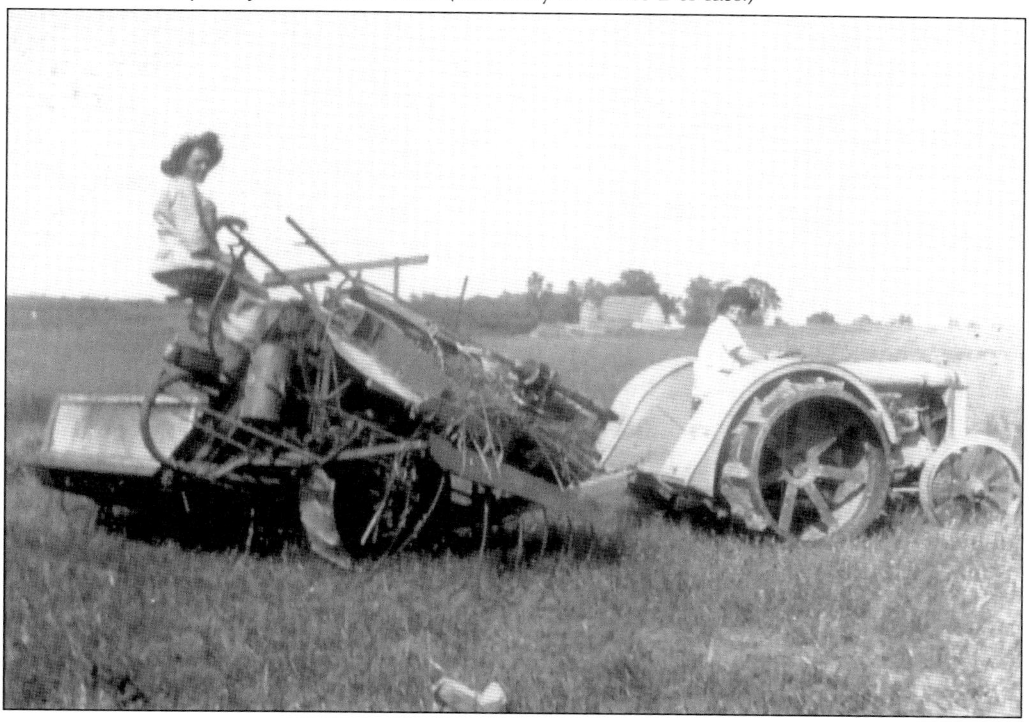

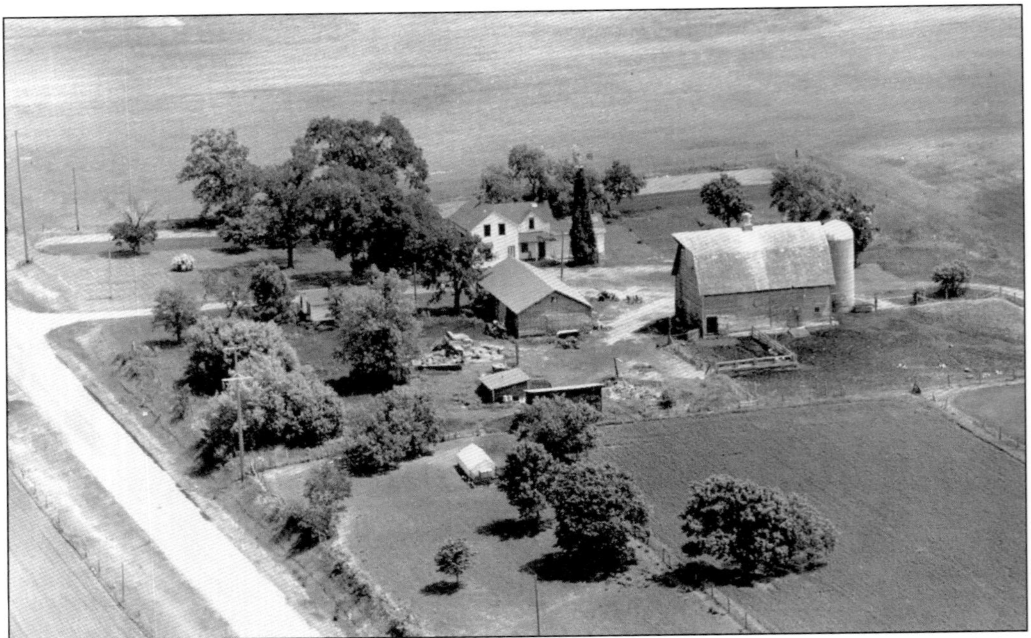

This aerial photograph is of the William Bell farm and the image below is of Bell with his daughter Bernice, taken in about 1930. Farming was a way of life for most residents of Otsego. When prices dropped in 1878, farmers turned to diversified crops and dairy cattle. The 1910 census revealed that 85 percent of the farms were operated by the owner; 49 percent were American born, and 51 percent were foreign born. Principle crops included corn, wheat, barley, flax, potatoes, oats, timothy, and alfalfa. The early settlers found an abundant supply of wild fruits, such as apples, grapes, plums, strawberries, choke cherries, raspberries, and blackberries. Some farmers transplanted the fruit trees and bushes in gardens. Michelle (Christian) Matchie remembered the berry bush in front of their home. Matchie was told the berries were poisonous so she would use them in mud pies. (Courtesy of John and Della [Bell] Anderson.)

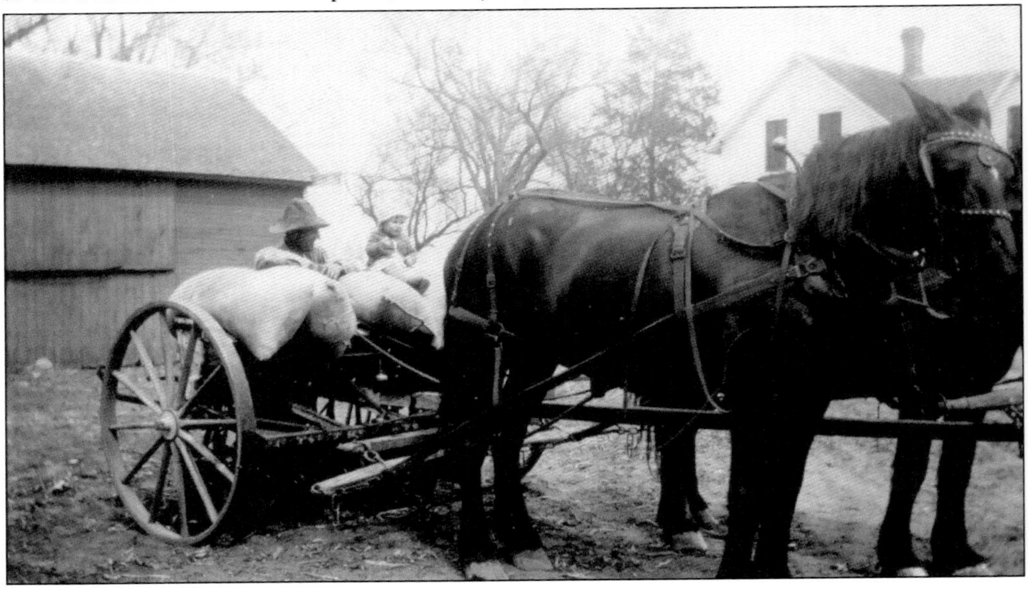

Food, clothing, petroleum products, and other such items were rationed during and after World War II. People were forced to conserve their use of common products to ensure enough supplies were available for the troops. Access to luxury items was severely restricted; however, there was a prevalent black market for those who could afford these items. Pictured here is a fuel oil ration for Raymond Carron, issued for the year ending August 31, 1945. As farmers had become used to the tractor, a dependency on petroleum products was created. Pictured below is a tractor restored by Bob Spencer. People can enjoy viewing a portion of Spencer's tractor collection at the annual local threshing shows. (Right, courtesy of Diane DeMars; below, courtesy of Bob Spencer.)

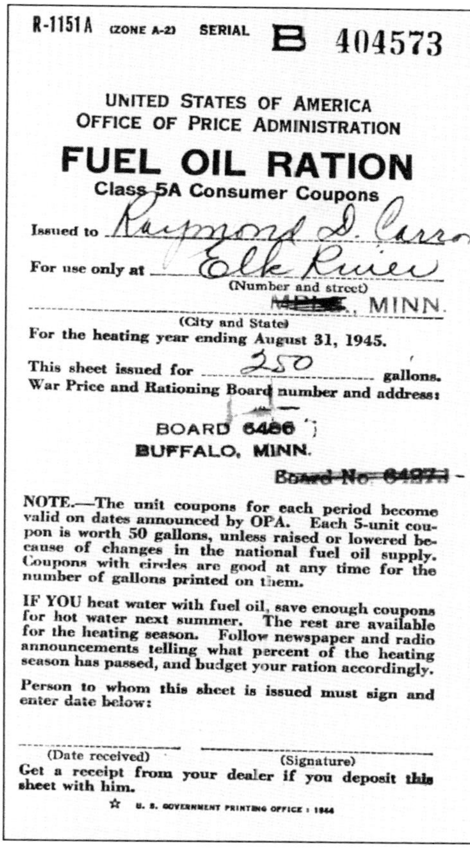

R-1151A (ZONE A-2) SERIAL B 404573

UNITED STATES OF AMERICA
OFFICE OF PRICE ADMINISTRATION

FUEL OIL RATION
Class 5A Consumer Coupons

Issued to Raymond D. Carron

For use only at Elk River
(Number and street)

MINN.
(City and State)

For the heating year ending August 31, 1945.

This sheet issued for 250 gallons.

War Price and Rationing Board number and address:

BOARD 6486
BUFFALO, MINN.

~~Board No. 6497~~

NOTE.—The unit coupons for each period become valid on dates announced by OPA. Each 5-unit coupon is worth 50 gallons, unless raised or lowered because of changes in the national fuel oil supply. Coupons with circles are good at any time for the number of gallons printed on them.

IF YOU heat water with fuel oil, save enough coupons for hot water next summer. The rest are available for the heating season. Follow newspaper and radio announcements telling what percent of the heating season has passed, and budget your ration accordingly.

Person to whom this sheet is issued must sign and enter date below:

(Date received) (Signature)

Get a receipt from your dealer if you deposit this sheet with him.

☆ U. S. GOVERNMENT PRINTING OFFICE : 1944

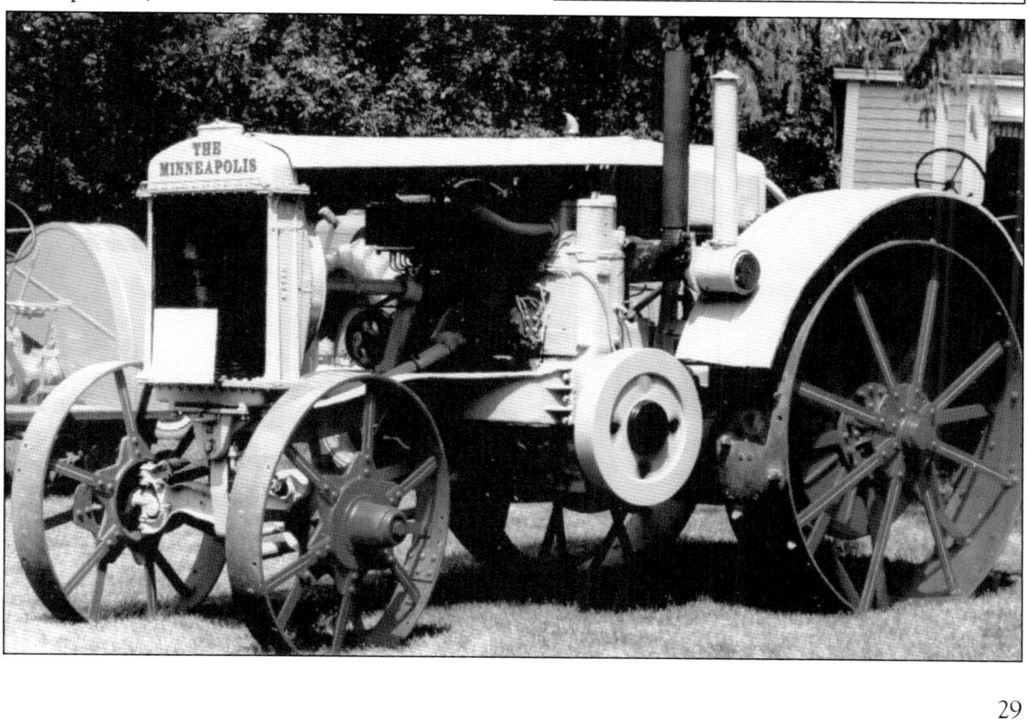

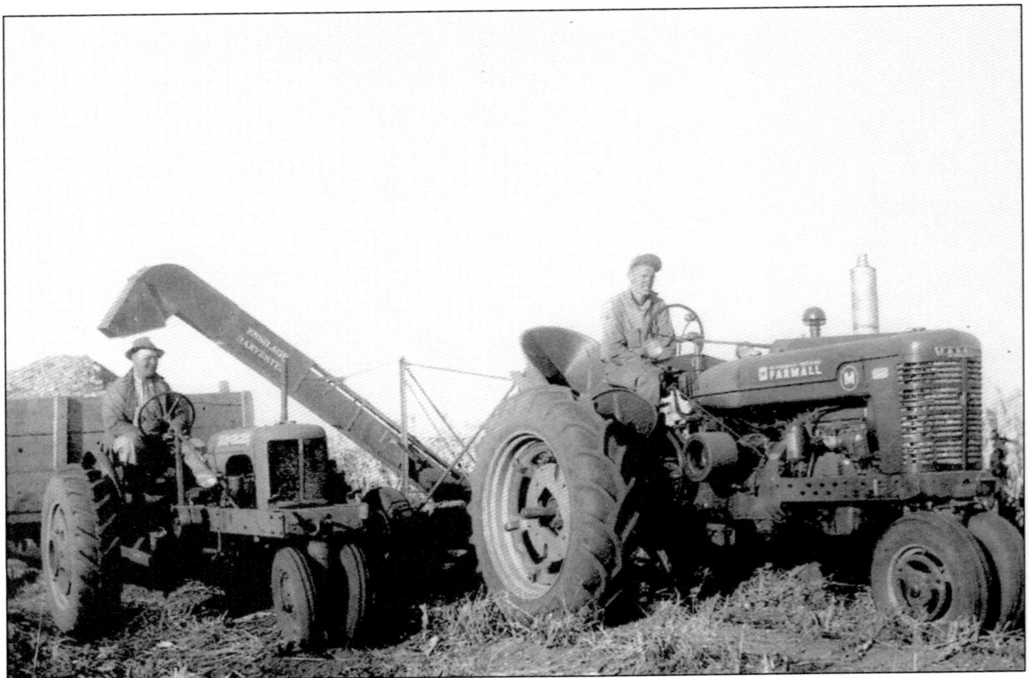

Elmer "Mike" Lefebvre and Eddie Lefebvre are pictured above in 1948 using a Farmall tractor. The aerial picture below is of the Lefebvre farm. With development comes change. Once a flourishing farm, much of the land in this picture has become retail business. Currently the land is home to Holiday Inn, Rockwoods Grill and Banquet Center, Riverview Bank, Otsego Café, Super America, and 101 Market. There are many strip malls peppered throughout the area as well. (Courtesy of Patty and Richard Lefebvre.)

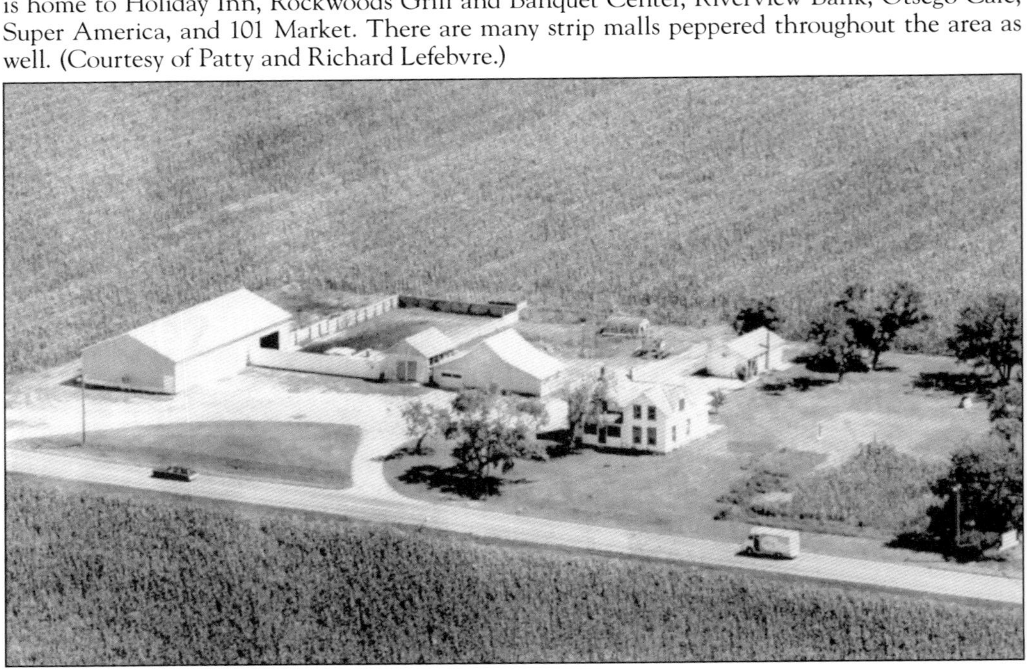

Three

A Place Called Home

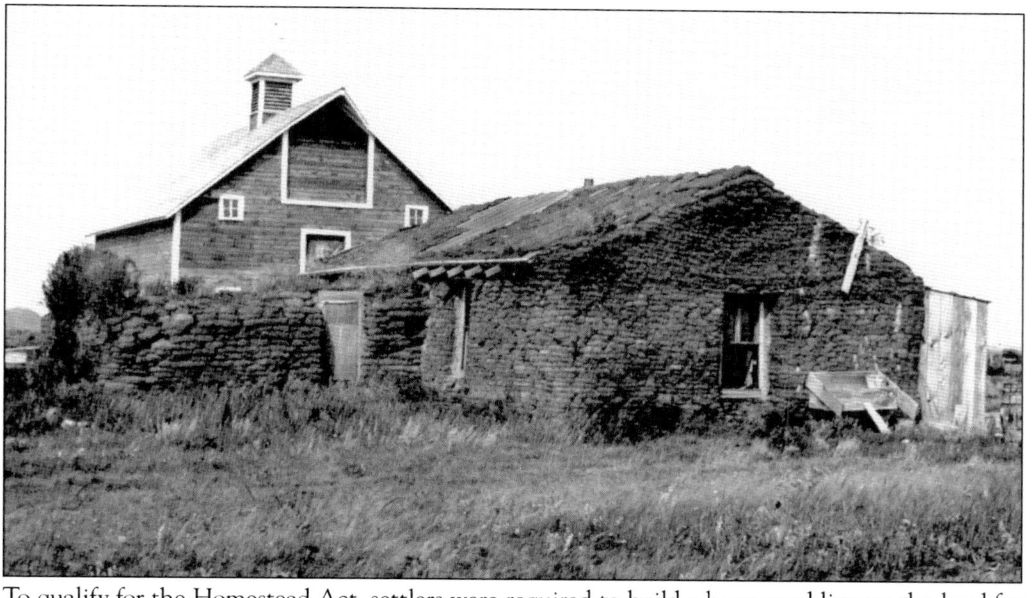

To qualify for the Homestead Act, settlers were required to build a house and live on the land for five years. Sod homes, like the one pictured here, and log cabins were the structures of choice. Trees cut from the "Big Woods" were used to build shelter and household furnishings. Animals were part of a family's livelihood, which is why a fight over a calf broke out between Philip Hoffman and Herman Trauch in 1881. The calf got into Trauch's meadow, and Trauch started to lead it away. Hoffman climbed the fence and told Trauch he would lead the calf back to the pasture. Trauch refused to give up the animal and struck Hoffman four times with a butcher knife. Hoffman died almost instantly. Trauch was tried in October 1881, found guilty, and sentenced to state prison for life. (Courtesy of Pamella Collins.)

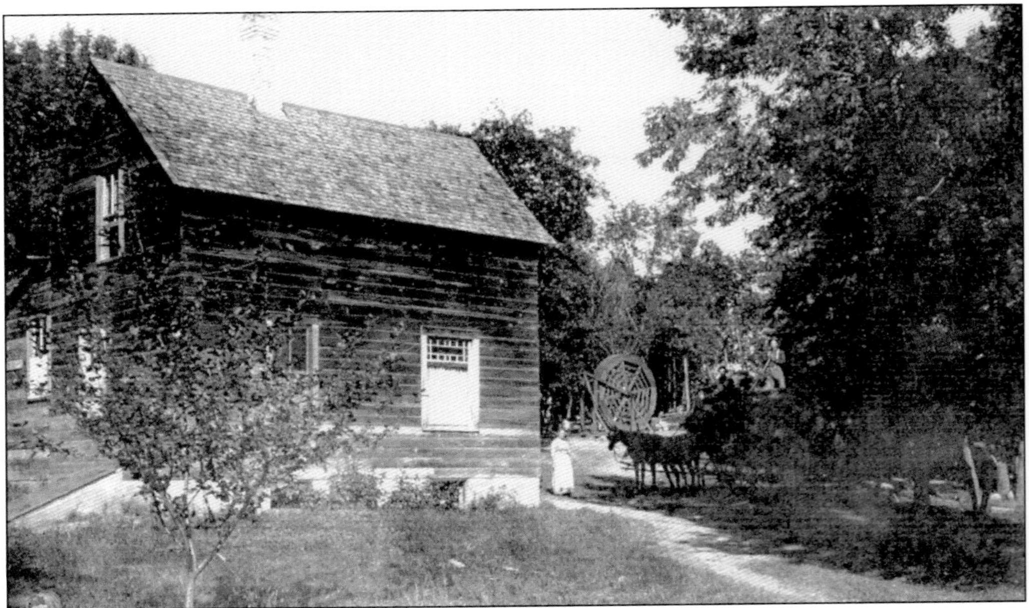

This wooden structure was the home of Willard and Alice (Holt) Mosman. Willard married Alice Louise Holt, daughter of Henry and Julia Frances (Ingersoll) Holt on November 17, 1883. They had eight children that attended the Lily Pond Grade School and Elk River High School. Notice the large treadmill towards the back of the image above. This treadmill, which was powered by a dog, pumped water from the well. Bob and Mae Spencer currently reside on this farm, which they have turned into the Clay Coupe, a pottery studio and site for restoring antique tractors. The picture of the brick house below is the home of Anna and Lorenzo Smith taken in about 1904. It is believed this home was built in 1861 using bricks produced at the Ingersoll Brick Factory. (Above, courtesy of Bob and Mae Spencer; below, courtesy of Arne Engstrom.)

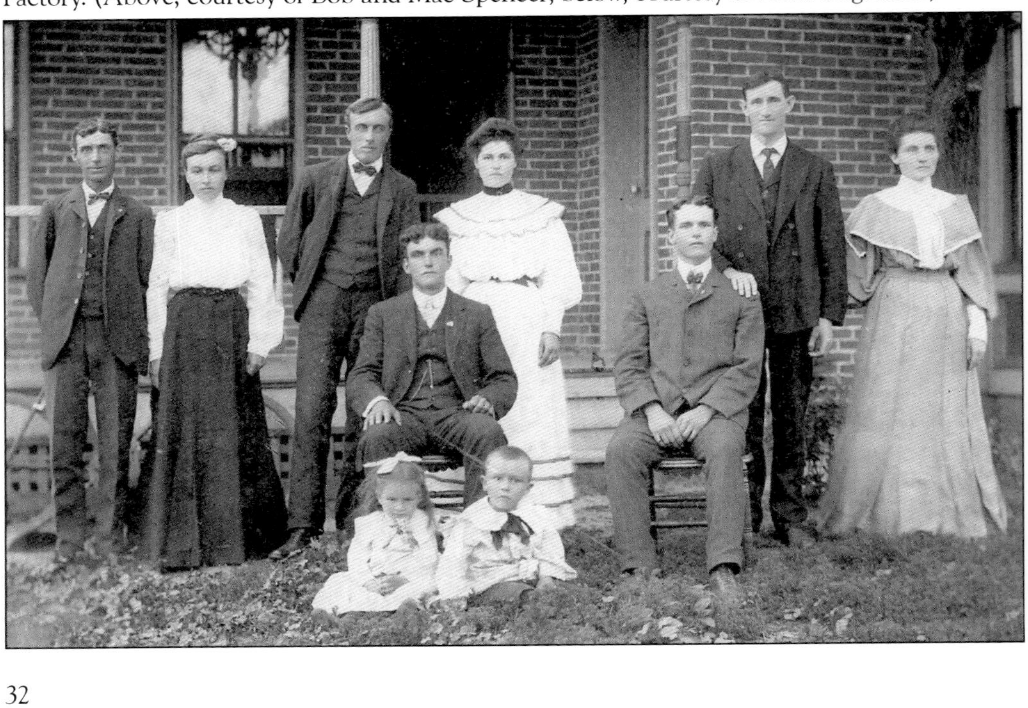

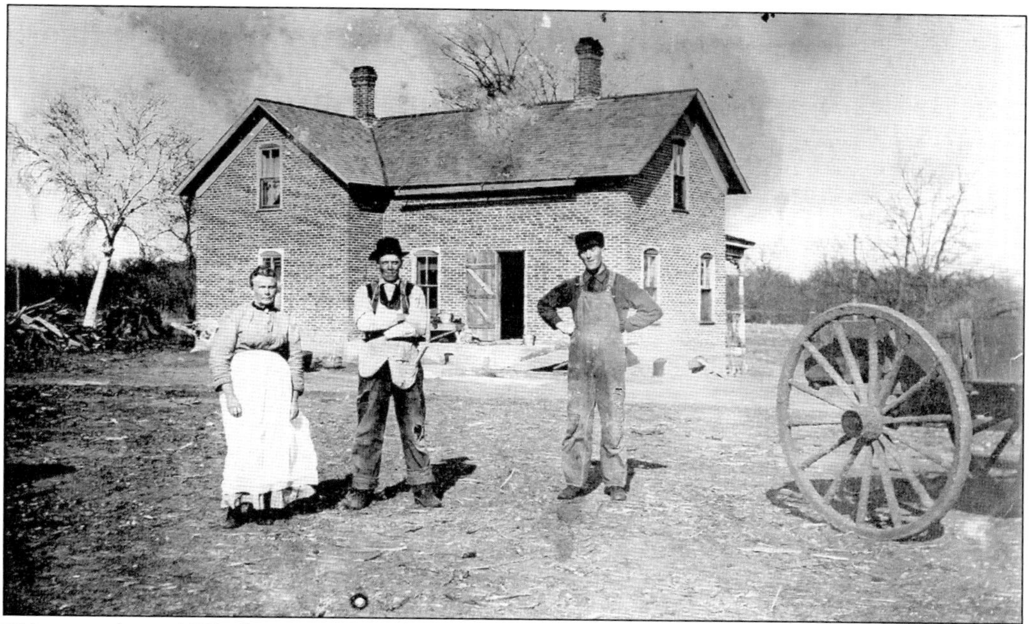

Taken in about 1875, these pictures of the Lorenzo and Anna Smith farm depict people hard at work. This particular day the crew was painting the barn. Their oldest son, Walter, assisted with the job. (Courtesy of Arne Engstrom.)

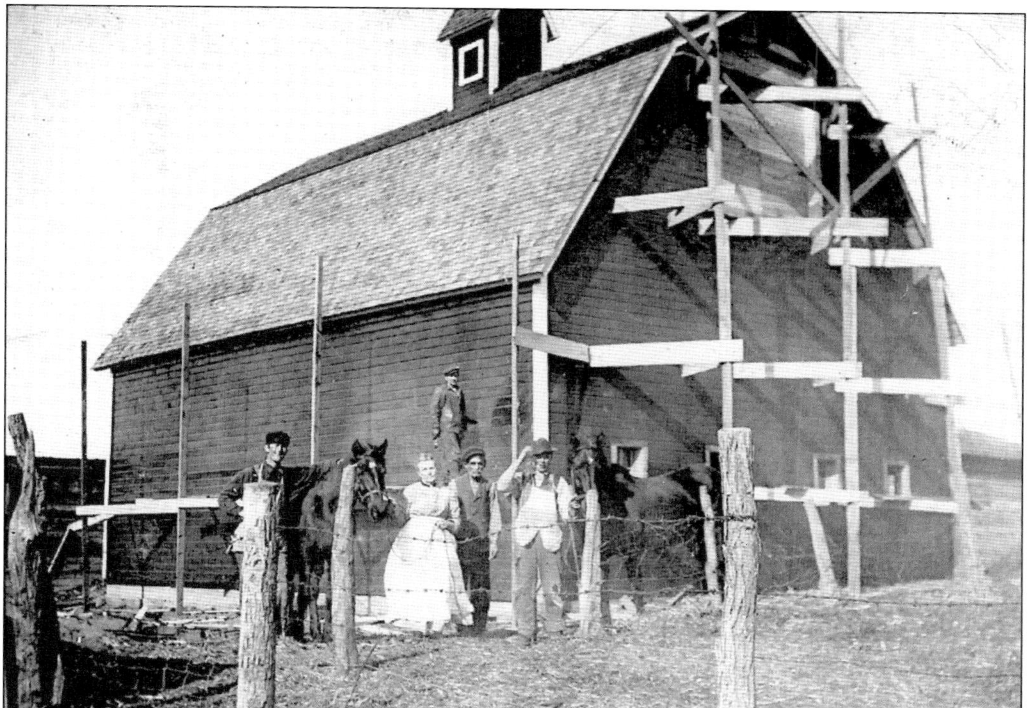

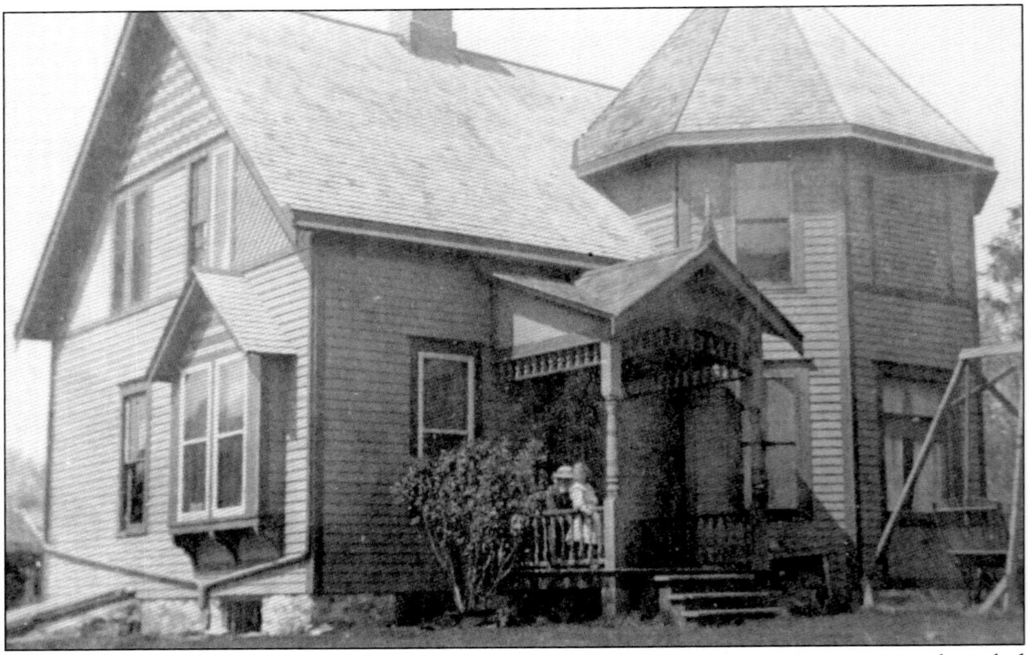

The Pepins and LaPlants came together from northern New York to Minnesota and settled northwest of the Mississippi and Crow Rivers in 1854. The land office record reflects that range 23 and sections 22 and 23 in Otsego Township were claimed by Charles LaPlant on May 26, 1856. Charles LaPlant was the fourth permanent settler to arrive in Otsego. Although some records list Eusebee (Ozier) LaPlant as the wife of Charles LaPlant, the 1860 census and each thereafter recorded Elizabeth LaPlant to be Charles's wife until her death on November 19, 1893. The LaPlant home shown above was quite ornate for the time and is still regarded as a treasure. Pictured below is the Cooley farm, which was later owned by the Hamlet family. (Above, courtesy of Bank of Elk River, Otsego; below, courtesy of Otsego Heritage Preservation Commission.)

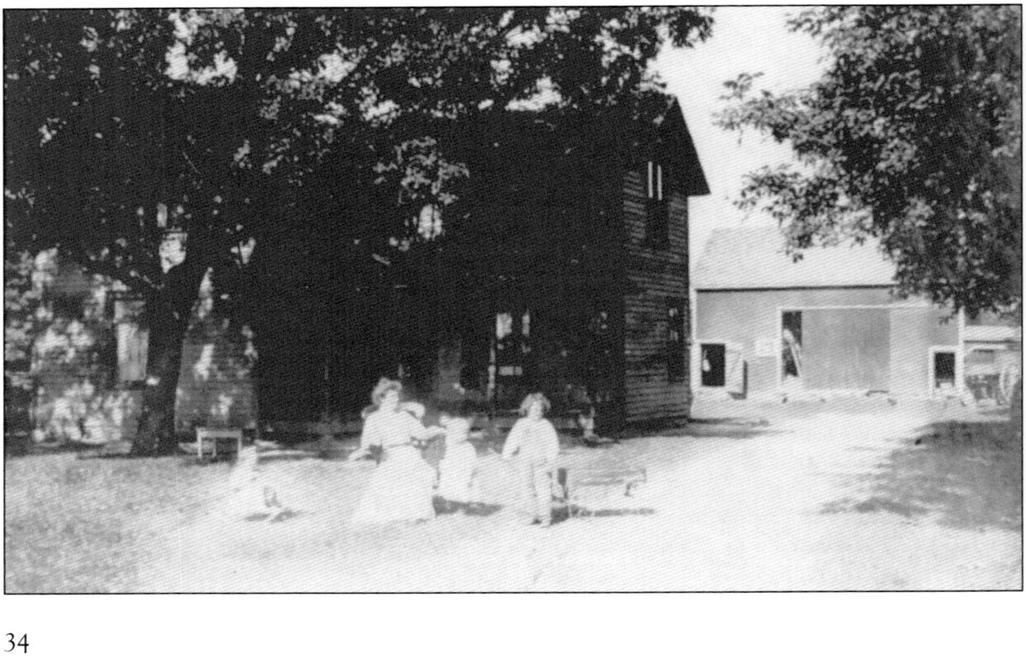

Seated on the front step of the John McDonald home in about 1910 are Orrin Peavey and grandmother Climena (Spencer) McDonald. The first marriage in Otsego was the union of Lewis McDonald and Climena Spencer on December 25, 1856, by O. H. Kelley, justice of the peace. Lewis and Climena's children were George; Joseph, who married Carrie Pickard; and Laura, who married Edmund Peavey. Orrin was the son of Laura and Edmund. Also shown here is the barn built by Frank Spencer in the early 1920s. Along with several others in the community, Spencer lost his farm during the depression. It was purchased by Fletcher Perrault. (Right, courtesy of Margaret Peavey; below, courtesy of John and Della [Bell] Anderson.)

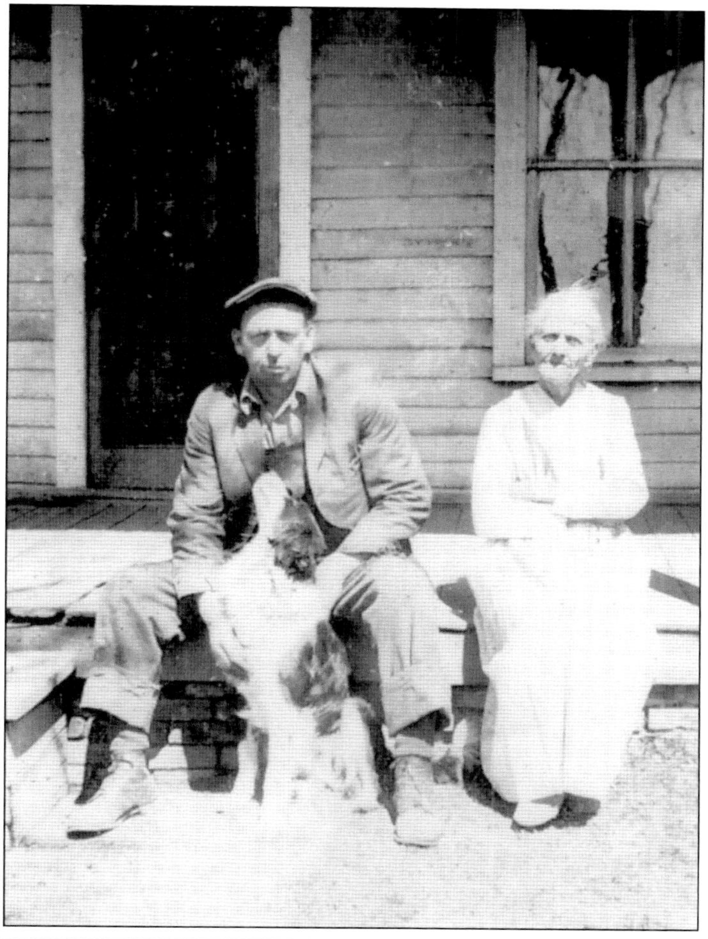

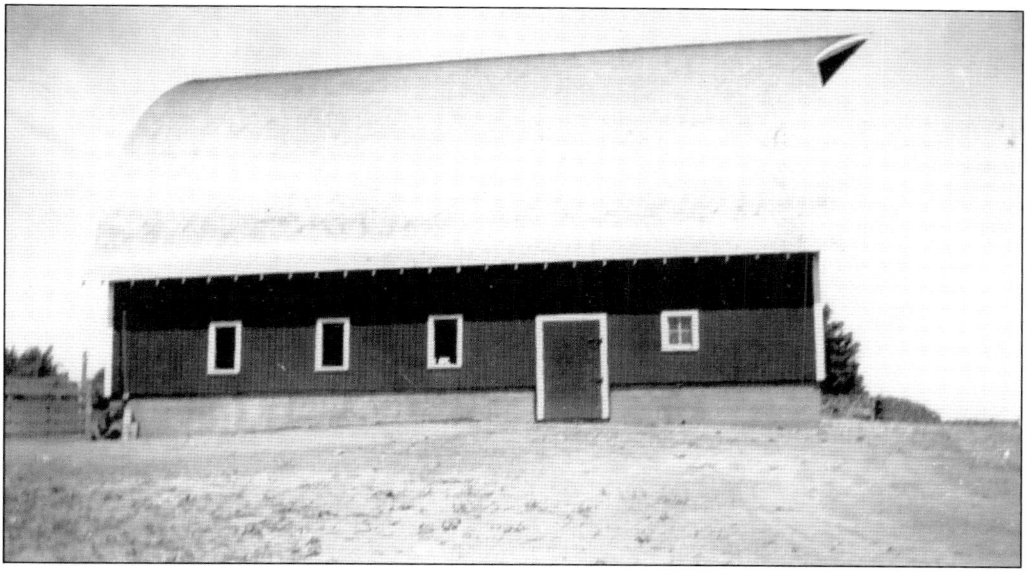

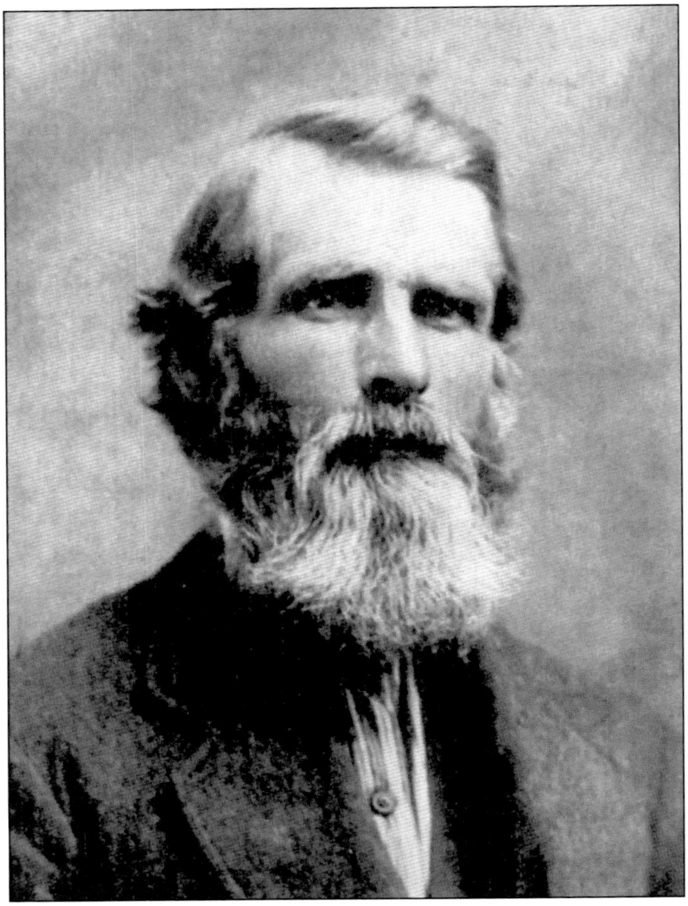

Pictured here is William Henry Holt, who married Julia Frances Ingersoll on August 27, 1859. They had 10 children, however, 2 of them died shortly after their births. Between 1873 and 1892, several families lost their children to specific diseases, such as scarlet fever, typhoid fever, and diphtheria, while many causes of death were simply recorded in general terms of fever and croup. Also shown is the Holt farm located at 8982 Mason Avenue northeast in Otsego. This picture was taken in 1930. (Left, courtesy of Otsego Heritage Preservation Commission; below, courtesy of Arne Engstrom.)

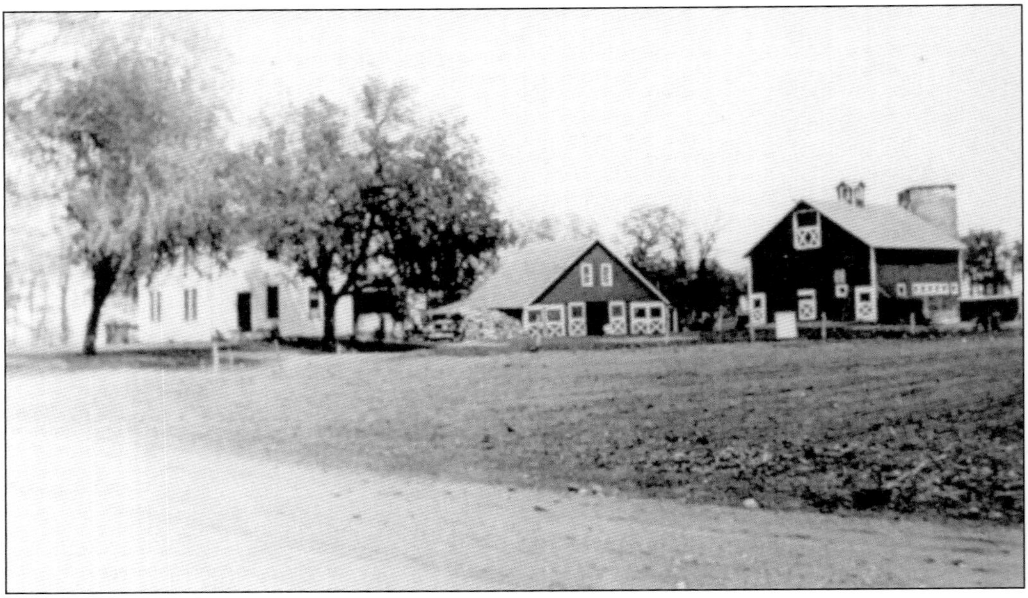

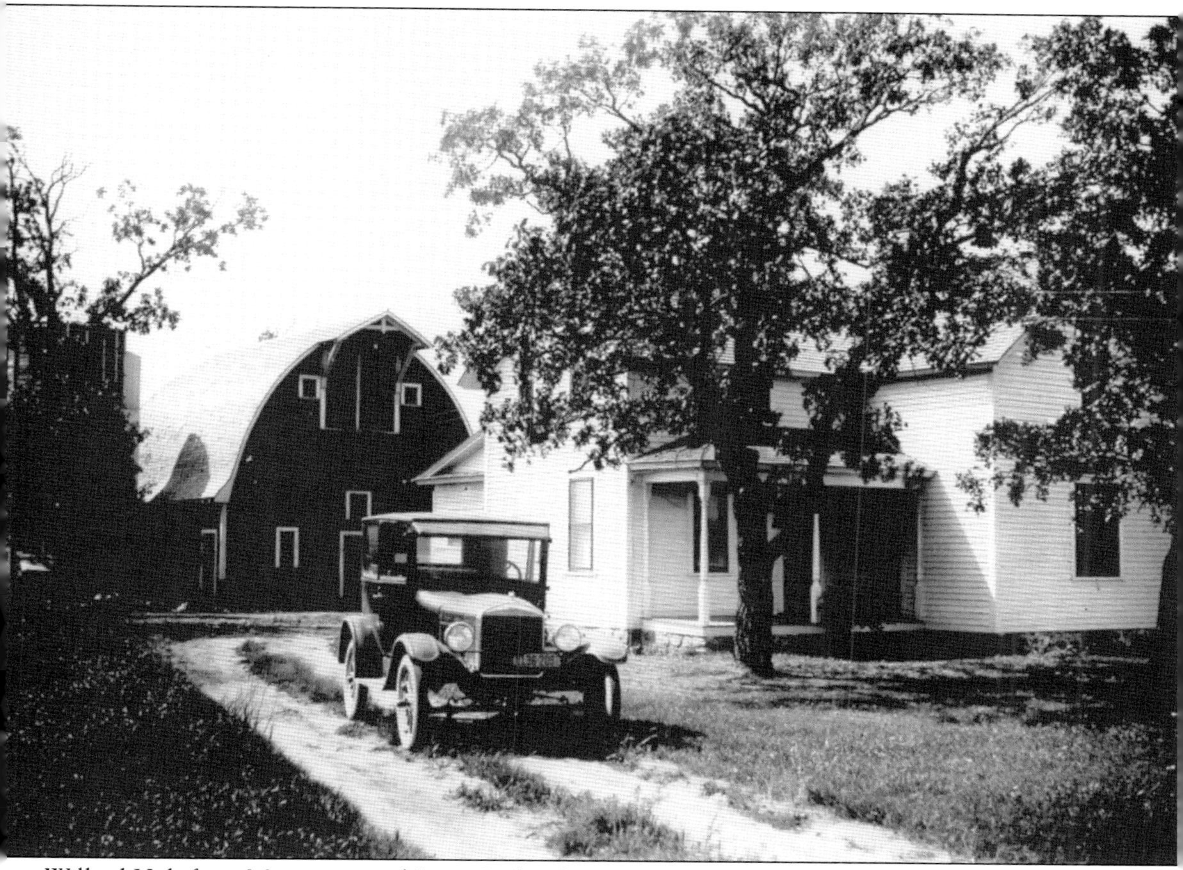

Willard Holt from Maine married Lizzie Parker from Canada. This picture, taken July 10, 1927, is of the Holt farm in Otsego, where Willard and Lizzie raised three sons, Ralph, Clifton, and Erwin. Ralph and his wife, Eva, lived on the farm prior to moving to a neighboring community. (Courtesy of Arne Engstrom.)

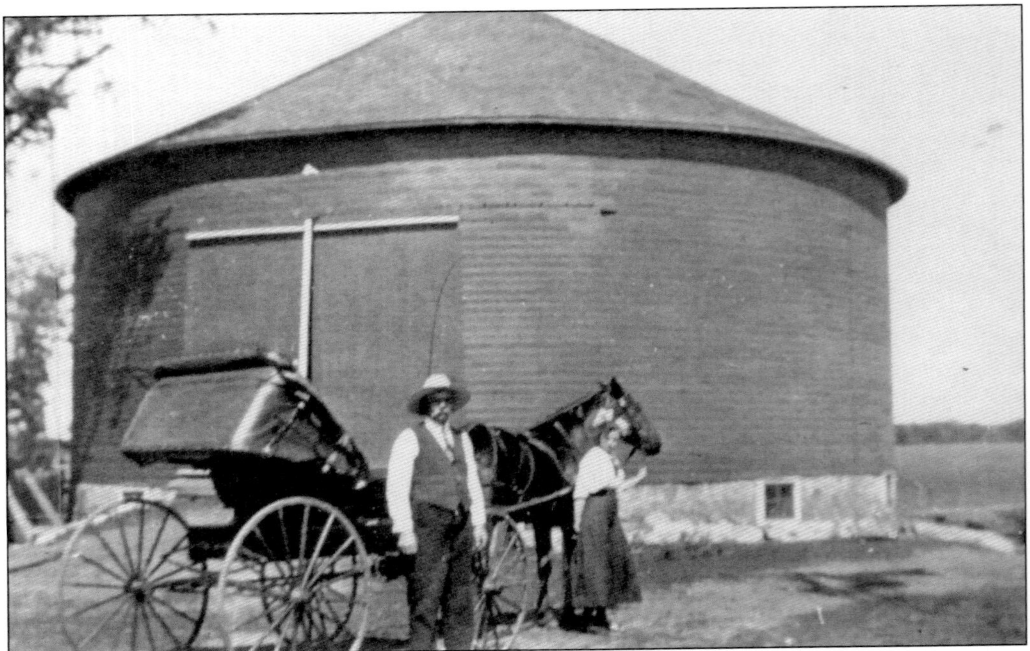

Joseph Lefebvre built this round barn located on Ferdinand Lefebvre's farm. When asked why the barn was round, Edward Lefebvre shared it was excellent for tending cattle. Hay was stored upstairs and thrown down to an area encircled by cows waiting to eat. Noel Lefebvre's youngest son, John, never married. He continued to farm and upon his death, passed the land to Edward's son Kevin, who lives there today. The Lefebvre family shared a story of when Johnnie Lefebvre, Ferdinand's son, bought a new buggy. Johnnie proudly stopped at the farm to show Ferdinand the purchase. Ferdinand was remembered saying the buggy was too good for Johnnie and exchanged it with a worn, but serviceable buggy. The story concludes with Emma, Johnnie's wife, not being pleased about the trade. Also pictured below is Richard playing at the Lefebvre farm in about 1937. (Above, courtesy of Mary Anne McNeil; below, courtesy of Patty and Richard Lefebvre.)

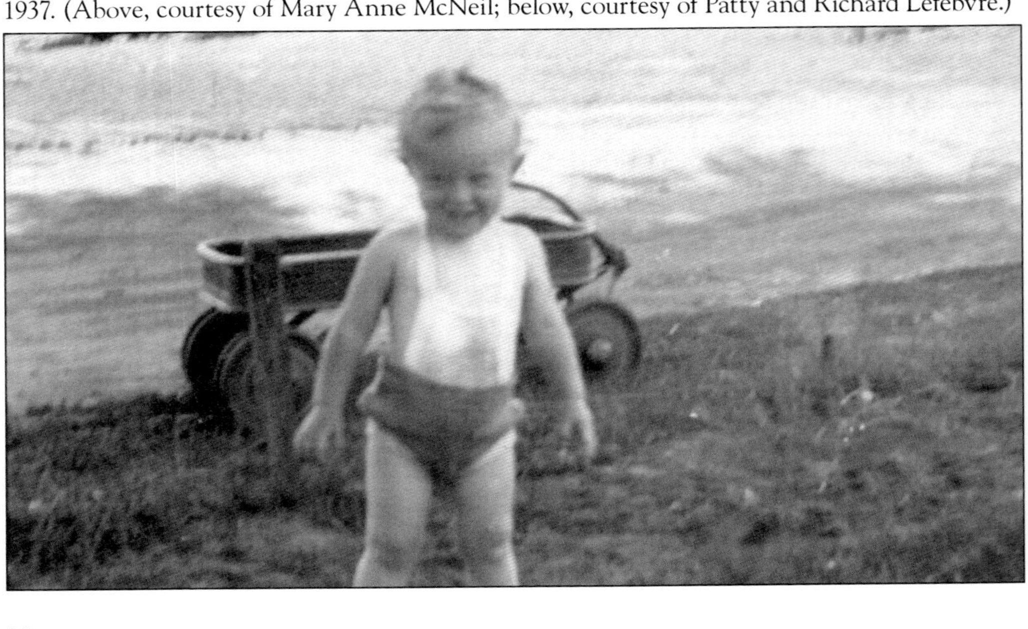

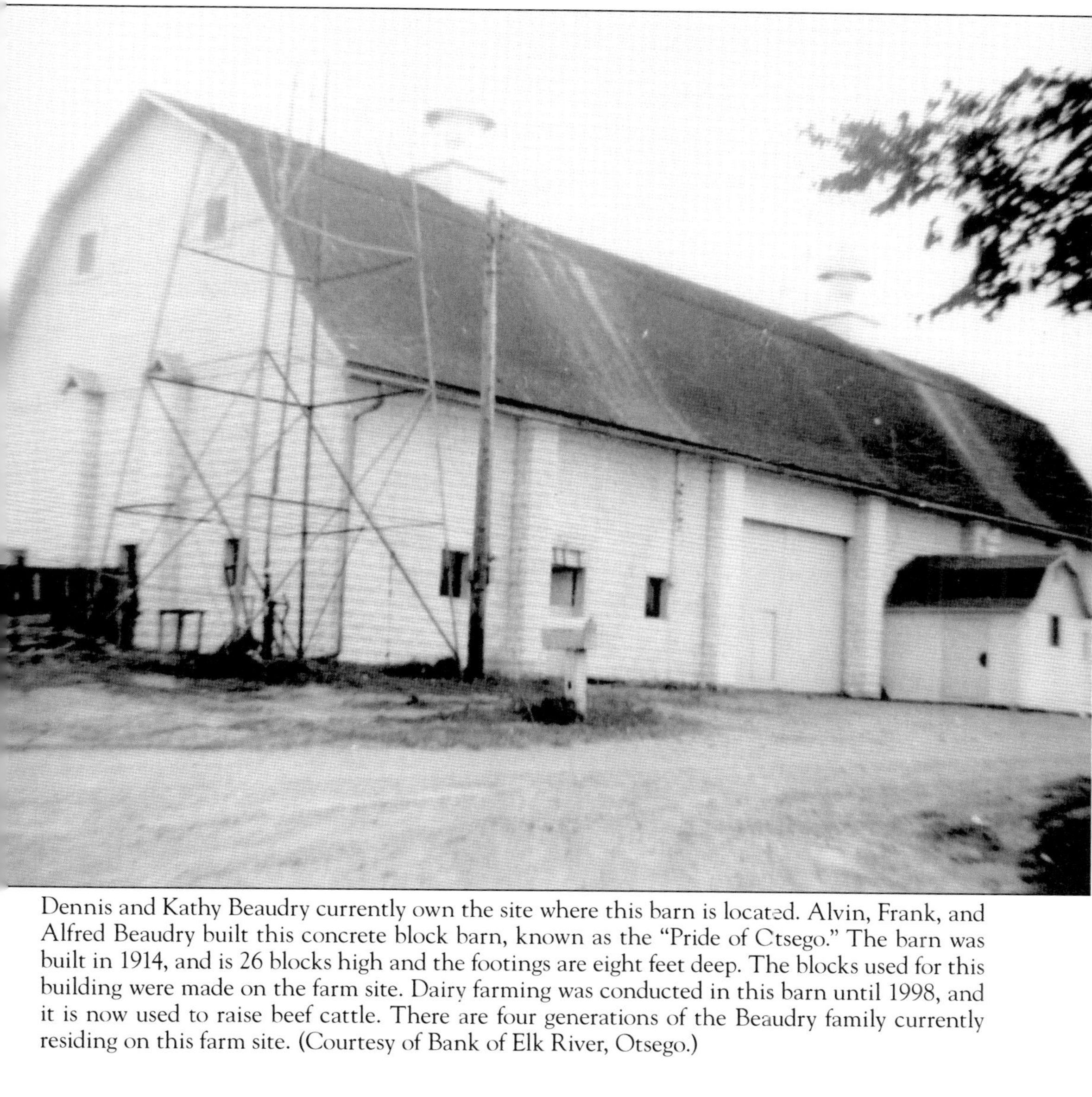

Dennis and Kathy Beaudry currently own the site where this barn is located. Alvin, Frank, and Alfred Beaudry built this concrete block barn, known as the "Pride of Otsego." The barn was built in 1914, and is 26 blocks high and the footings are eight feet deep. The blocks used for this building were made on the farm site. Dairy farming was conducted in this barn until 1998, and it is now used to raise beef cattle. There are four generations of the Beaudry family currently residing on this farm site. (Courtesy of Bank of Elk River, Otsego.)

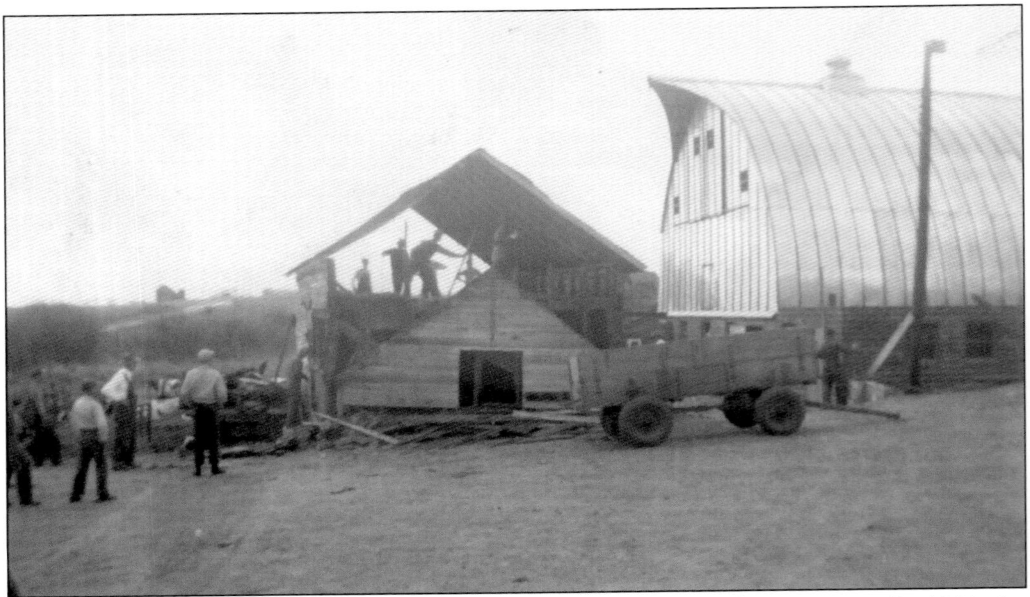

Out with the old and in with the new seems to be the theme of these pictures. In 1944, the Lefebvre family built the foundation for a new barn. When contractors from Anoka were contacted to determine what the best roof option would be, the recommendation was steel. The Lefebvres agreed and this one-of-a-kind barn was created. When the day came to begin filling it with hay, all the contractors came to the farm to watch the christening of the building. The barn withstood the weight of the hay and everyone celebrated. Gordy Lefebvre shared this barn is still standing, but will likely come down sometime soon. He is considering recycling the steel roof for other projects. (Courtesy of Gordy Lefebvre.)

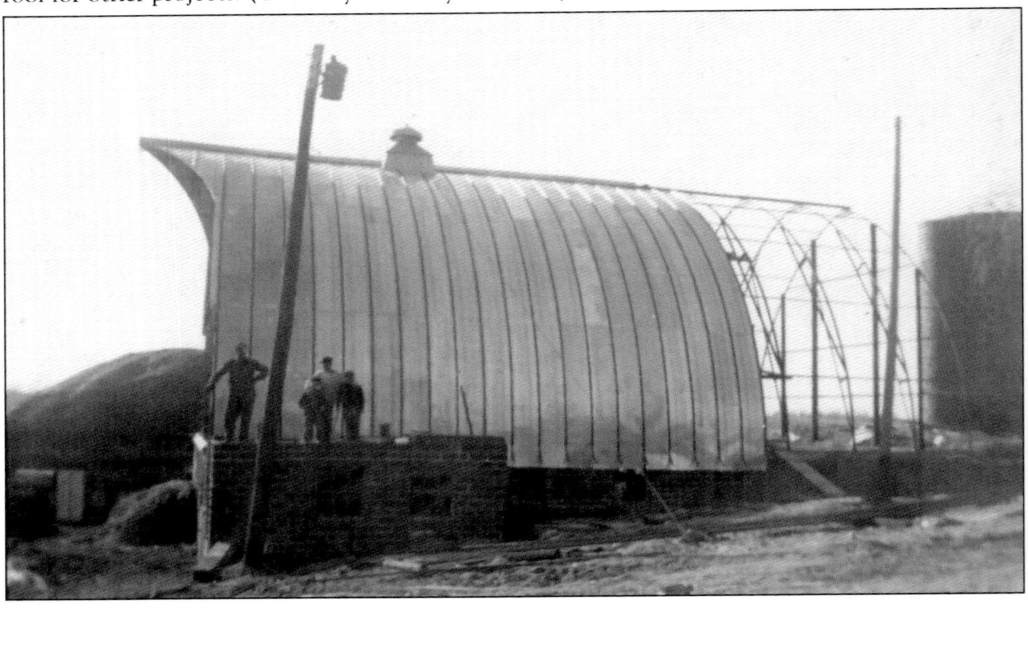

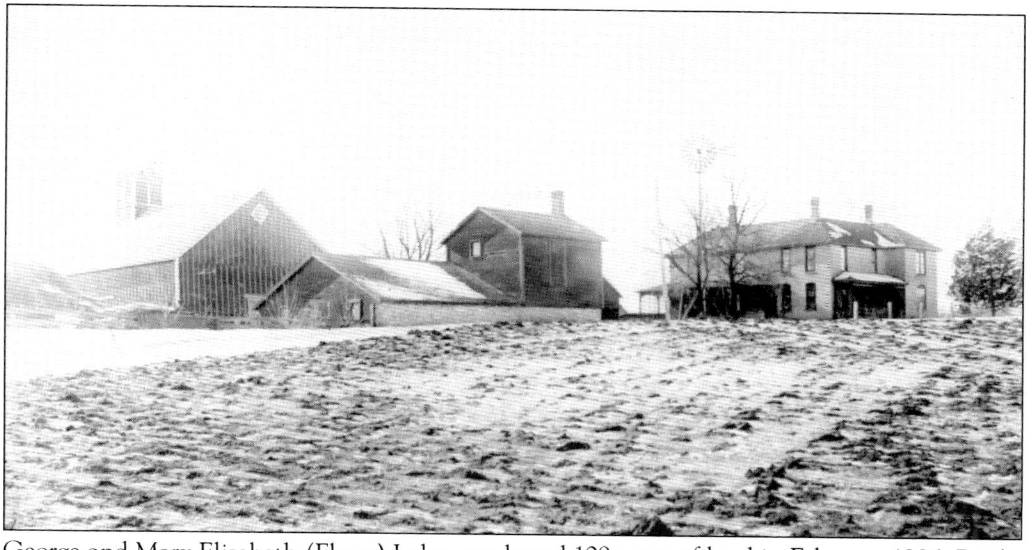

George and Mary Elizabeth (Ebner) Lahn purchased 109 acres of land in February 1886. Bricks from the nearby Vassar and Company brickyard were used to build the house. This picture of the farm site was taken in 1912, and the close up of the house was taken in 1914. In August 1910, telephone service was delivered to the house for three dollars a year, an indoor bathroom was installed May 1920, electricity was supplied by a home plant gasoline generator in May 1926 and provided by Northern States Power in 1938. George died in 1901, which meant that his widow was quite resourceful at providing for the family. Ralph Lahn, a son, fixed things for people, and the business grew. Many refer to Ralph's shop as the blacksmith's shop, but his daughter Wenda (Lahn) Duerr was not positive Ralph had been an actual "blacksmith." (Courtesy of Wenda [Lahn] Duerr.)

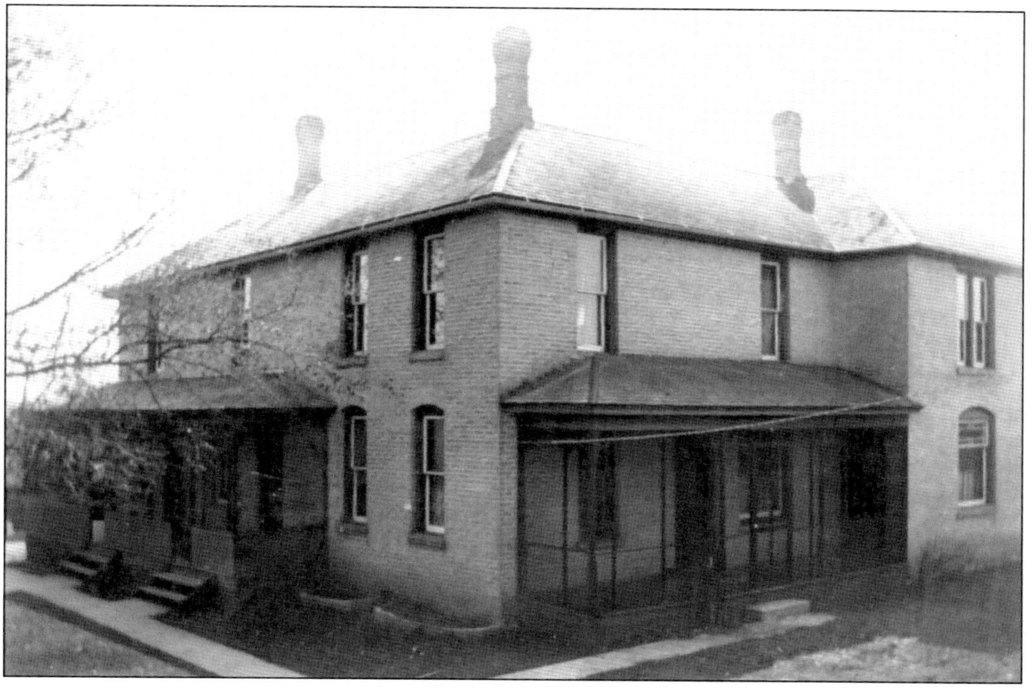

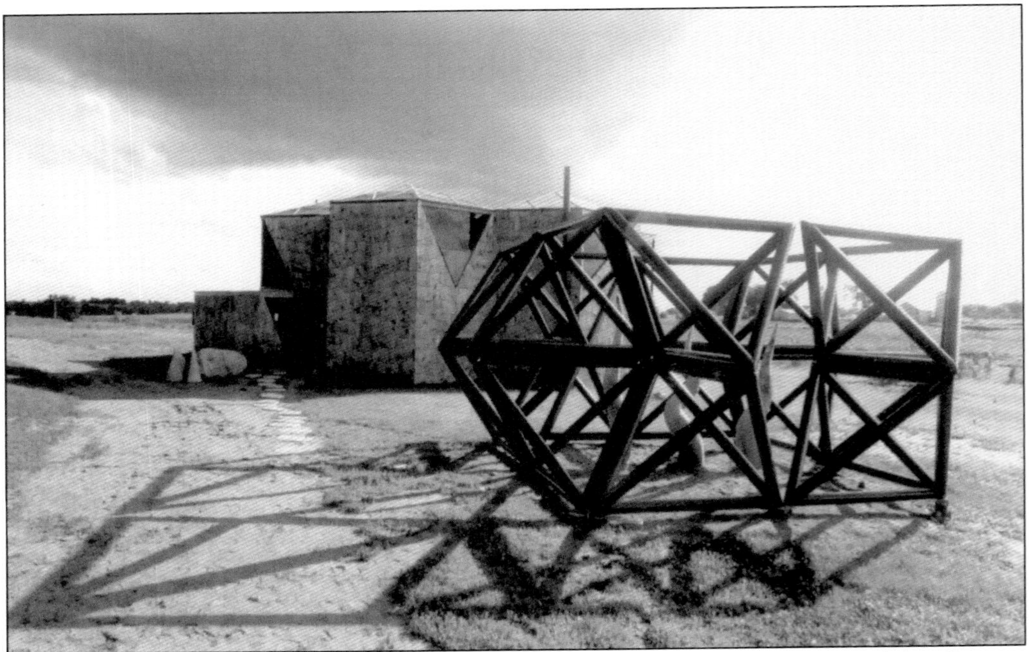

Located on the outskirts of Otsego was a leading-edge facility constructed by Stewart Turnquist, Bob Saxon, and Arlene DeCandia-Turnquist. The team had a vision of creating an evolving earthwork that would serve as an environment for studying visual patterns in nature. Patternstation was 48 acres of land, two houses, and a studio located along the Mississippi River. The structures were created using hexagons as the basic cellular building unit just as many plants are formed. Creating a visual and emotional house-to-land-to-human contact was the purpose for these buildings. Turnquist had built several hexagon houses for others until he changed his focus to turning the sculpture studio into a conference center. The location of Patternstation has become the Riverwood Inn and Conference Center. (Courtesy of Bob Saxon.)

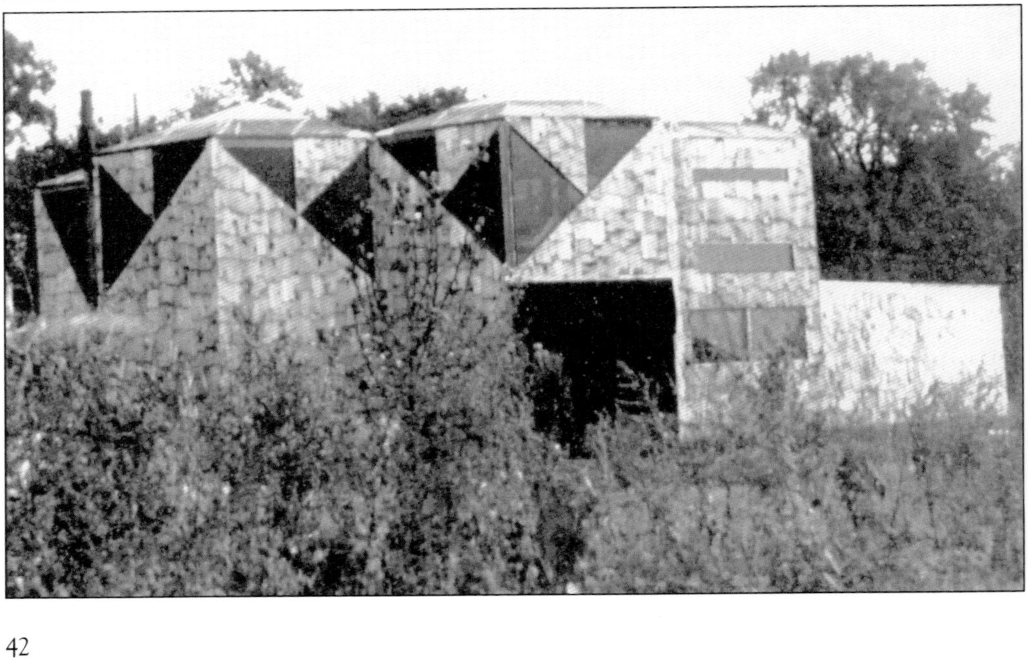

Four

Hometown Heroes

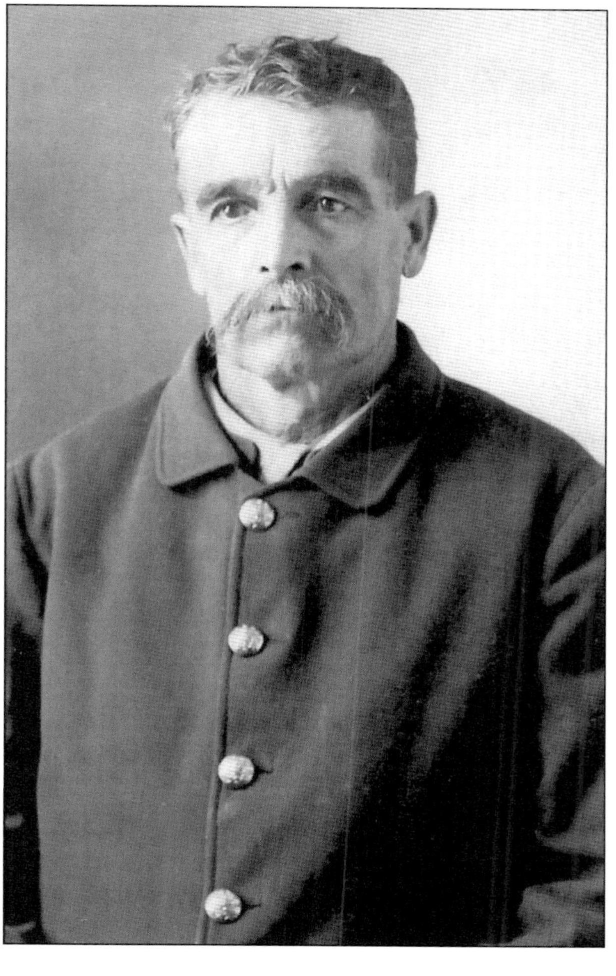

Lorenzo Smith, pictured here in his Civil War uniform, moved with his wife, Anna, and their child from Jamesport, Maine, to Otsego after the Civil War. In April 1861, the war beckoned many warriors from Otsego. Orson Washburn enlisted, and in less than two short years was laid to rest in a soldier's grave. On August 14, 1862, Edson Washburn enlisted in Company E, 8th Minnesota Volunteer Infantry. Leaving from Fort Snelling about the time the Sioux Massacre occurred and the Indian War broke out, Edson's infantry fought the Native Americans and then marched south to fight the Confederates. Edson was mustered out of Fort Snelling after three years of soldiering and returned to Otsego to look for a farm. (Courtesy of Arne Engstrom.)

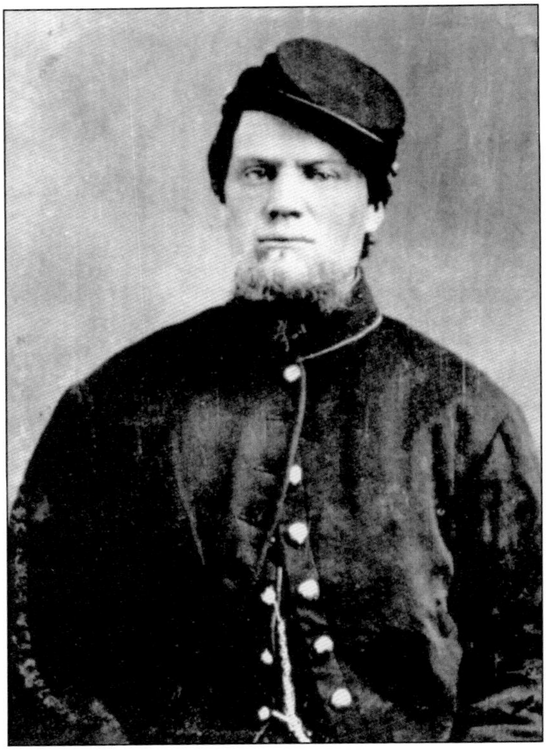

Charles H. Spencer served in the Civil War from August 14, 1862, until August 24, 1865, as a private in the 9th Minnesota Volunteer Infantry. On June 10, 1864, Spencer was captured at the battle of Brice's Crossroads and spent several months in Andersonville, or Camp Sumter as it was officially known. Although the 9th Minnesota Volunteer Infantry lost almost half its force, Spencer survived the experience and was freed on April 15, 1865, through an exchange process; one Union prisoner of war was exchanged for a Confederate prisoner of war at Vicksburg. During his imprisonment, Spencer suffered tremendously from malnutrition, but found the strength to walk from Mississippi to Missouri where his unit was stationed. With his regiment, he then walked to Fort Snelling in Minnesota. Pictured below is his wife, Mary Elizabeth "Libbie" (Slater Richardson) Spencer. (Courtesy of the Spencer family.)

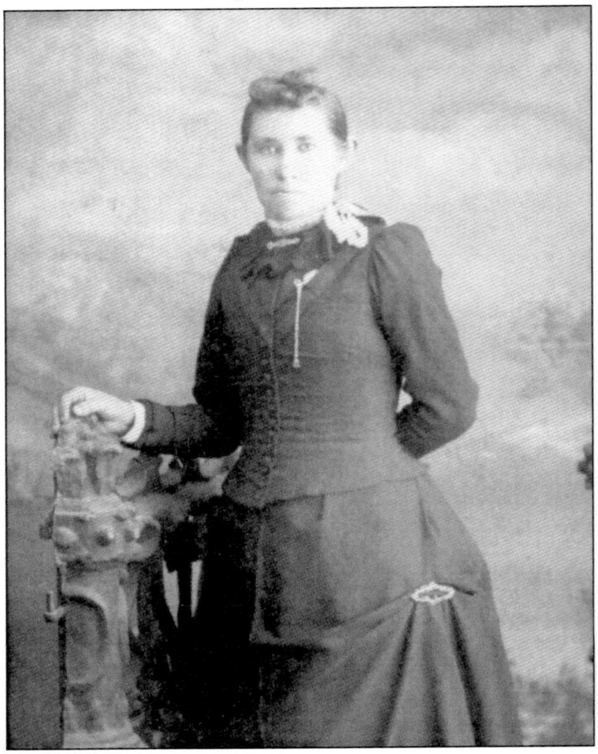

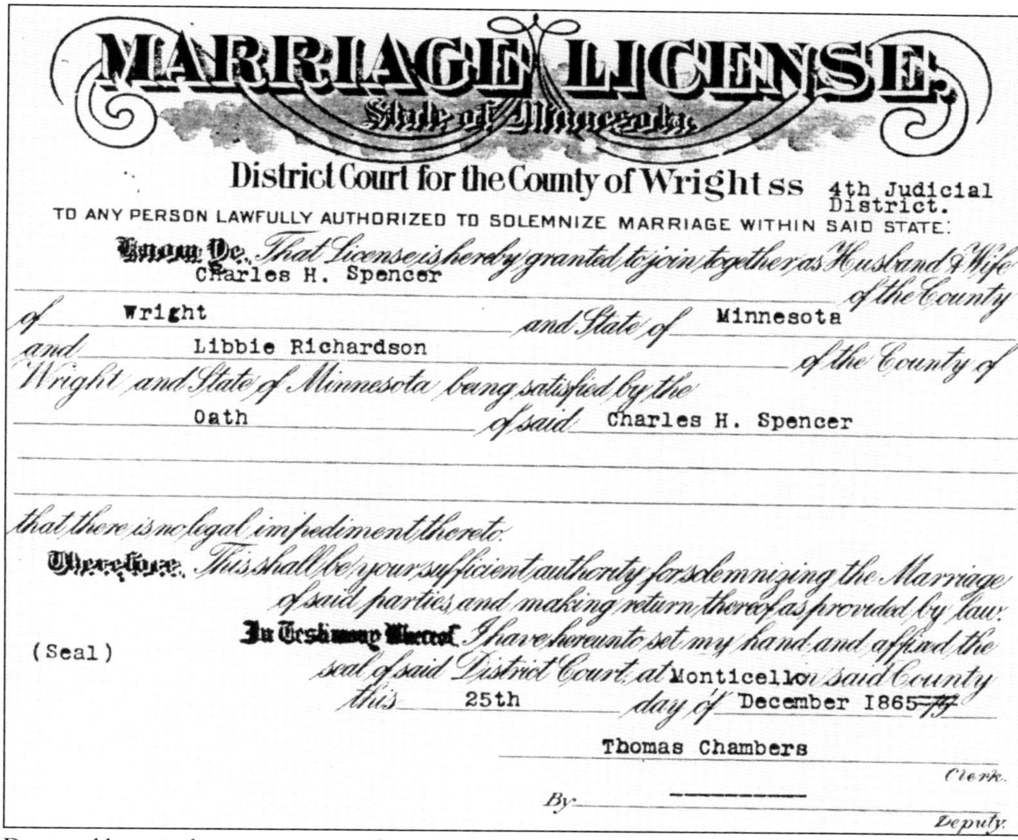
MARRIAGE LICENSE
State of Minnesota
District Court for the County of Wright ss 4th Judicial District.
TO ANY PERSON LAWFULLY AUTHORIZED TO SOLEMNIZE MARRIAGE WITHIN SAID STATE:
Know Ye, That License is hereby granted to join together as Husband & Wife Charles H. Spencer of the County of Wright and State of Minnesota and Libbie Richardson of the County of Wright and State of Minnesota being satisfied by the Oath of said Charles H. Spencer that there is no legal impediment thereto.
Therefore, This shall be your sufficient authority for solemnizing the Marriage of said parties, and making return thereof as provided by law.
(Seal) In Testimony Whereof, I have hereunto set my hand and affixed the seal of said District Court, at Monticello in said County this 25th day of December 1865
Thomas Chambers
Clerk.
By ______
Deputy.

Depicted here is the marriage certificate and marriage license for the union between Charles H. Spencer and Libbie (Slater) Richardson on December 25, 1865. They were married by justice of the peace Hiram K. Hill. Libbie's first husband, Richardson, was killed in the Civil War. Listed here are some of the many Otsego residents that served the United Army: Myron Bartlett, Alexander Borthwick, John Bowers, J. M. Burgan, B .F. Cooley, John Victor Daniels, George Henry Dillaber, Ripley Goodwin, William Henry Holt, Frank Johnson, Joseph McDonald, Lewis McDonald, John N. Morrell, Vernon R. Morrell, Charles Frederick Parker, Gerald Peavey, Leonard Snow Sr., Martin Spencer, and many more. (Courtesy of the Spencer family.)

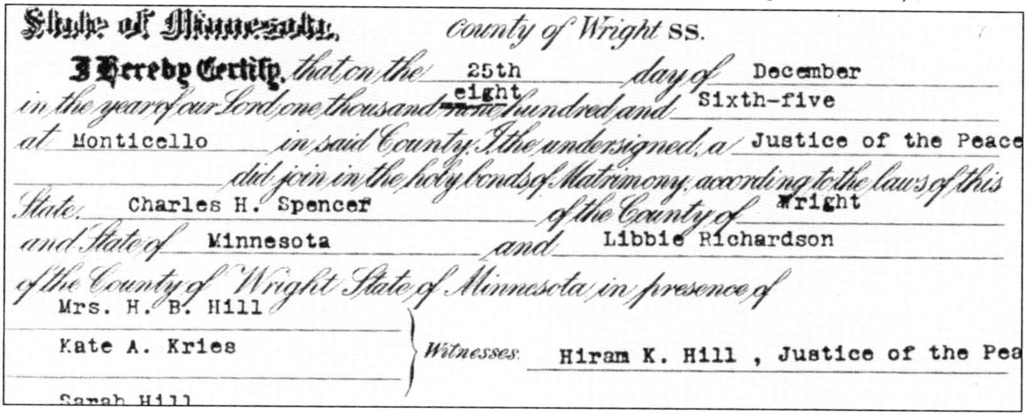
State of Minnesota, County of Wright ss.
I Hereby Certify, that on the 25th day of December in the year of our Lord one thousand eight hundred and Sixth-five at Monticello in said County, I the undersigned, a Justice of the Peace did join in the holy bonds of Matrimony, according to the laws of this State, Charles H. Spencer of the County of Wright and State of Minnesota and Libbie Richardson of the County of Wright State of Minnesota in presence of
Mrs. H. B. Hill
Kate A. Kries
Sarah Hill
Witnesses. Hiram K. Hill , Justice of the Pea

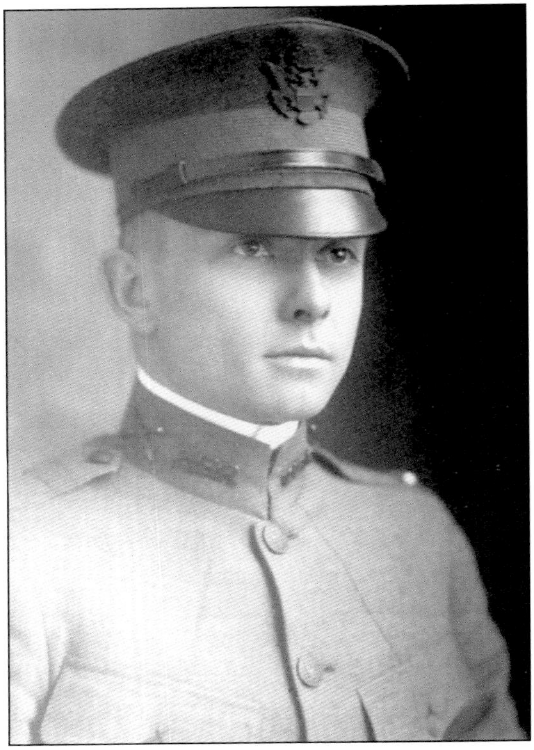

Pictured at left is Kenneth Orton, son of Adelia (Holt) Orton, in his World War I uniform. Pictured below are Mervin "Bud" and Verna (Joyer) Hauan taken in 1945. Hauan knew he was going to get drafted, so he contacted Earl Joyer in the Merchant Marines. Hauan and Verna Joyer rode with Joyer's uncle Joseph and aunt Louise Goodin to California so they could share gas coupons since gas was rationed. Hauan was called to duty and joined the U.S. Navy. Hauan and Joyer were married on May 17, 1944. Hauan's ship, the USS *Lowry*, was part of the second invasion of the Philippines. When the war was over, Hauan's ship escorted the USS *Missouri* into Tokyo Bay, where on September 2, 1945, Gen. Douglas McArthur and Gen. Yoshijiro Umeza signed the surrender aboard the USS *Missouri*. (Left, courtesy of Otsego Heritage Preservation Commission; below, courtesy of Merle and Mary Ann [Hauan] Eden.)

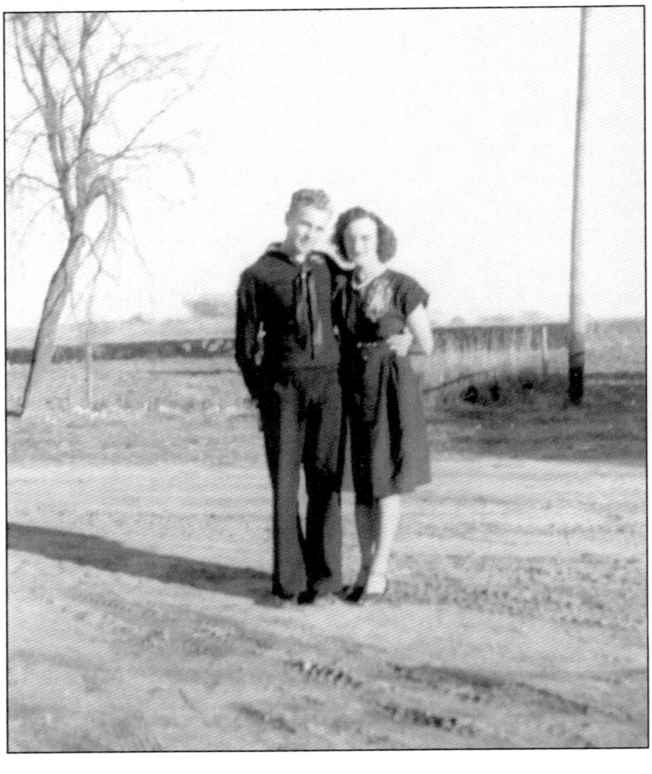

Five

School Days

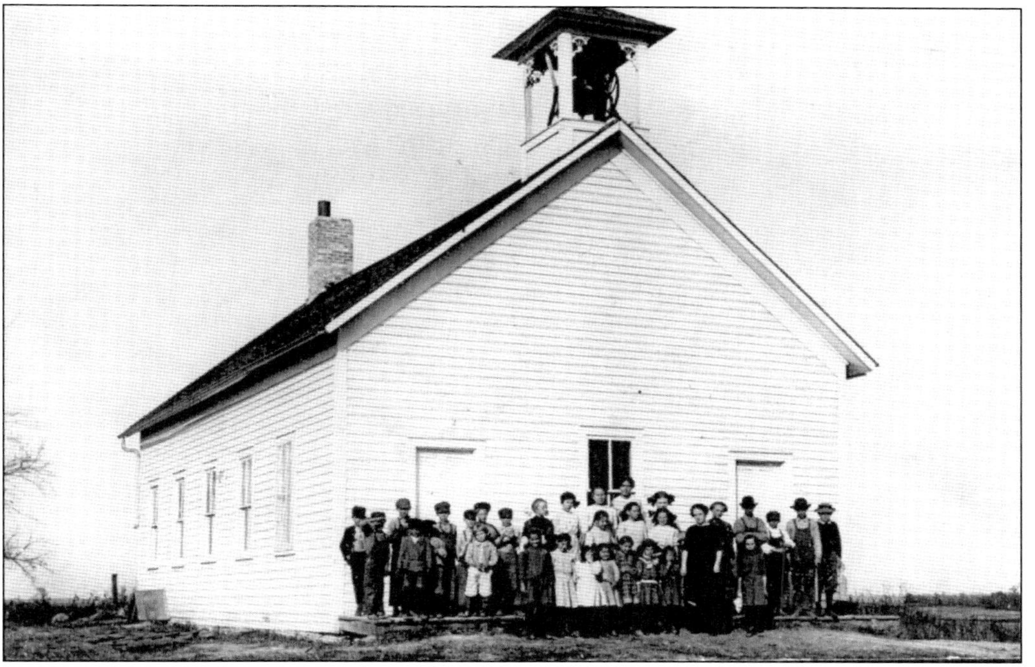

Land for School District No. 11, better known as Lily Pond, was dedicated in about 1870. The original school building burned down in 1913 and a new structure was built in 1914. After the school burned, classes were held in the church until the new school was ready for educating. Lily Pond closed in 1955, and its population was consolidated with the Elk River and Monticello school districts. The Lily Pond building is still in use today. After extensive remodeling, the building has been transformed into a home, but it remains an icon in the community. (Courtesy of Otsego Heritage Preservation Commission.)

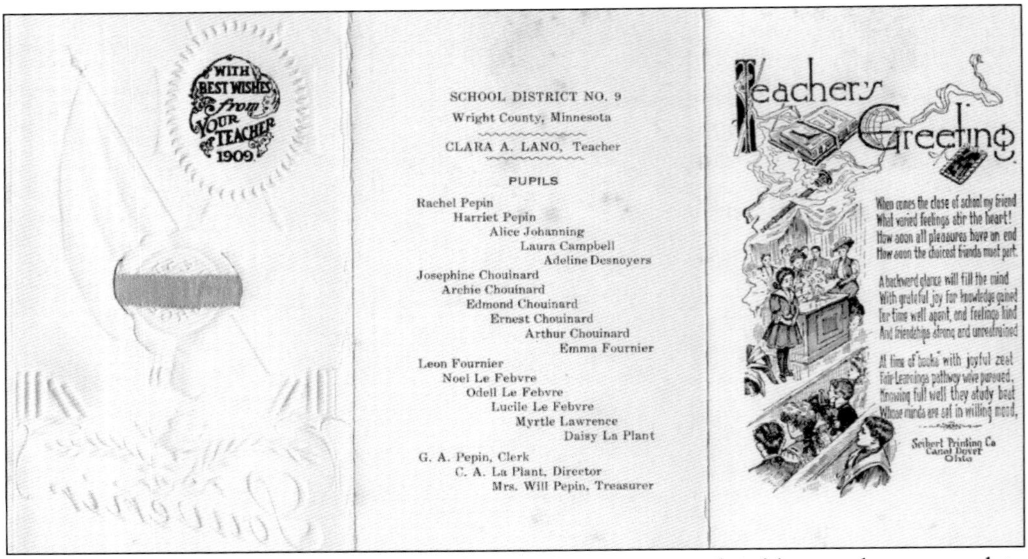

The teacher of School District No. 9, Clara A. Lano, gave each of her students a card in 1909 as a keepsake of the year together. A picture of the teacher was on the front of the card. Students in this class included Rachel and Harriet Pepin; Alice Johanning; Laura Campbell; Adeline Desnoyers; Josephine, Archie, Edmond, Ernest and Arthur Chouinard; Emma and Leon Fournier; Noel, Odell, and Lucille Lefebvre; Myrtle Lawrence; and Daisy LaPlant. School District No. 9 was closed in 1947, and its students were consolidated with Elk River. (Above, courtesy of David Stewart; below, courtesy of Otsego Heritage Preservation Commission.)

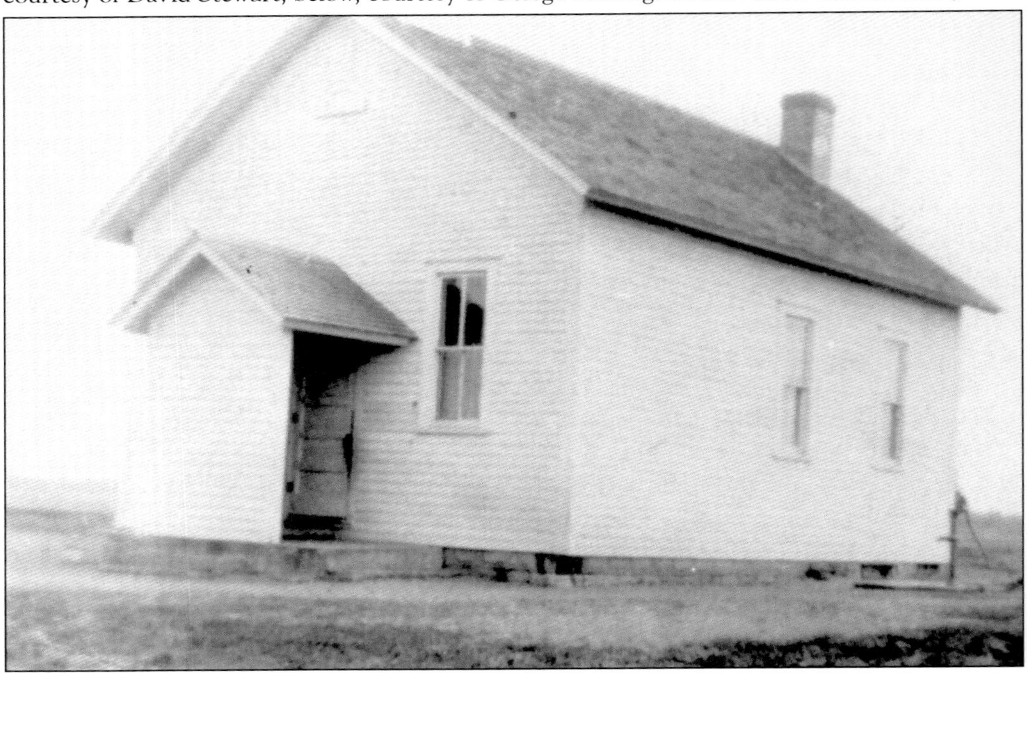

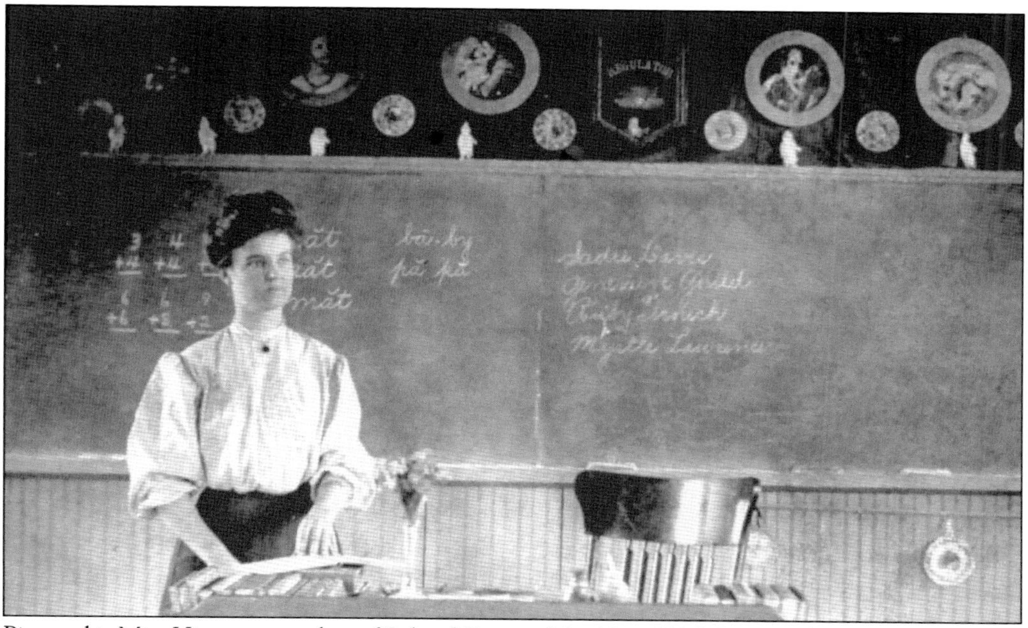

Pictured is Miss Hitsman, teacher of School District No. 10 in 1906. During the years of one-room schoolhouses, children started school when they were six years old. Kindergarten did not exist. Usually these country schools taught first through eighth grades. Some students went on to high school in Elk River or other neighboring communities; however many stayed on the farm to work. In the early years, children learned writing, orthography, reading, and arithmetic. By eighth grade, the spectrum included reading, grammar, spelling, arithmetic, history, elementary citizenship, penmanship, physiology, and current events. In one year, a single teacher taught nine subjects to the oldest students, while also teaching six or seven other subjects to younger students. Teachers were very competent and showed great dedication. School District No. 10, also known as the Otsego School, was closed in 1950, and students were transferred to Elk River. (Above, courtesy of Otsego Heritage Preservation Commission; below, courtesy of Wright County Historical Society.)

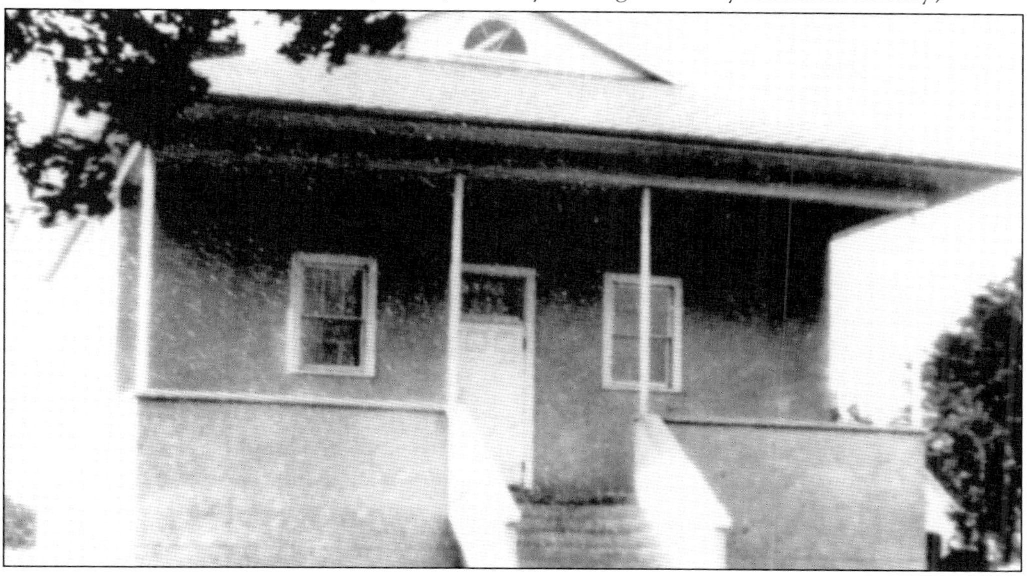

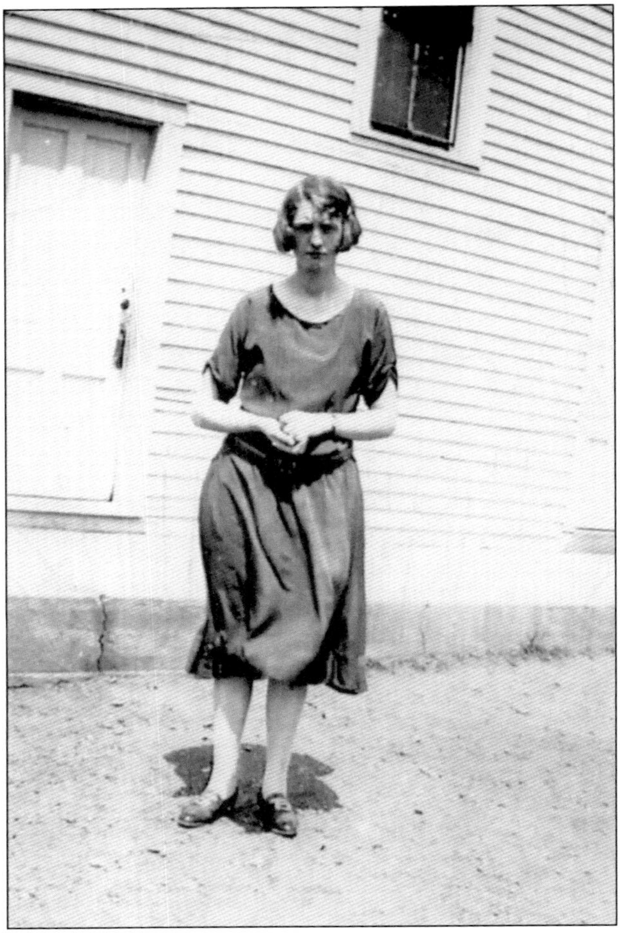

Pictured is School District No. 10's teacher for the 1925–1926 school year, Marie Taplin. The photograph below of the class was taken in June 1926. Some students included in this class were Rich Cooley, Bernice DeMars, Mildred Stroner, Laura Peavey, Dorothy Rambler, Leona Counter, Harry DeMars, Alveda Lefebvre, Marion Davis, Vernon Rich, Margaret Cooley, Florence Peavey, Lorene Stroner, Frances Counter, Verna Burkhart, Harold Burkhart, Bernard Vail, Gene Cooley, Everet Millhouse, Elmer Peavey, Roy Tenterson, Evelyn Rich, Lavern Rich, Lillian Lefebvre, Eugrega Counter, Edith Kiichli, Blanche Milhouse, Agnes Lefebvre, Irene Stroner, Joe Peavey, Gordon Cooley, and Art Cooley. (Left, courtesy of Otsego Heritage Preservation Commission; below, courtesy of Wright County Historical Society.)

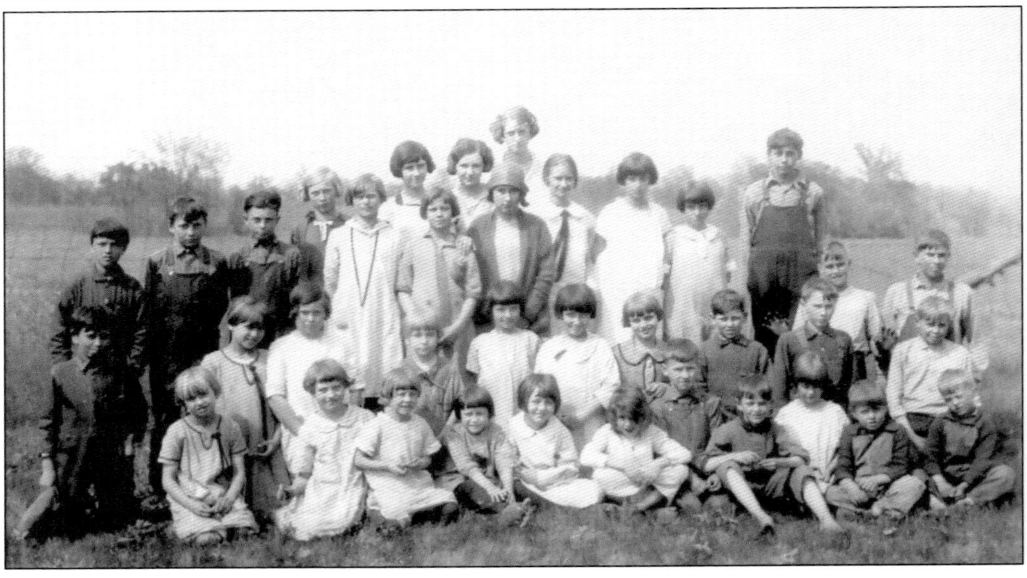

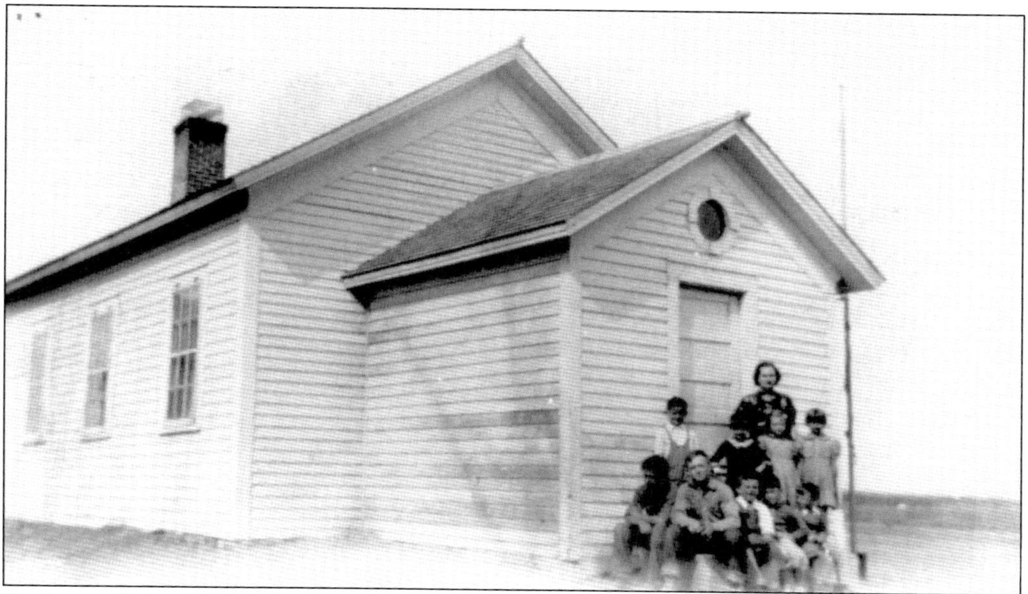

Students of the Greeninger School (School District No. 30) are huddled above on the front stoop for the class picture. This school closed in 1941. The lower photograph has Delphine Lefebvre posing with her class on September 29, 1926. Lefebvre taught at School District No. 12. She is the daughter of Johnnie and Emma (Martin) Lefebvre. Marie Corbin shared that some of the teachers held plays at their schools. Corbin fondly remembers when she got to play the character Mrs. Boggs. She did not remember the name of the play, but did remember she had to laugh a lot. (Above, courtesy of Otsego Heritage Preservation Commission; below, courtesy of Mary Anne McNeil.)

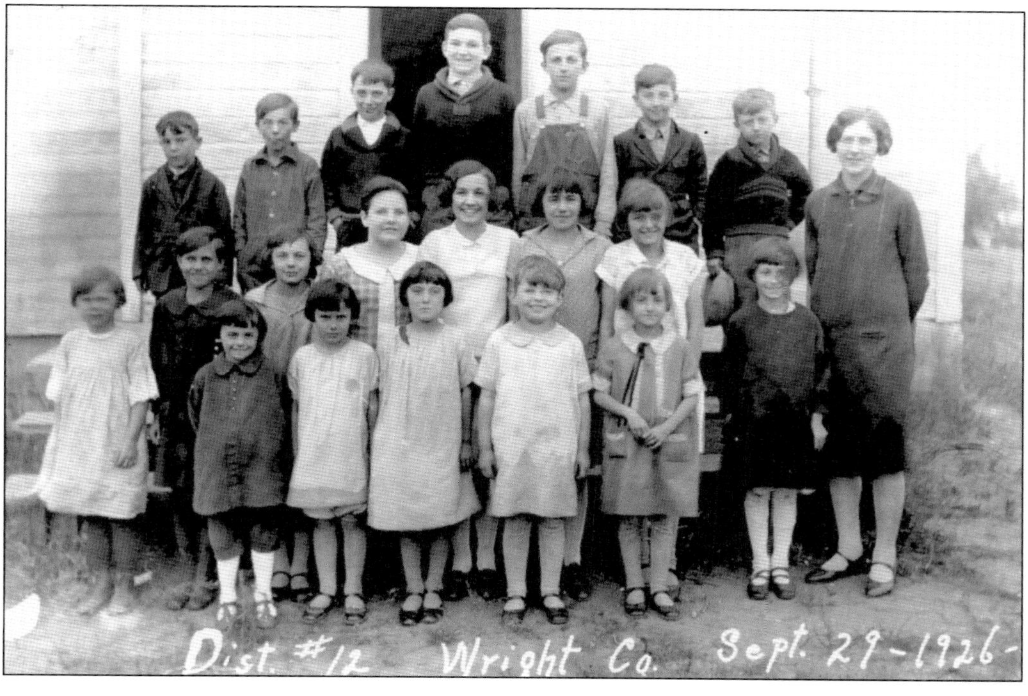

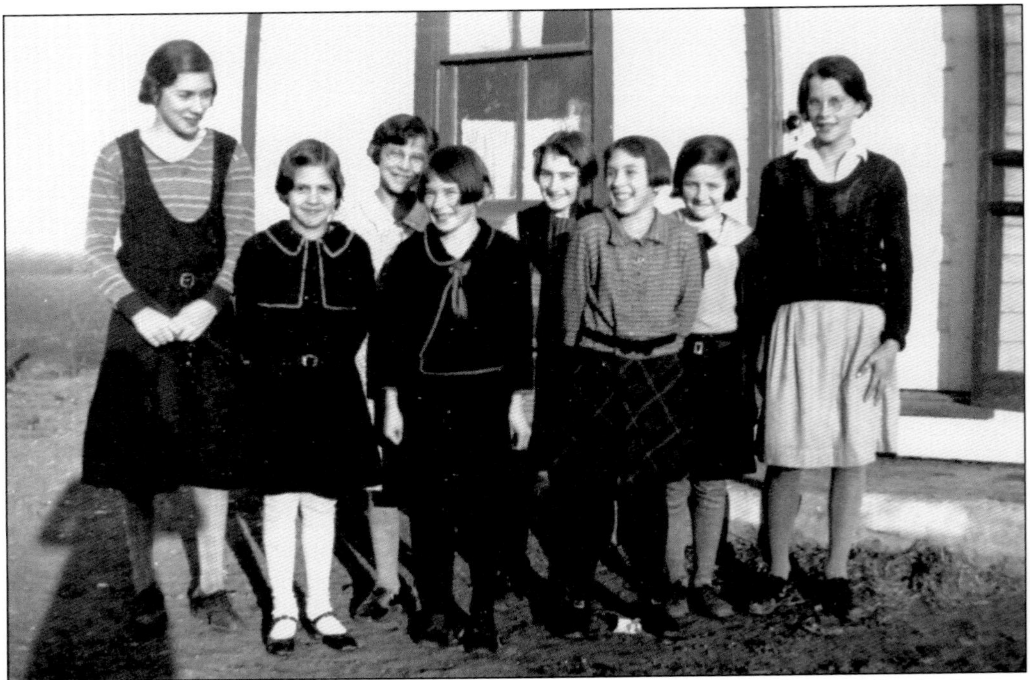

The teacher is taking the picture above of the students attending school district 112, also known as Richter School. They are, from left to right, (first row) Leah Barthel, Laverna DeMars, and Doris DeMars; (second row) Beatrice DeMars, Ellen Beaudry, Vivian DeMars, Dorothy Bistodeau, and Elma Hagel. This school was closed after the 1943–1944 school year. Erwin Specht had the contract to drive the high school students from Otsego to Elk River. Specht was known to pick up elementary students on his way by and deliver them to the appropriate school at no charge; he told the children he would make up the money when he transported them to high school in a few years. The photograph below was taken in 1937. (Courtesy of Elma [Hagel] Pouliot.)

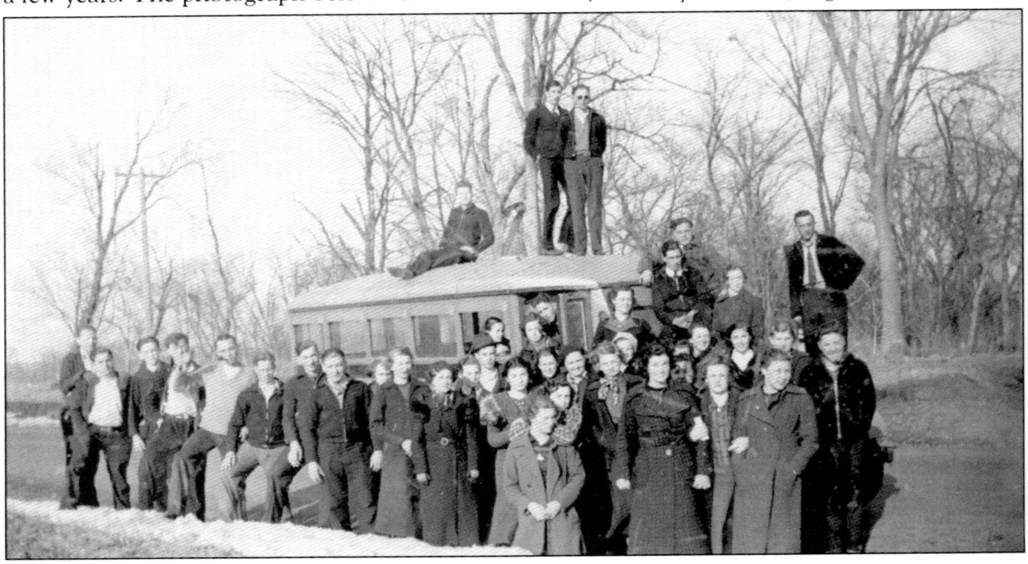

Six

COMMUNITY FUN

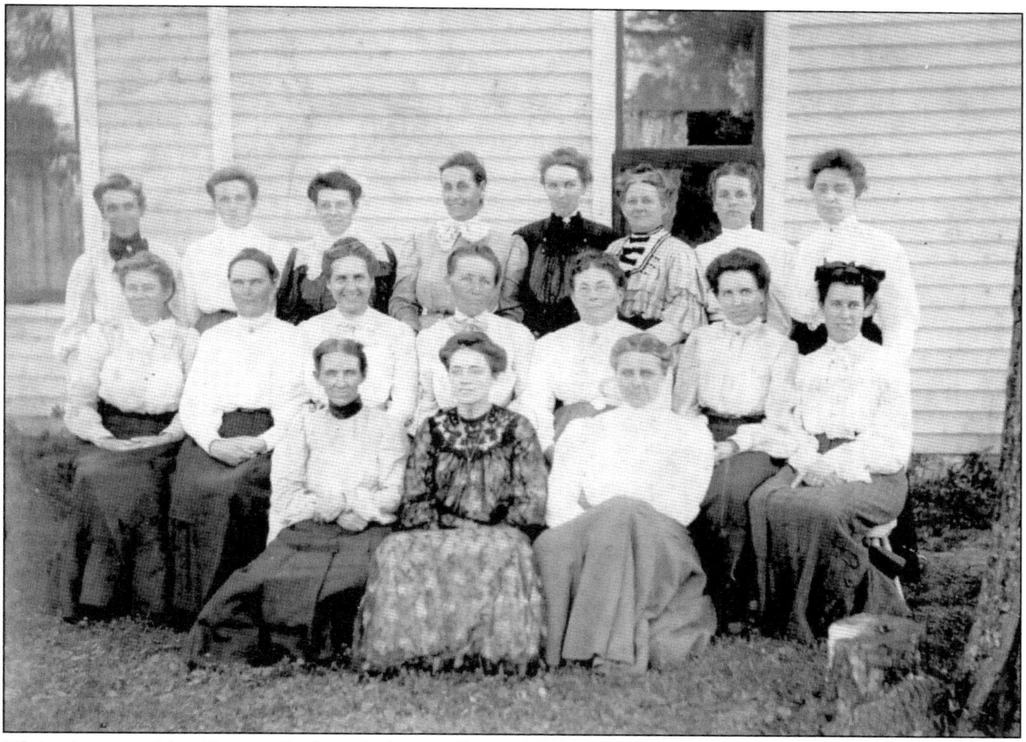

This picture of the Otsego Ladies Aid was taken on July 5, 1906. Women active in the community, such as Mattie Millhouse, Minnie Kiichli, Leone Bell, Ellen DeMars, Bess Mossman, Cora Bell, Addie Snow, and Nellie Spencer, to name a few, were members of the local ladies aid. This group was responsible for organizing community events and coordinating celebrations held at the church. These events included a Memorial Day parade and picnic and Thanksgiving Day meal. Life in Otsego evolved around the church and schools. (Courtesy of Otsego Heritage Preservation Commission.)

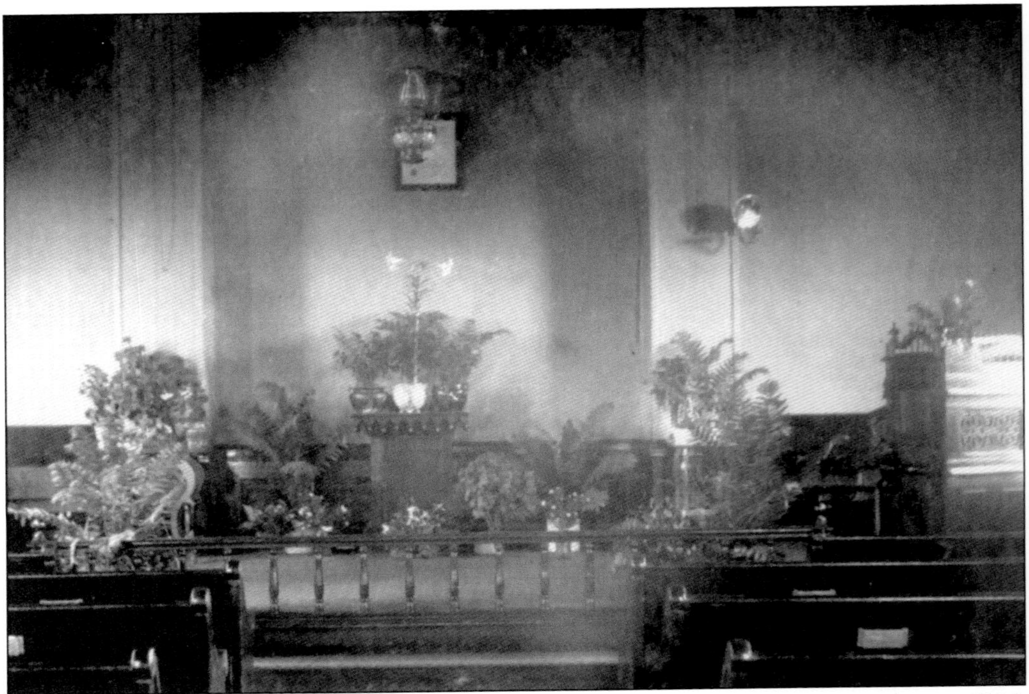

This interior picture of the Methodist Episcopal Church decorated for Easter was taken in 1906. Pictured below in the same year is a Sunday school class posed on the front steps of the church. Treasured photographs like these and the ones shown on the opposite page would have been lost if not for dedicated community members. Loretta Moos graciously provided these images to the Otsego Heritage Preservation Commission for the enjoyment and education of the community. (Courtesy of Otsego Heritage Preservation Commission.)

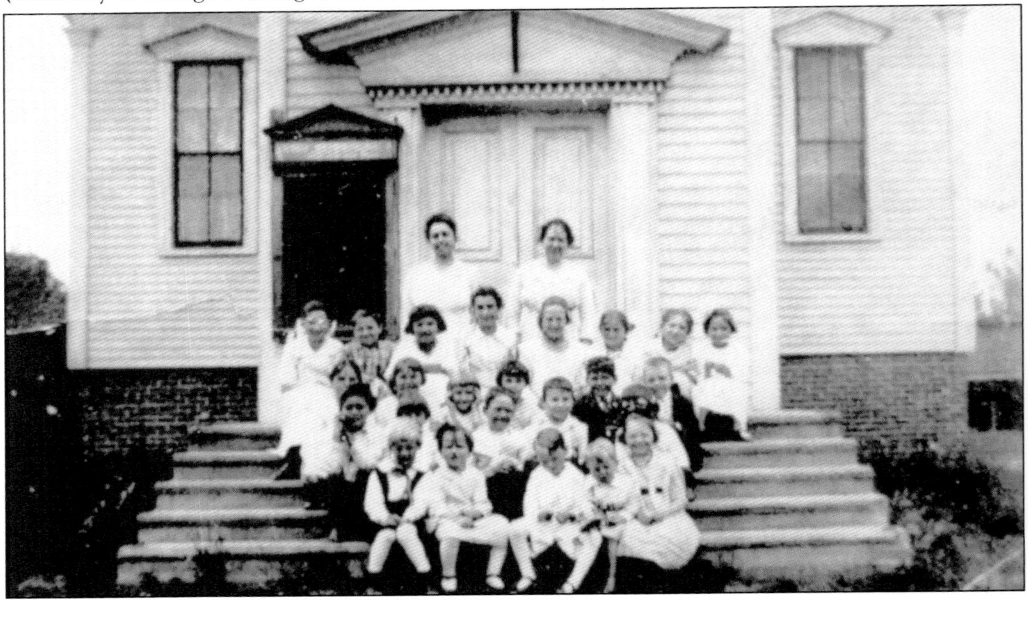

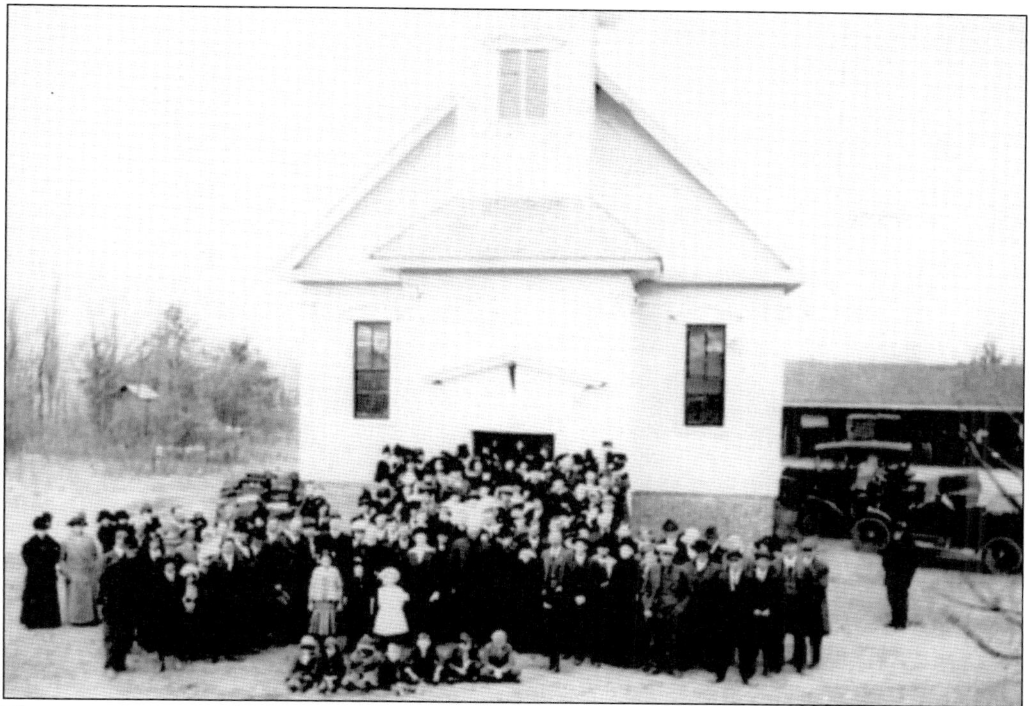

These pictures were taken in 1914. The community was celebrating Thanksgiving Day with a feast at the Methodist Episcopal Church. Families enjoyed sharing the holidays together. Events like this were often coordinated by the ladies aid. (Courtesy of Otsego Historic Preservation Commission.)

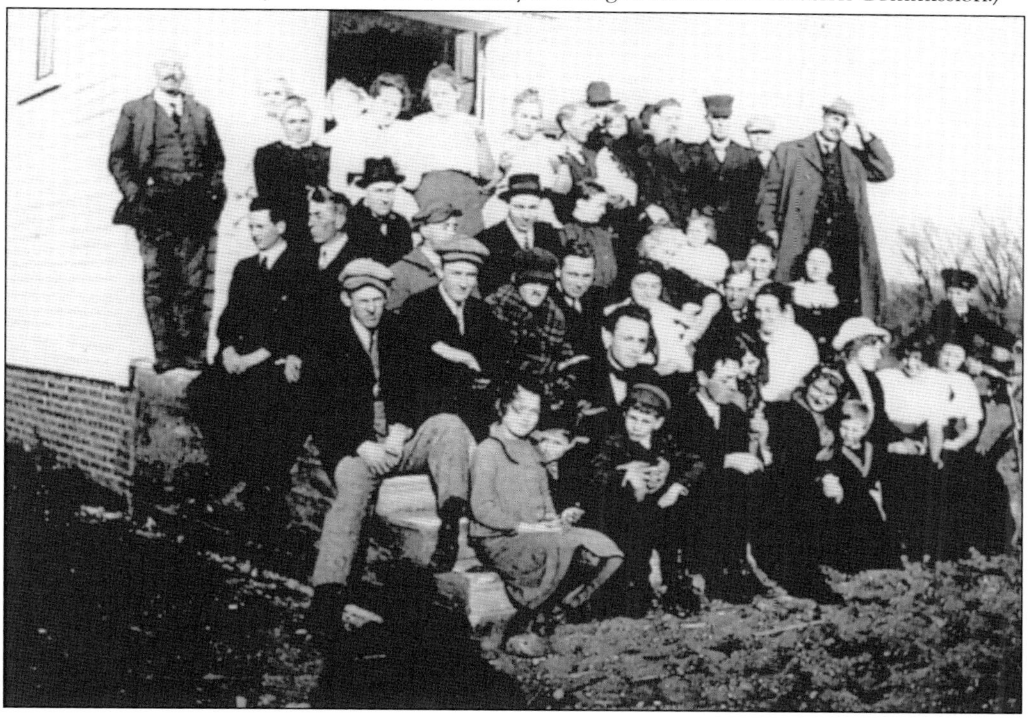

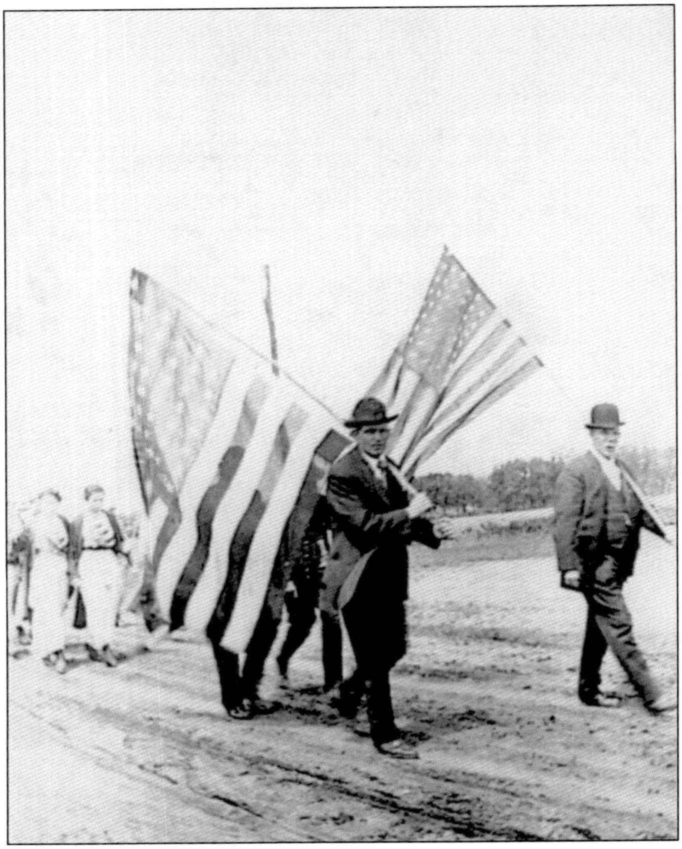

The Memorial Day celebration of 1915 is captured in these pictures. Orville Harrington is shown at left carrying a flag, while his wife, Mary, is pictured below working with the ladies aid to ensure the community enjoyed the day. Orville settled on a 120-acre farm in 1906, where he made extensive improvements, erected a sturdy home, and developed an excellent farm. Orville held the role of town constable, and for three years served as the director of School District No. 10. Orville married Mary Hayward on April 26, 1906. Aunt Mary, as she was lovingly called by community members, was well respected. Mary was active in the church and enjoyed assisting with social activities. (Courtesy of Otsego Heritage Preservation Commission.)

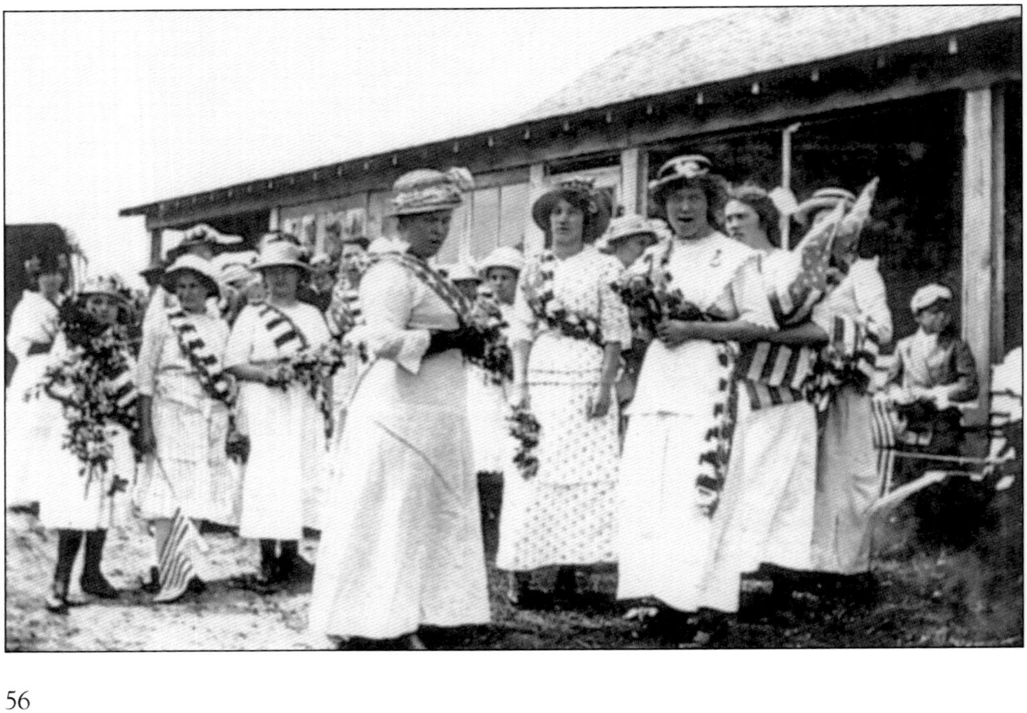

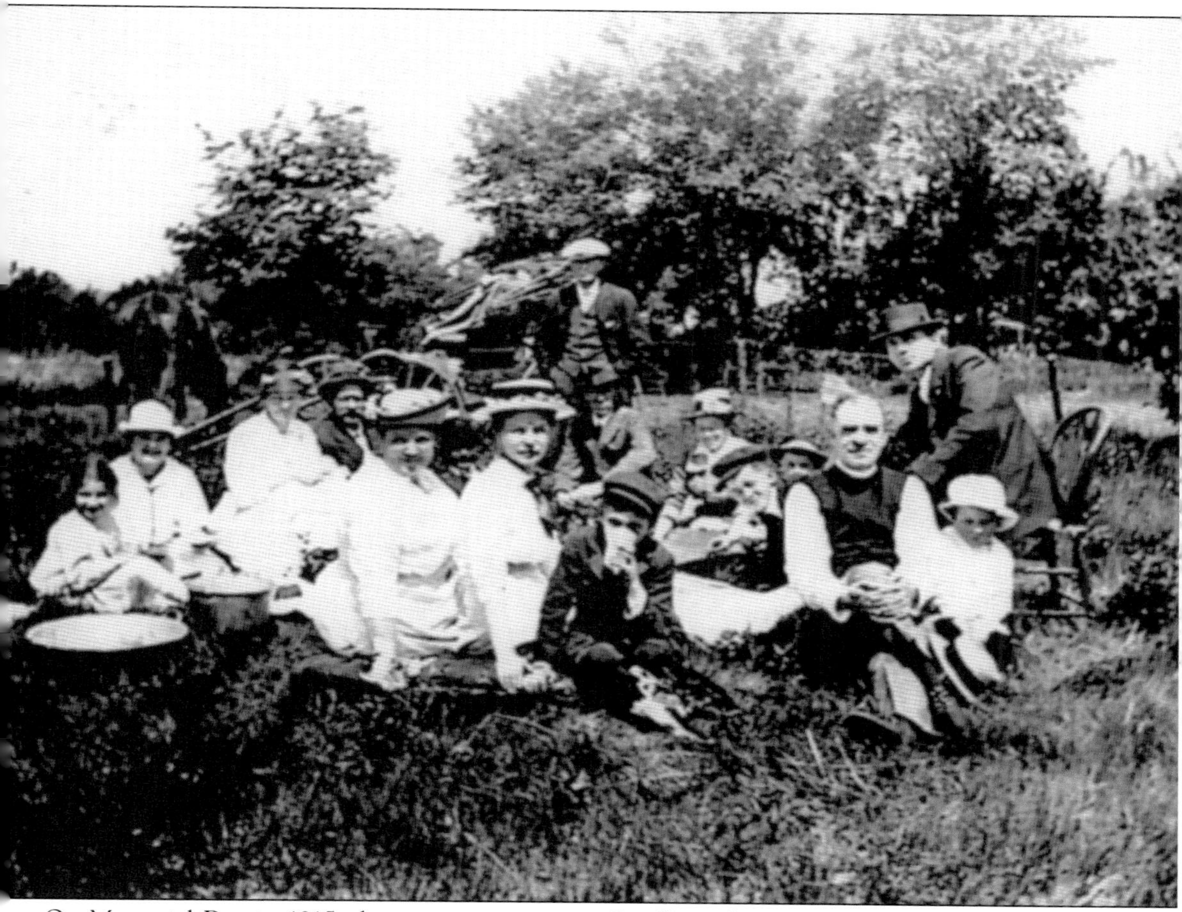

On Memorial Day in 1915, the community met at Orville and Mary Harrington's home and paraded to the church where they held services. After the service concluded, the community members walked to the cemetery to decorate the soldiers' graves. There was a community dinner held at the church. (Courtesy of Otsego Heritage Preservation Commission.)

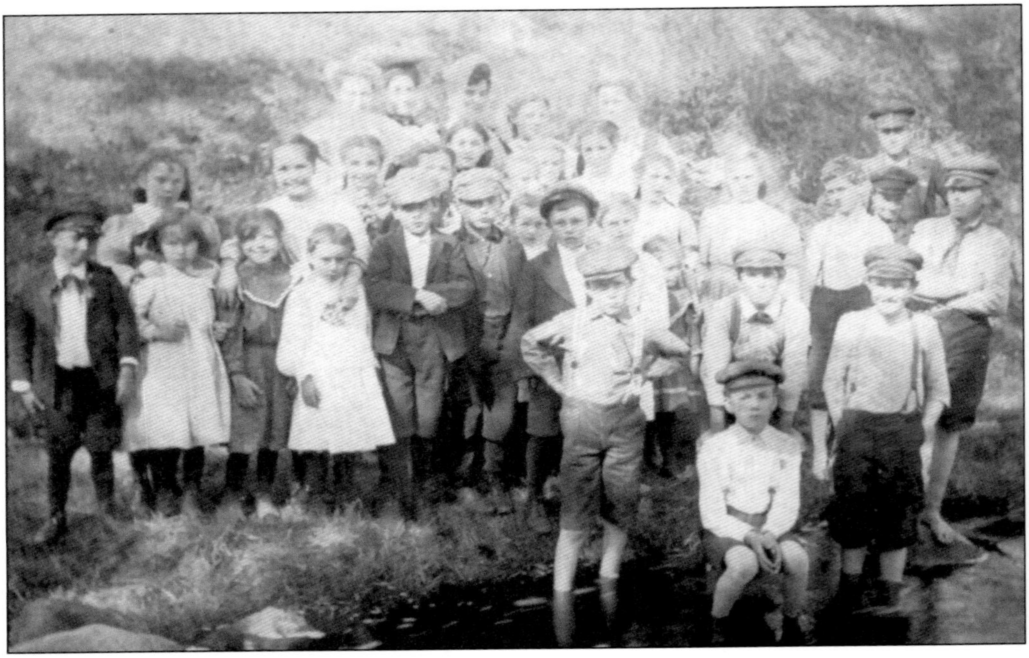

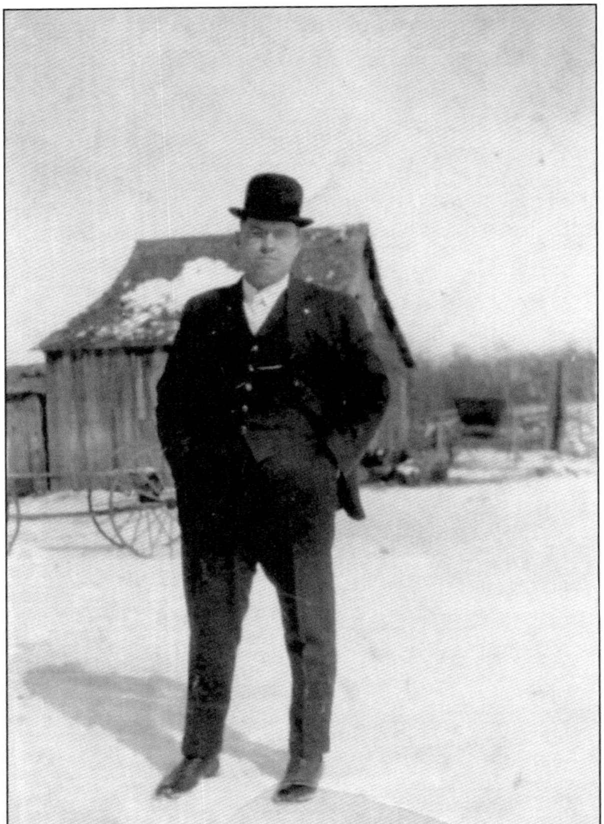

Seen above, Otsego children gather for an outing to the Otsego creek by the old city hall during Sunday school. The kids loved to play in the creek. It is believed the Methodist and Baptist families shared the community church. Pictured at left is Reverend Carr, the minister at Otsego Methodist Episcopal Church. (Courtesy of Otsego Heritage Preservation Commission.)

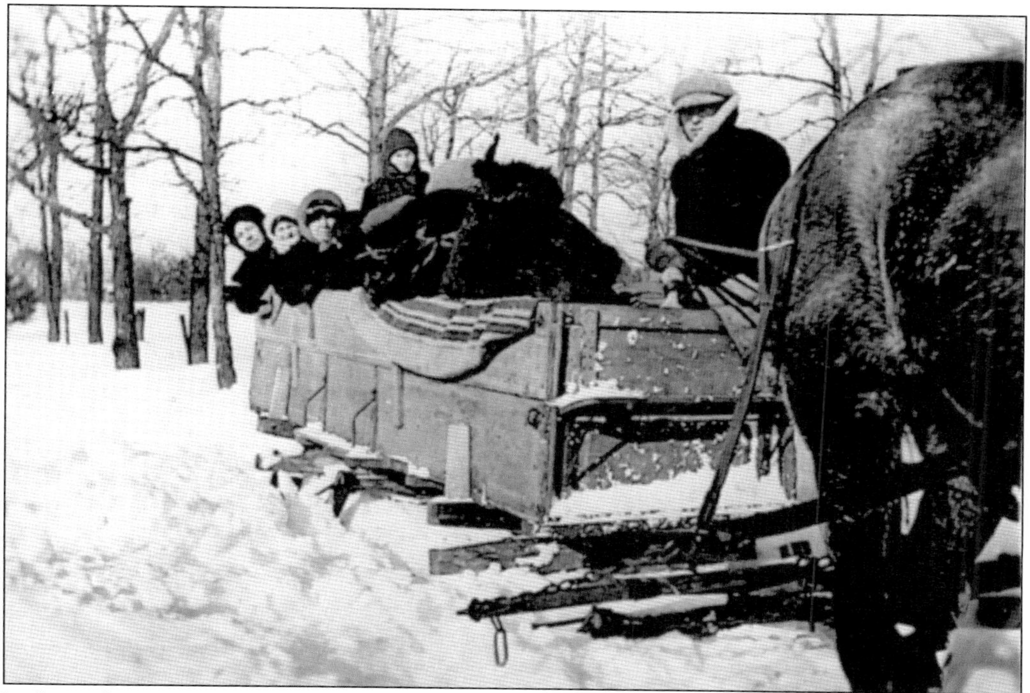

Ladies aid was a social club for the women in the community. They met on a regular basis at the church. Pictured above are several of the members on their way to a ladies aid meeting in 1916. Also pictured below is Pastor John Walker with his wife and sons in a photograph taken in 1916. (Courtesy of Otsego Heritage Preservation Commission.)

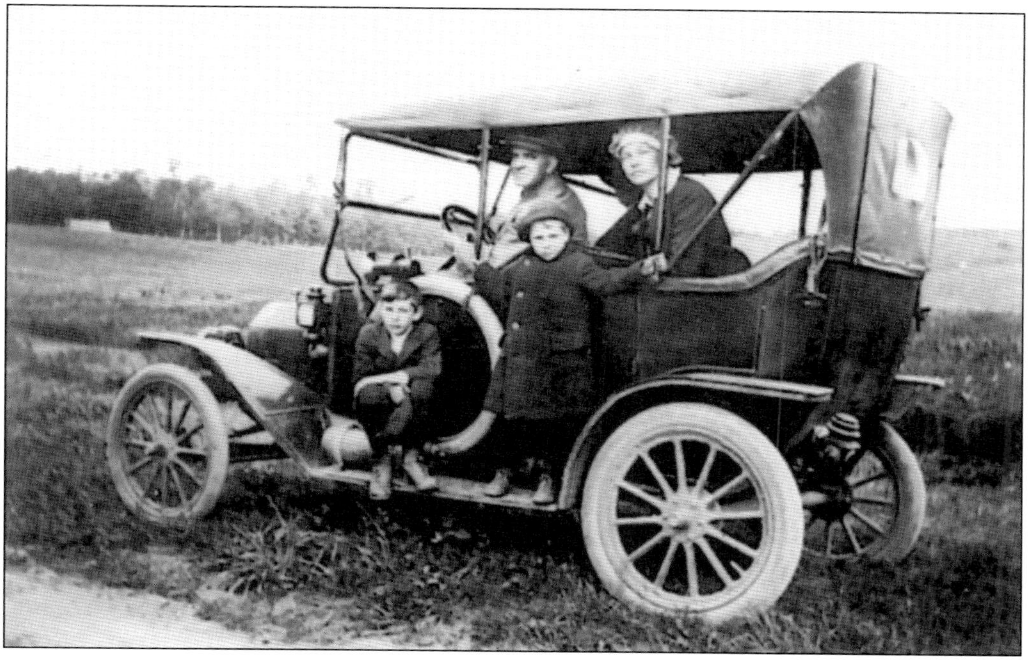

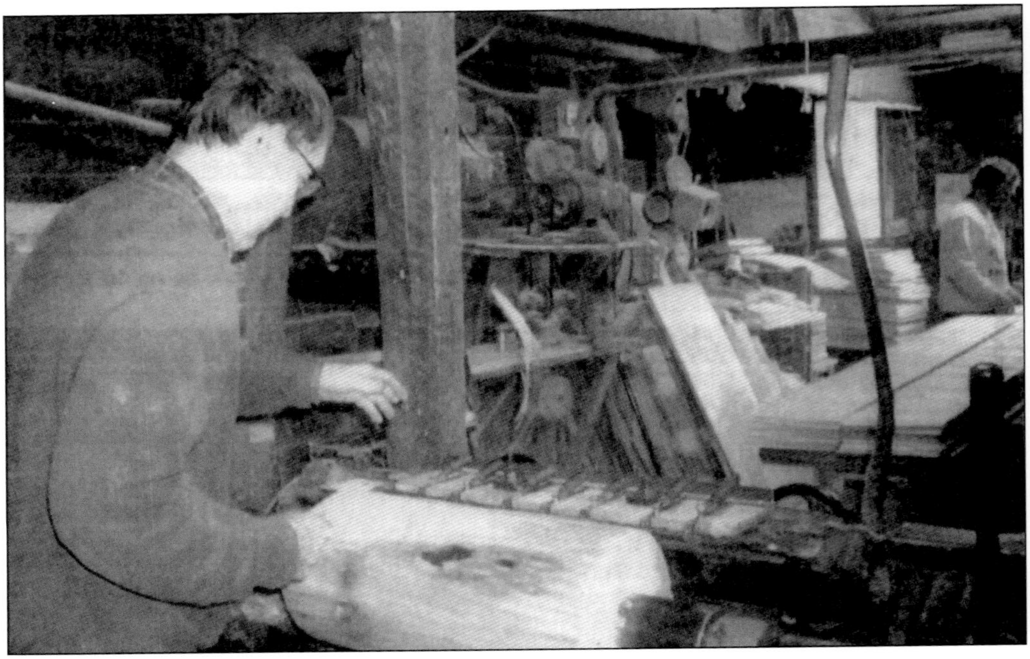

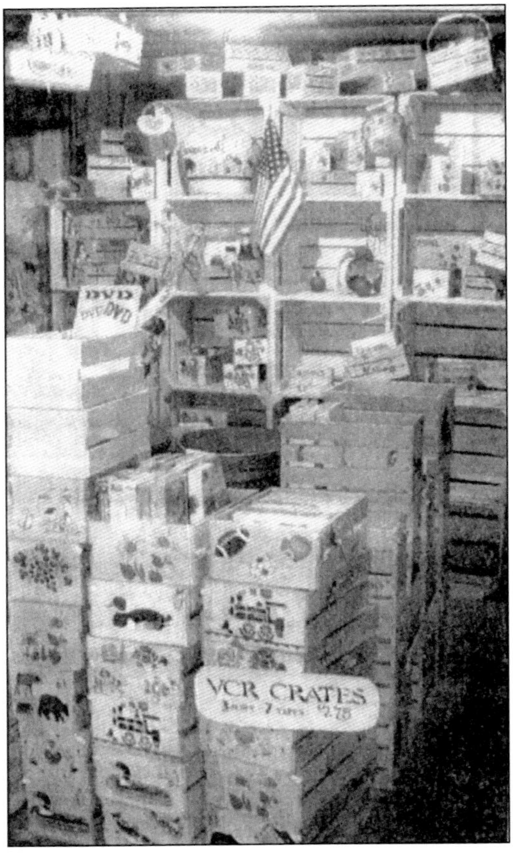

William Ebner and his children lived with his sister for two years after the passing of his wife, Margaret. Two houses were built across the road and east from the George Lahn home. Eventually these houses were renovated to form one home, which still exists today. The houses were built as shelter for the box factory workers. According to Ralph Lahn, Ebner's nephew, Ebner ran the box factory right on the bank of the Crow River, until the factory burned in 1910. Ebner left the area for about two years. After returning, he rebuilt the box factory in its current location, which was in about 1912. (Courtesy of the Drummer.)

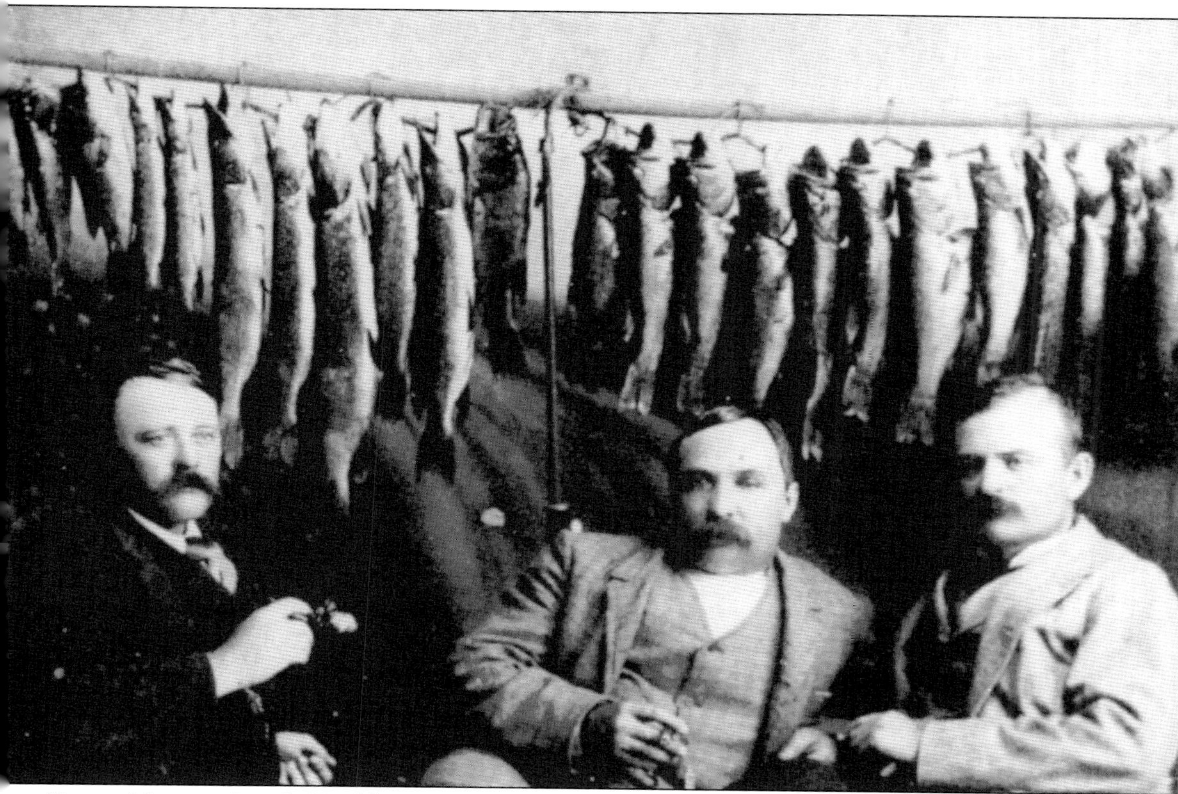

Pictured here is Joseph Kiichli Sr., smoking cigars with two of his friends after a successful fishing trip. Fishing and trapping were forms of fun and relaxation, yet they were necessary to survival as well. (Courtesy of Otsego Heritage Preservation Commission.)

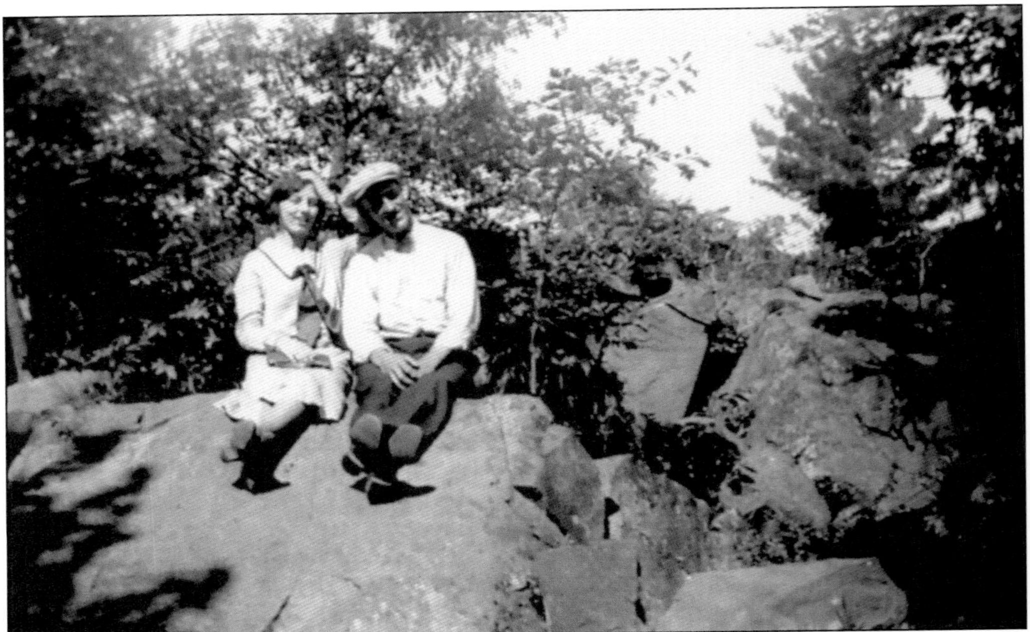

Pictured above are Willy Bell and Leona Loekwood enjoying the day in 1927. Also pictured (below) are the three Plude sisters, from left to right, Marie Anne Cyr, Leone "Tudy" Mack, and Betty Lou Segner. (Above, courtesy of Otsego Heritage Preservation Commission; below, courtesy of Lloyd and Marie Anne Cyr.)

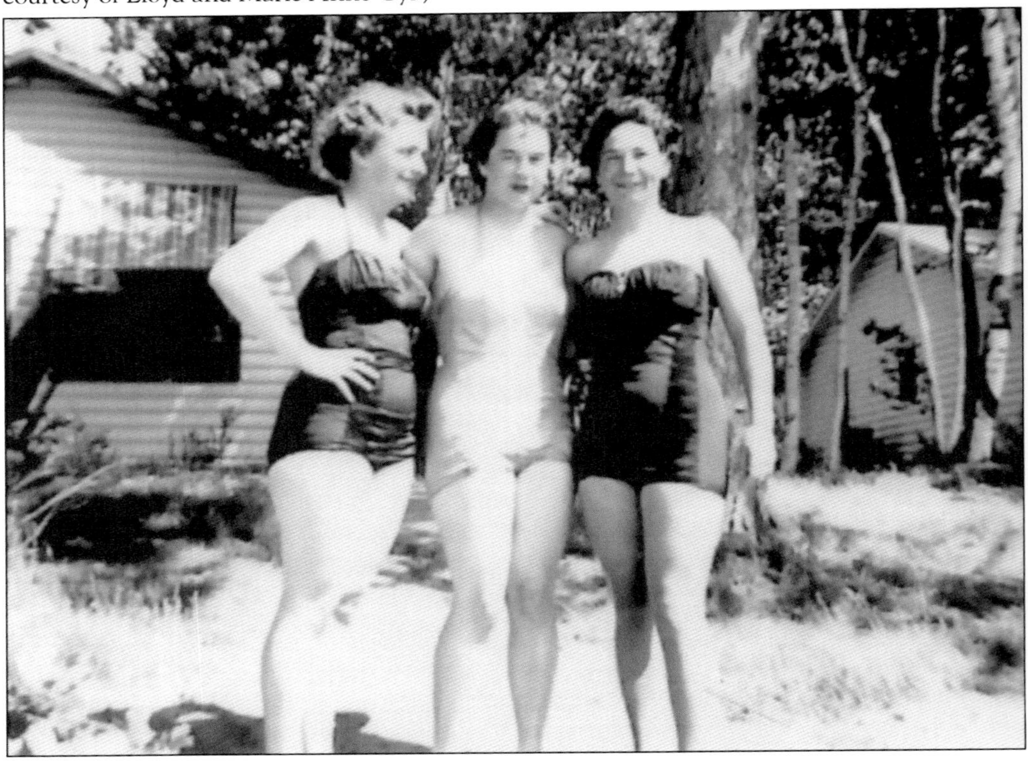

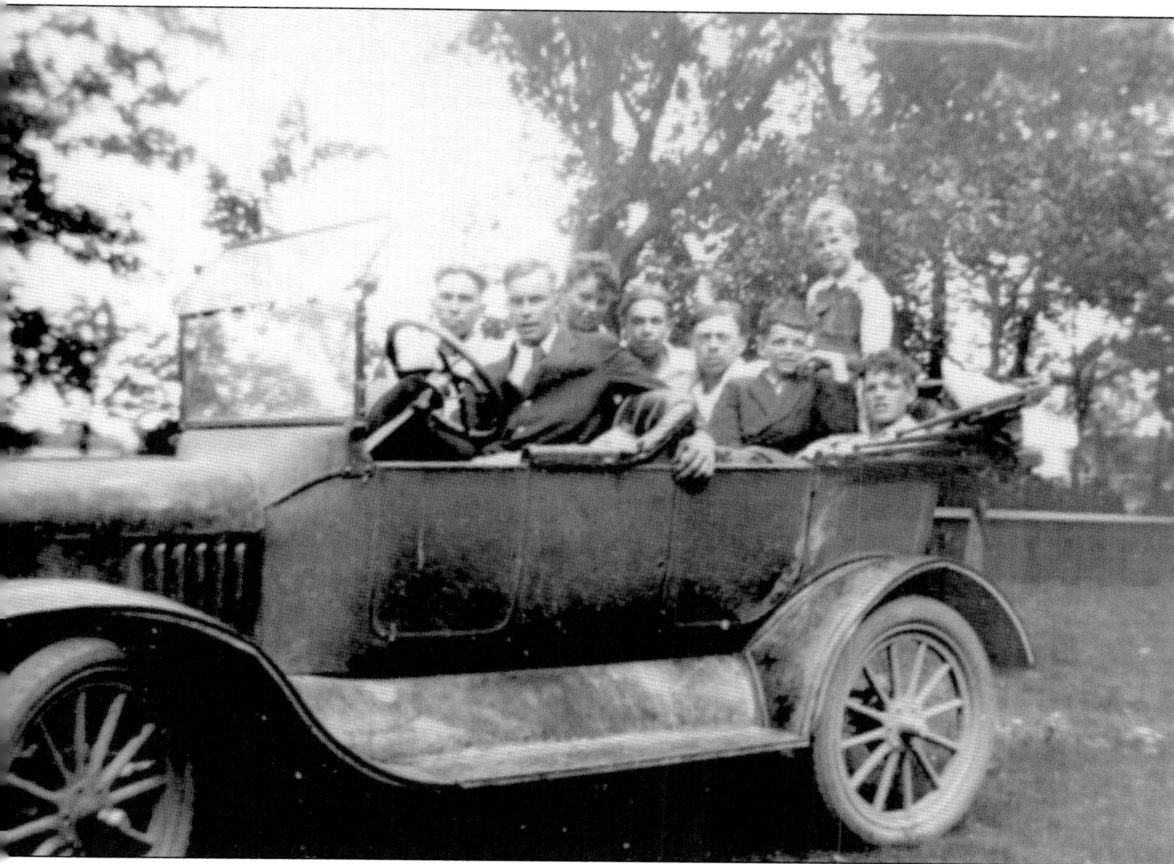

In the early 1900s, motor vehicle speed limits in closely built-up portions of town, village, or city was 10 miles per hour, 15 miles per hour passing through residential sections, and 25 miles per hour on public highways outside a built-up city. Drivers had to slow to 6 miles per hour going around curves. Whoever operated a motor vehicle while in an intoxicated state would be found guilty of a misdemeanor and forfeit their license to drive for three months. Anyone found riding or driving faster than a walking pace upon any bridge would be fined $10. Despite the strict rules, automobile accidents were prevalent in the early years. Pictured in the 1930 Model T touring car are, from left to right, Arthur Cooley, Gordon Cooley, Dave McMahon, Eugene Cooley, Garold Peavey, Mike McMahon, Robert Cooley, and John McMahon. (Courtesy of Otsego Heritage Preservation Commission.)

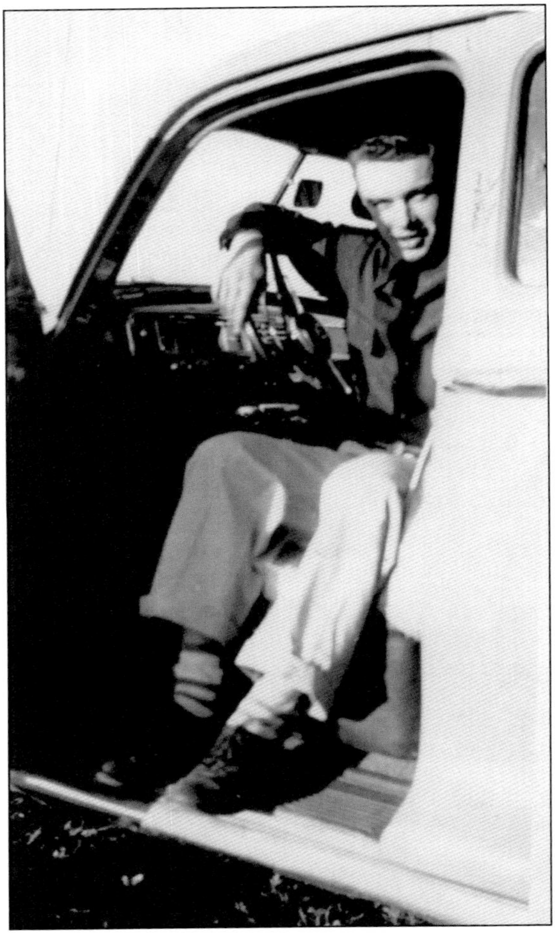

Richard Lefebvre enjoys visiting neighboring communities with his friends. Lefebvre is pictured at left in one of his first cars. The picture below is a group of Otsego residents out for a joy ride. Time was much slower and more peaceful then. (Left, courtesy of Richard and Patty Lefebvre; below, courtesy of Mary Anne McNeil.)

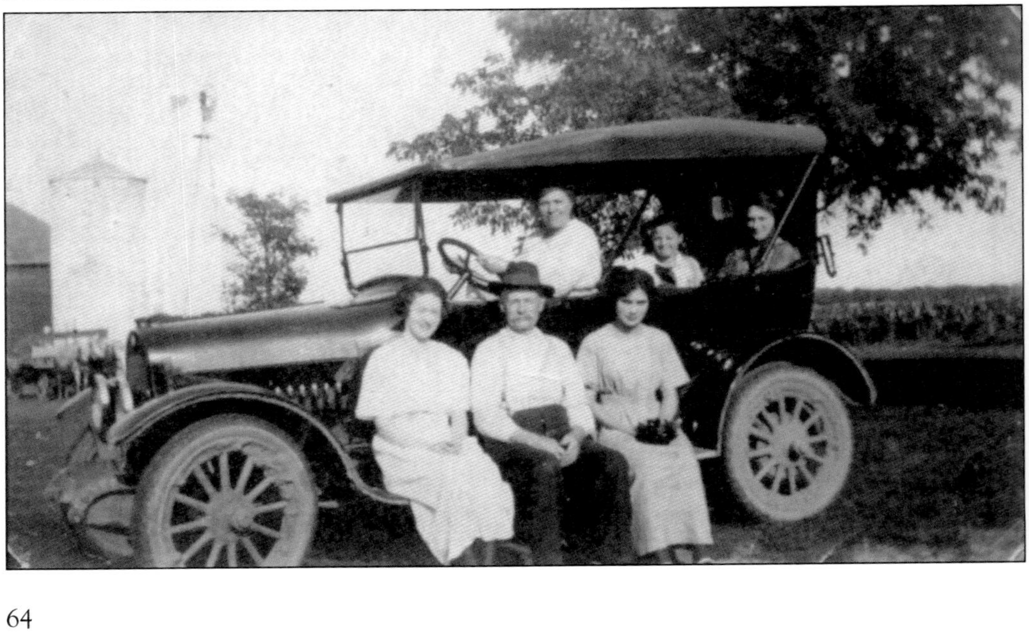

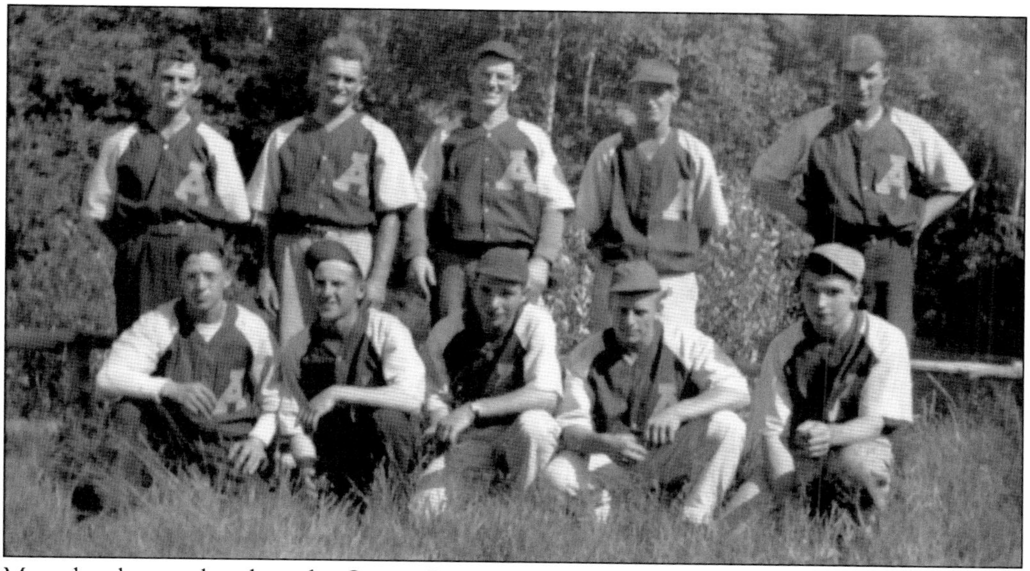

Many local men played on the Otsego Bone Crushers baseball team. Pictured above are, from left to right, (first row) H. Milless, A. Barnier, Ray Zachman, D. Corbin, and Leon Zachman; (second row) Bob Dehne, H. Gonyea, Ray Dehne, Bob Franklin, and G. Heuring. Baseball was a Sunday afternoon pastime. Another form of fun was playing cards. Patty and Richard Lefebvre, along with Mary Anne McNeil, reminisced about the fun the card club has had over the past 47 years. The card club would get together once a month to play 500, and later the men would play smear. Pictured below are, from left to right, Darry McAlpine, Catherine McAlpine, Richard Lefebvre, Patty Lefebvre, Rita Lefebvre, Jim Lefebvre, Yvonne Thibodeau, Emerick Thibodeau, and Pat McNeil. Taking the picture is Mary Anne McNeil. (Above, courtesy of Marie Corbin; below, courtesy of Mary Anne McNeil.)

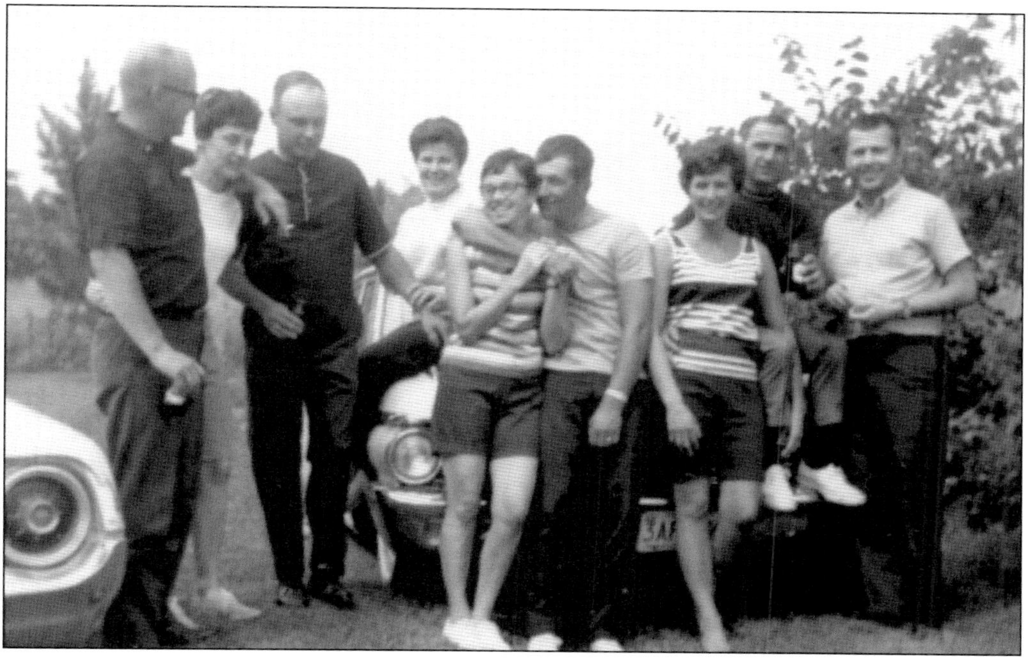

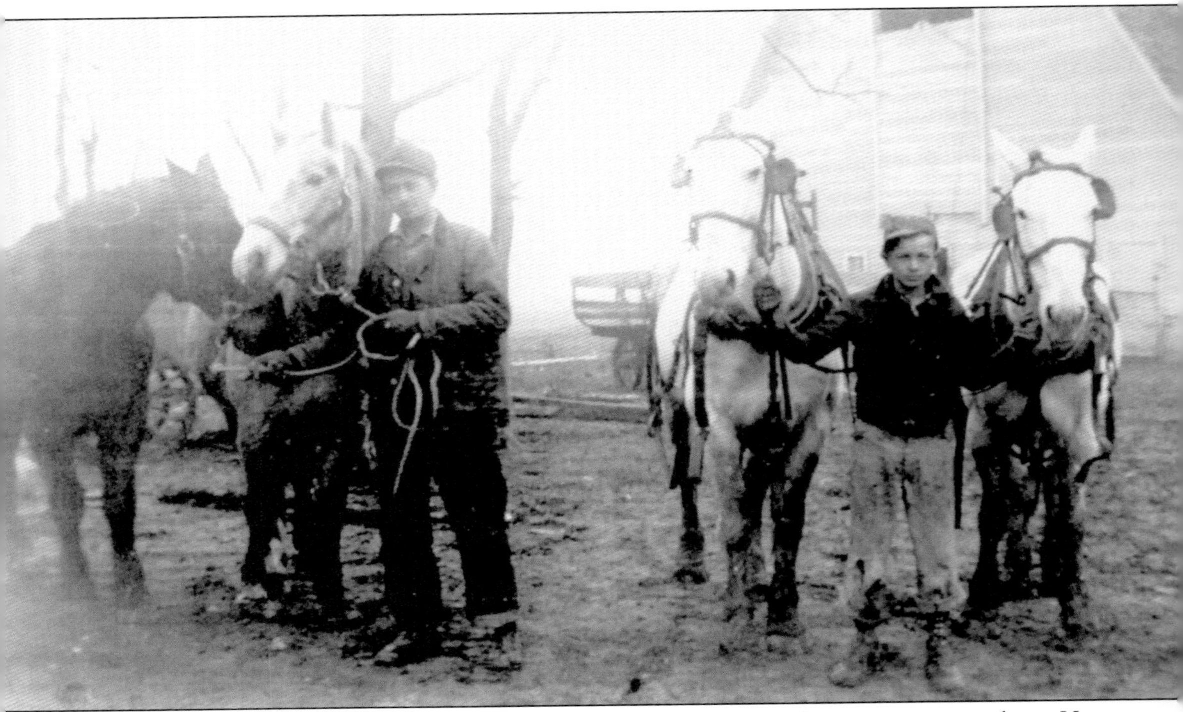

It was normal for families to have horses, even after tractors became commonplace. Harvey Hauan shared stories about how their family usually had Indian ponies on the farm. Hauan remembered when friends from Dayton would ride bikes to his farm so they could ride the ponies. This gave the Hauan children a chance to ride the bikes. Hauan explained that there was a time when they did not have horses, so they rode steers and pigs. Richard Lefebvre shared that he was too little to ride the family's Indian pony because it was too fast; however, Eugene Lefebvre rode the pony a lot. Richard remembered when some of the local residents arranged for the Lefebvre pony to challenge a racehorse; the little Indian pony won. The horse was sold to Arne Beaudry. (Courtesy of Mary Ann [Hauan] Eden.)

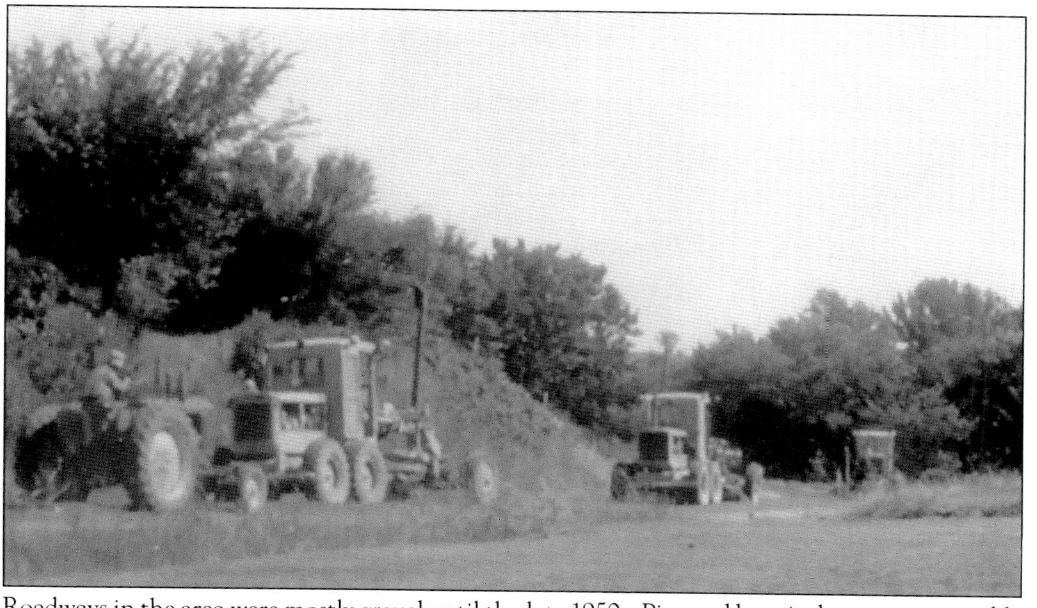

Roadways in the area were mostly gravel until the late 1950s. Pictured here is the crew responsible for paving County Road 36 in 1957. Lloyd and Marie Anne Cyr moved into their home in 1954; County Road 39 runs right past the Cyr home. Also pictured are Lou and Robert Lefebvre resting with friends. Notice the haystack between the trees. Work on the farm was never done, but at least tractors and automobiles made it easier. (Above, courtesy of Lloyd and Marie Anne Cyr; below, courtesy of Gordy Lefebvre.)

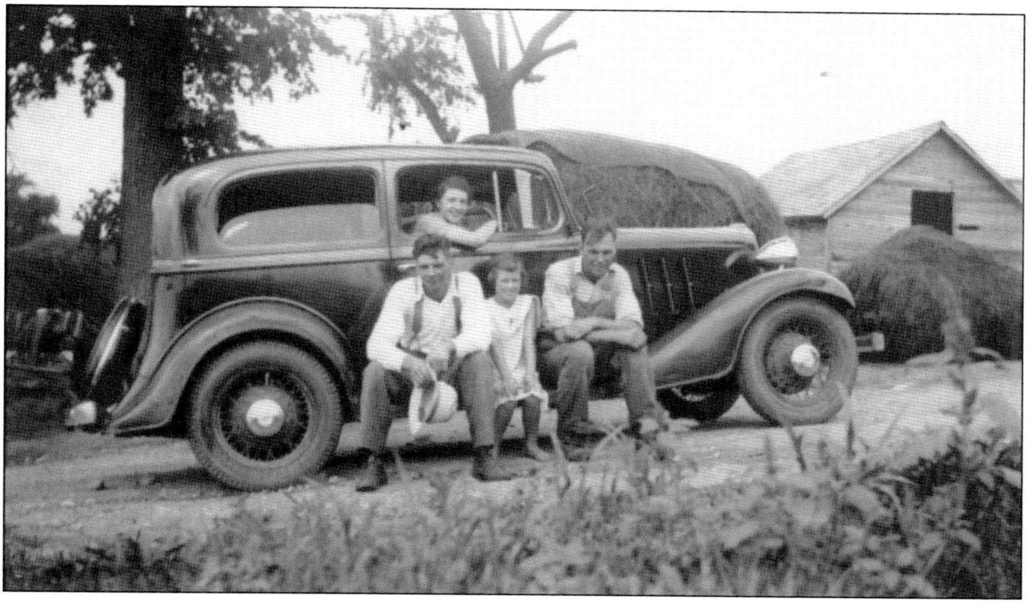

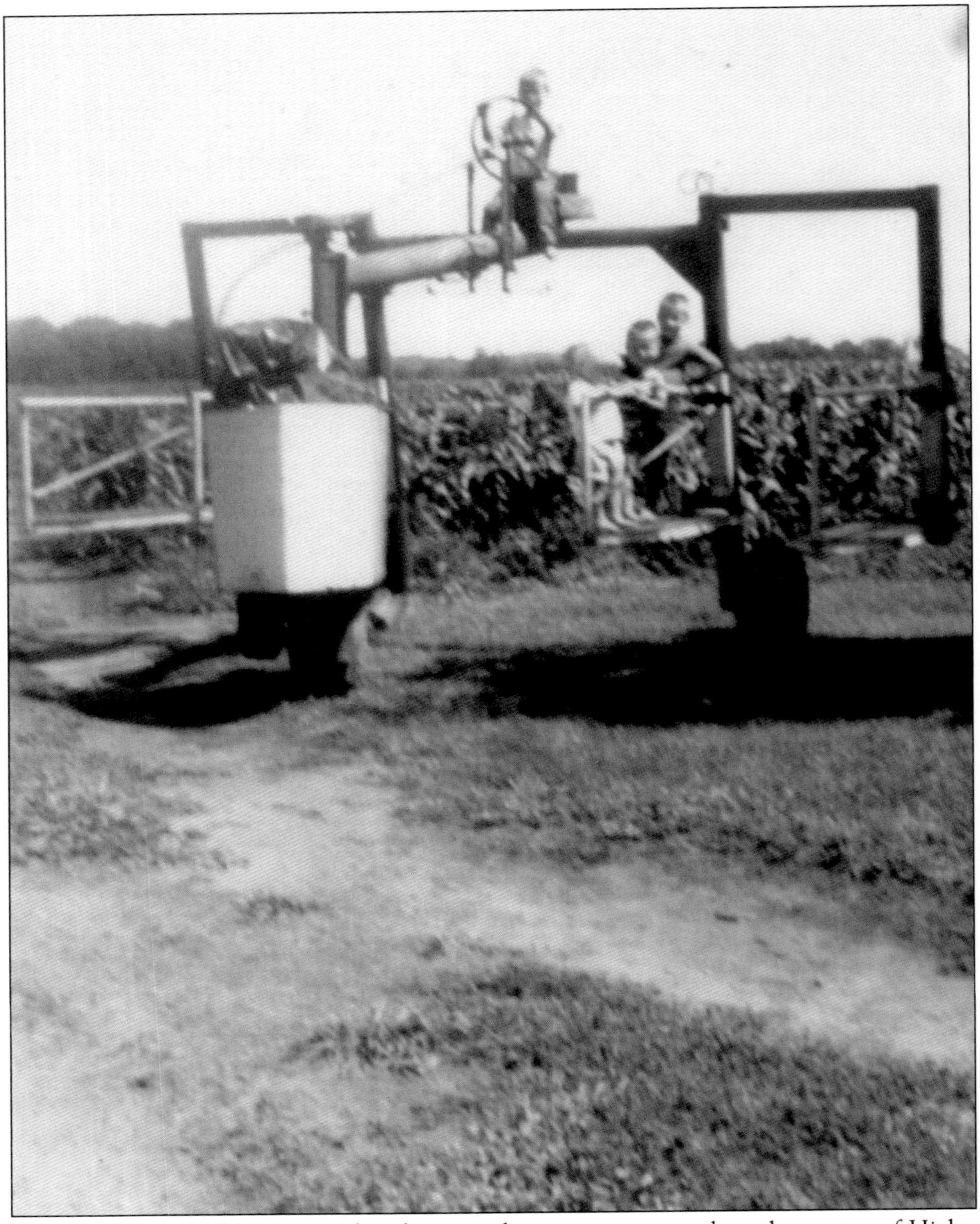

Richard and Patty Lefebvre owned and operated a sweet corn stand on the corner of Highway 101 and County Road 39. People in the area claimed it was the best corn in the country. Patty said that people would drive by the stand and see the rows of corn and watch the children pick the ripe ears, and they knew it was fresh. At times, there were cars lined up to get corn before the stand was even open. People kept coming back for more because they knew the corn was ripe and fresh and because they often received 13 or 14 ears of corn rather than just a dozen. The business grew to cover 80 acres. The Lefebvres even supplied fresh sweet corn to local super markets. Progress has turned the once corn fields into a retail center, but the Lefebvre family and many local residents still remember the fun the field provided. Pictured is a detasseling machine run by Lefebvre children in July 1964. (Courtesy of Patty and Richard Lefebvre.)

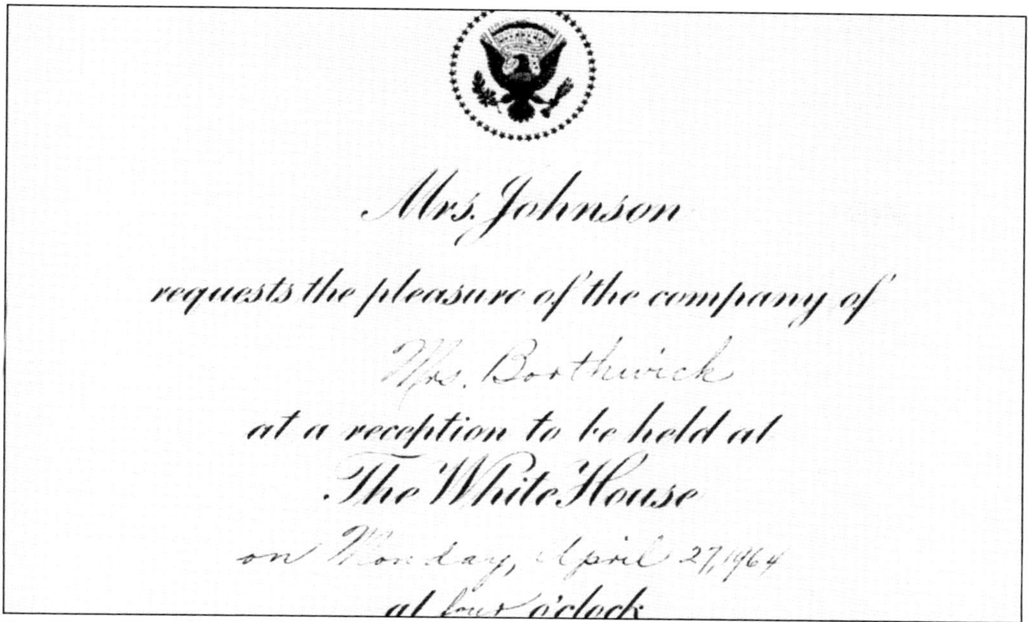

Mrs. Johnson

requests the pleasure of the company of

Mrs. Borthwick

at a reception to be held at

The White House

on Monday, April 27, 1964

at four o'clock

Dr. Harry Humphrey and Dr. Harry Borthwick once lived in Otsego; their interest in plant pathology, however, took them around the world. Humphrey is credited with over 50 scientific publications, and his work contributed to the development of disease-resistant cereal grains. Humphrey was Borthwick's uncle and mentor. Borthwick studied at the University of Minnesota and then Stanford University, majoring in botany. Borthwick is credited with writing over 100 scientific publications and joined the research staff of the United States Department of Agriculture in Maryland. Here are two of the many invitations the Borthwick family received from the White House. (Courtesy of Otsego Heritage Preservation Commission.)

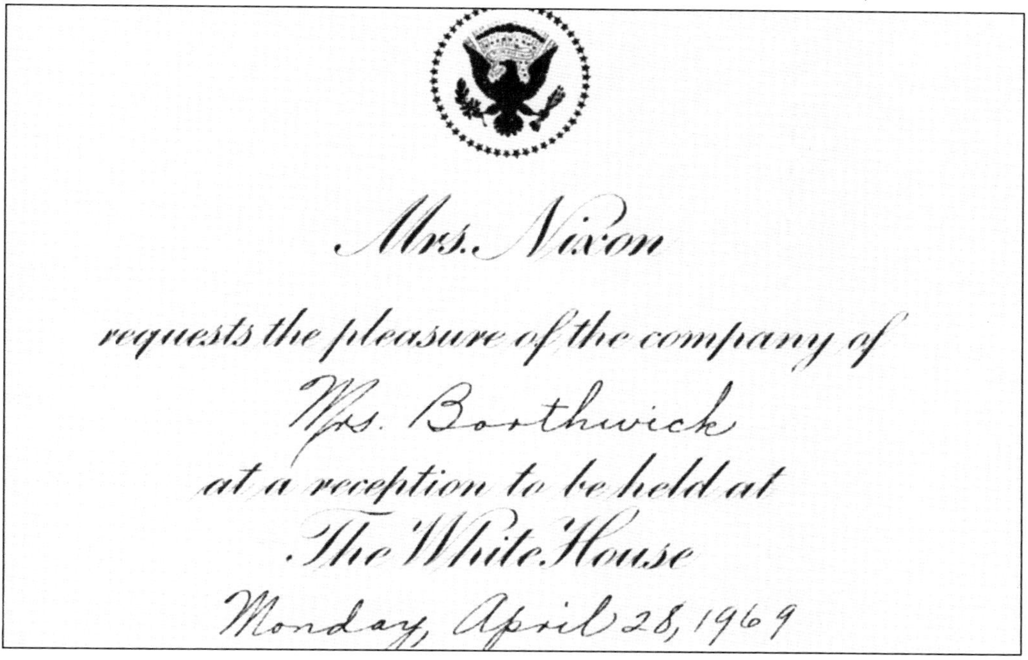

Mrs. Nixon

requests the pleasure of the company of

Mrs. Borthwick

at a reception to be held at

The White House

Monday, April 28, 1969

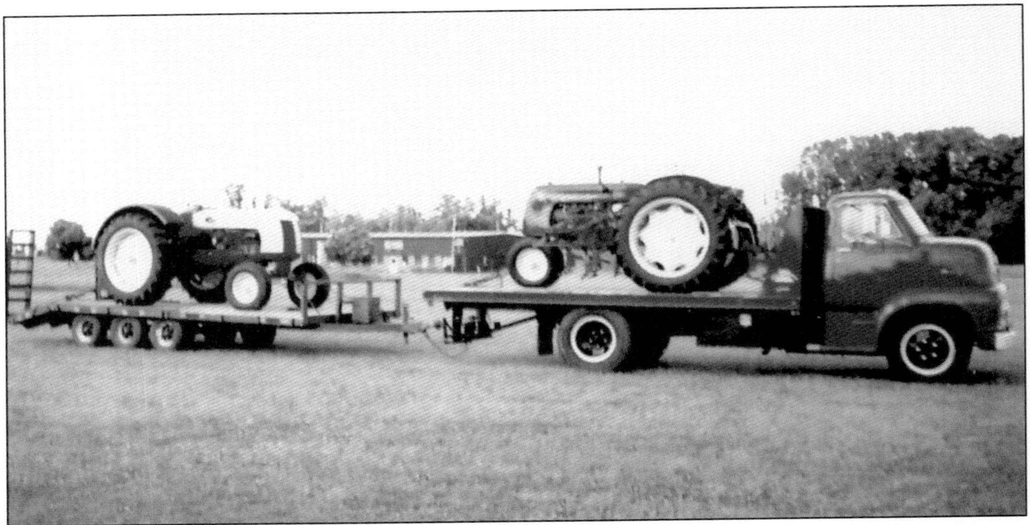

Jim, Richard, Gordy, and Eddie Lefebvre formed an antique tractor club. Each of the Lefebvres restored a different type of tractor, which provides for some fun family rivalry. Shown here are a few of the machines Gordy has restored. People can see the restored tractors and trucks in local parades. (Courtesy of Gordy Lefebvre.)

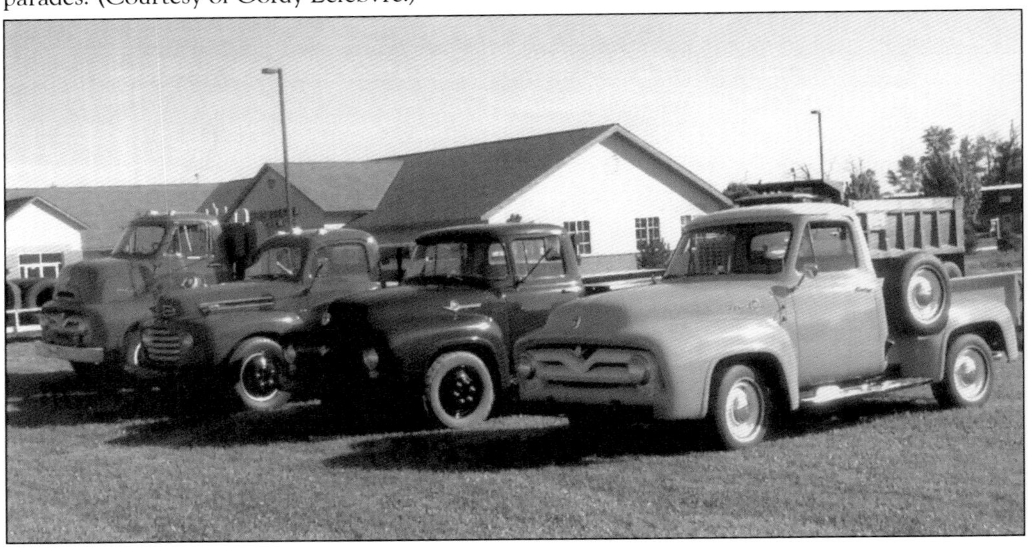

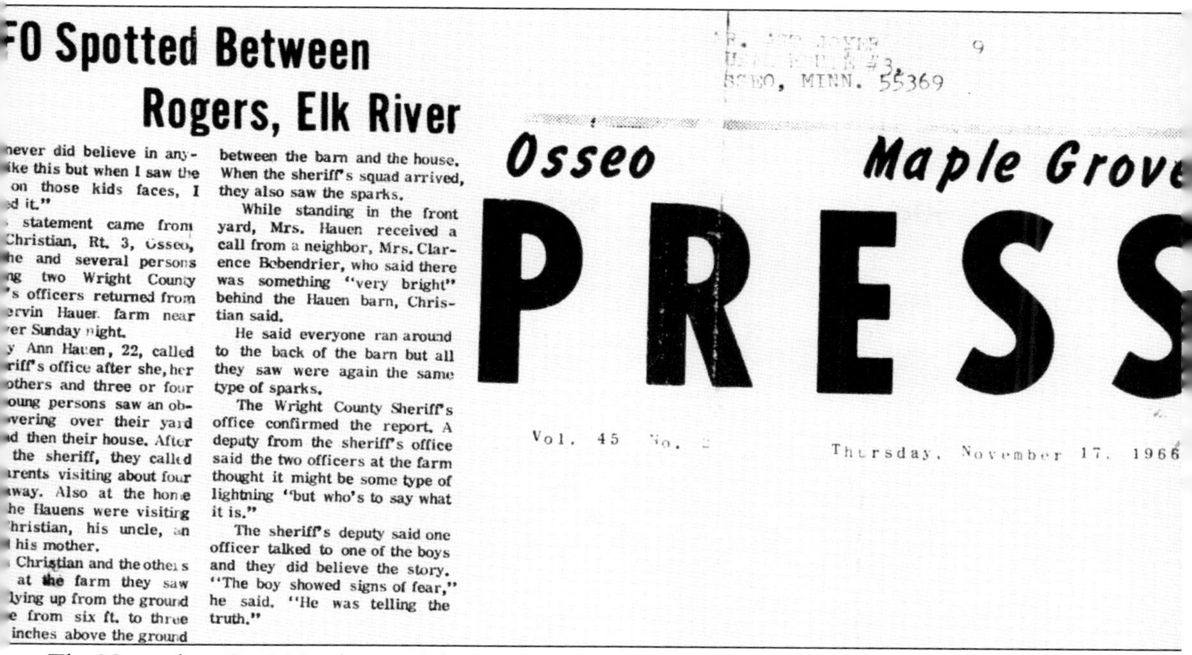

FO Spotted Between Rogers, Elk River

never did believe in any- ike this but when I saw the on those kids faces, I ed it."

statement came from Christian, Rt. 3, Osseo, he and several persons ng two Wright County 's officers returned from ervin Hauer. farm near er Sunday night.

y Ann Hauen, 22, called riff's office after she, her others and three or four oung persons saw an ob- overing over their yard d then their house. After the sheriff, they called arents visiting about four way. Also at the home he Hauens were visiting hristian, his uncle, an his mother.

Christian and the others at the farm they saw lying up from the ground e from six ft. to three inches above the ground between the barn and the house. When the sheriff's squad arrived, they also saw the sparks.

While standing in the front yard, Mrs. Hauen received a call from a neighbor, Mrs. Clarence Bebendrier, who said there was something "very bright" behind the Hauen barn, Christian said.

He said everyone ran around to the back of the barn but all they saw were again the same type of sparks.

The Wright County Sheriff's office confirmed the report. A deputy from the sheriff's office said the two officers at the farm thought it might be some type of lightning "but who's to say what it is."

The sheriff's deputy said one officer talked to one of the boys and they did believe the story. "The boy showed signs of fear," he said. "He was telling the truth."

OSSEO, MINN. 55369

Osseo Maple Grove PRESS

Vol. 45 Thursday, November 17, 1966

The November 17, 1966, edition of the *Osseo Maple Grove Press* carried a story that frightened many. Mary Ann (Hauan) Eden was home doing the dishes when she spotted a UFO. Eden was looking toward the barn and saw flashing lights. Eden called for her brother Eugene to see if he knew what it was. He saw the same thing and was frightened too. The flying object moved very fast and then stopped instantly. The flashing lights were faster than anything Eden had ever seen. The object hovered over the ground leaving burn marks in its wake. The saucer-shaped object also hovered over power lines; Hauan thought it was collecting energy. Soon the object moved towards Elk River and all of a sudden it was gone. A person driving from Elk River and a neighbor also saw the phenomenon. The Wright County Sheriff's office was called and responded. When their cousin Dave Christian reached the farm there were still sparks on the ground; the police saw the sparks too. (Courtesy of Crow River News.)

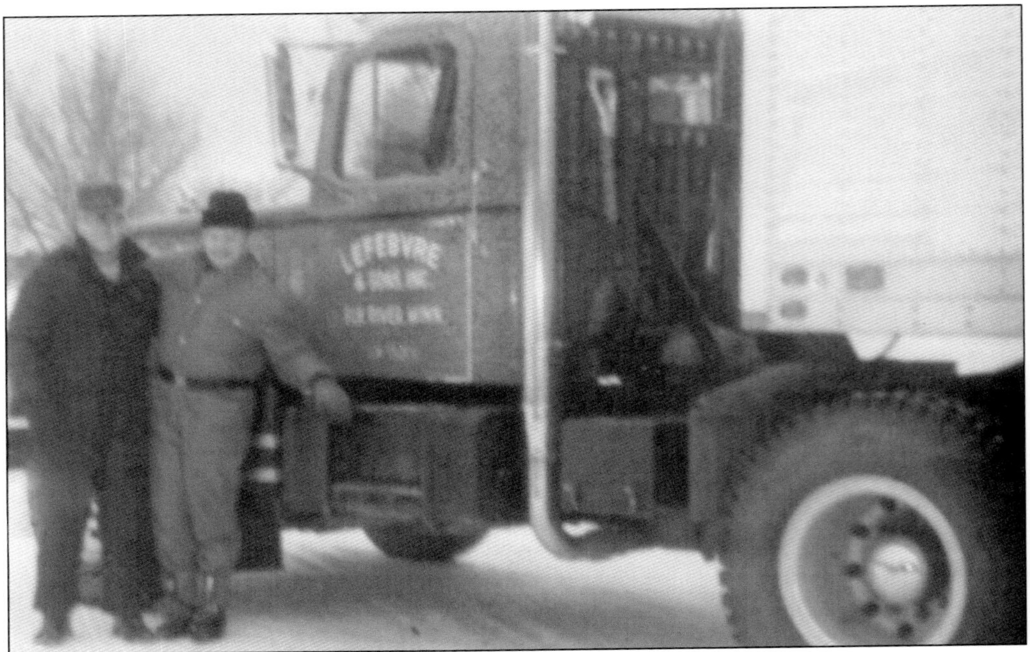

In the early 1970s, the Lefebvre family and friends bought snowmobiles and spent long weekends at the Breezy Point Resort near Brainerd. Members of the group would rent cabins and enjoy fun in the snow. One year, the Lefebvres loaded all the machines in a Lefebvre and Sons Trucking semi truck. There were a lot of snowmobiles packed in the trailer, and the family sure did get noticed when they arrived at the resort. The Lefebvres would also snowmobile locally and stop at establishments, such as Millside Tavern, Monte Club, and Daytona. (Courtesy of Patty and Richard Lefebvre.)

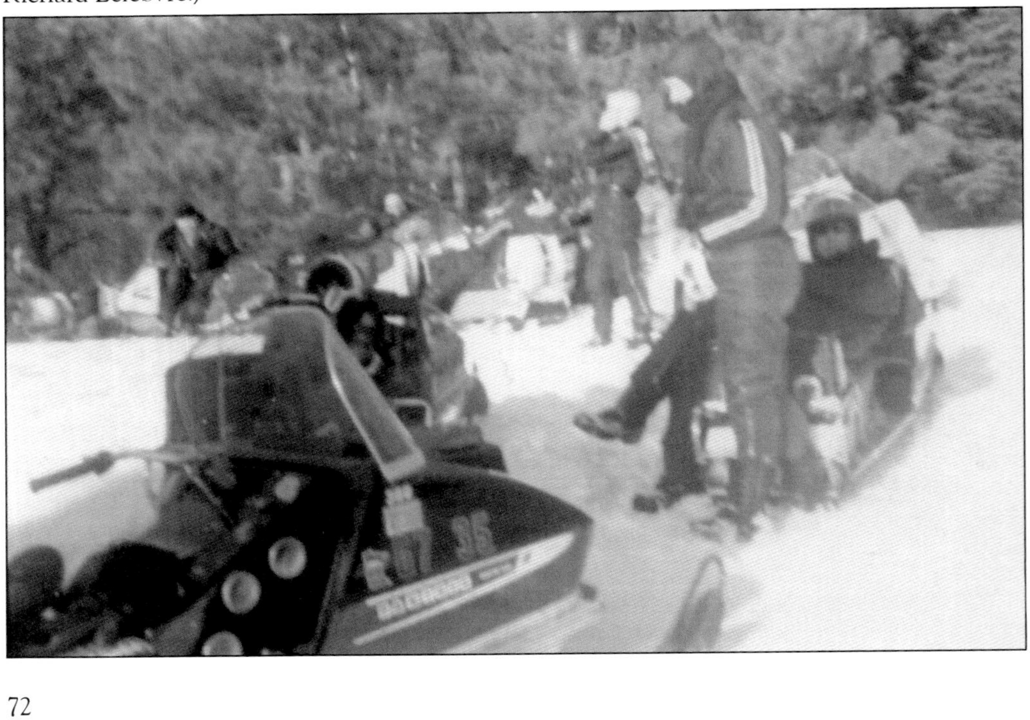

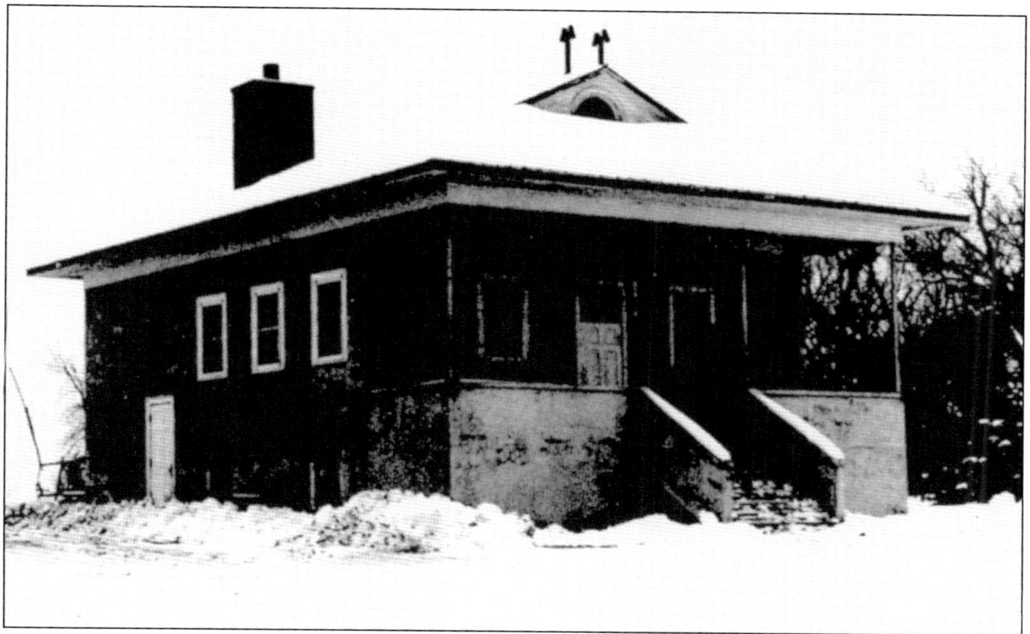

In 1950, the building that had served as School District No. 10 became the Otsego Town Hall. On September 21, 1990, the Minnesota State Municipal Board proclaimed that Otsego would be Minnesota's 885th city. On November 6, 1990, Otsego held elections for the first city council. The newly elected council was sworn in on November 15, 1990: Mayor Norman Freske and council members, Ron Black, Larry Fournier, Douglas Lindenfelser, and Floyd Roden. Town hall is pictured here all decked out in patriotic celebration. (Courtesy of Otsego Heritage Preservation Commission.)

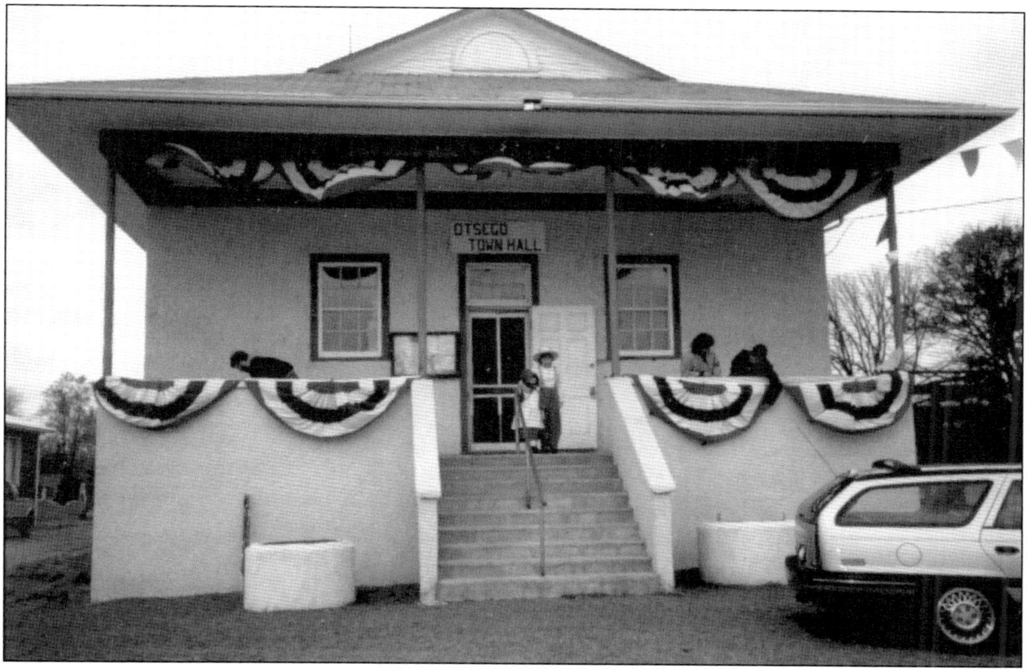

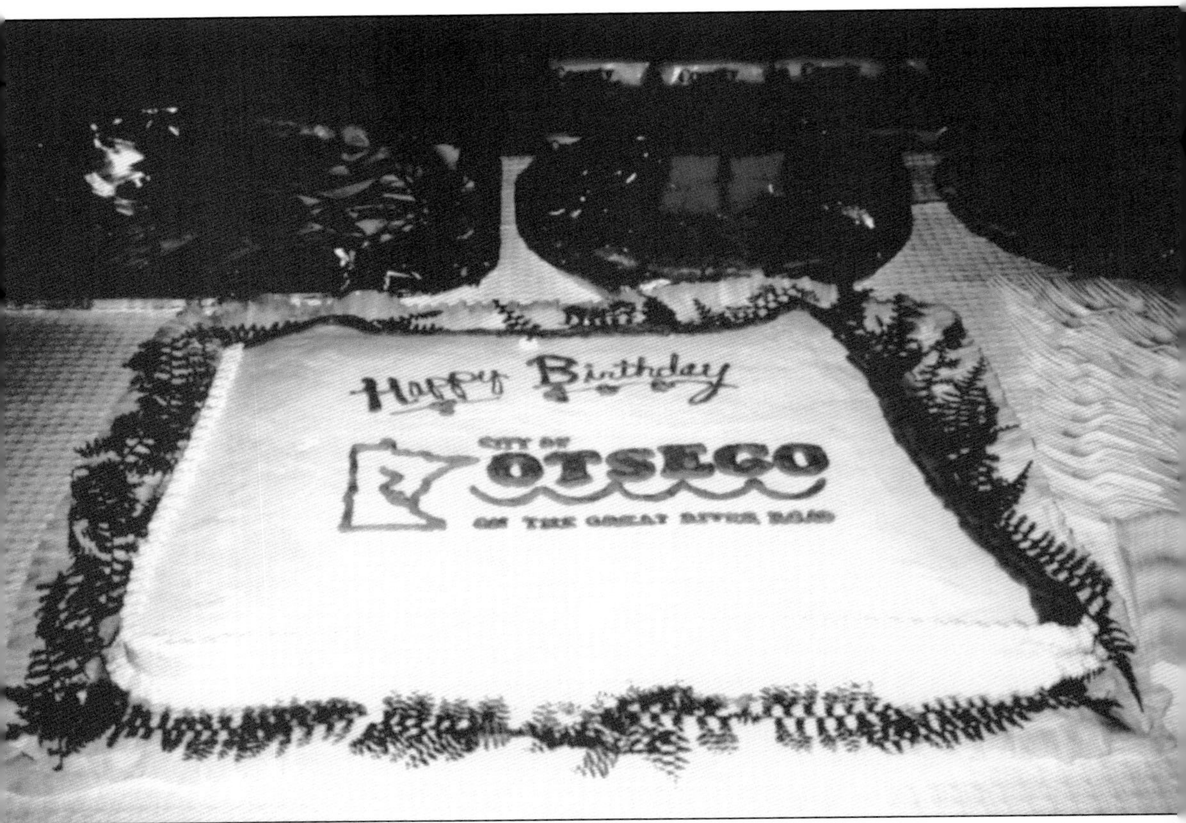

Town hall was decorated in honor of Otsego becoming a city. A proclamation was given by Gov. Rudolph Perpich declaring November 15, 1990, as Otsego Day. Outgoing city representatives were presented with plaques of appreciation by Senator Betty Adkins. Special recognition was given to Jerome Perrault for 43 years of service as the Otsego town clerk. This birthday cake was shared by many residents that enjoyed the celebration. (Courtesy of Otsego Heritage Preservation Commission.)

Seven

FLOODS OF 1965 AND 1966

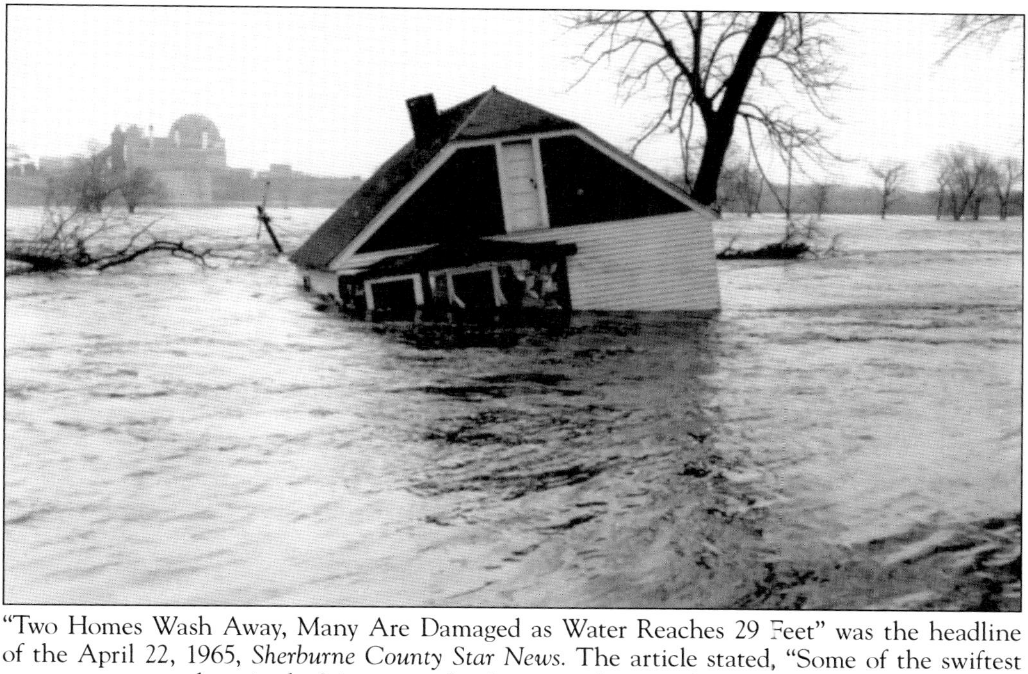

"Two Homes Wash Away, Many Are Damaged as Water Reaches 29 Feet" was the headline of the April 22, 1965, *Sherburne County Star News*. The article stated, "Some of the swiftest current seen anywhere in the Minnesota flood areas and a record crest on Good Friday gave the angry old Mississippi River the power to cut a new channel across what has become known as the Ebnerville peninsula." Pictured here is a summer home owned by Victoria Olson Rouse of Brainerd. It was carried away and finally stopped when it hit a tree in front of the Jay Hetrick home. The river level, recorded at 15 feet on April 9, 1965, rose to 29 feet in just one week. (Courtesy of Otsego Heritage Preservation Commission.)

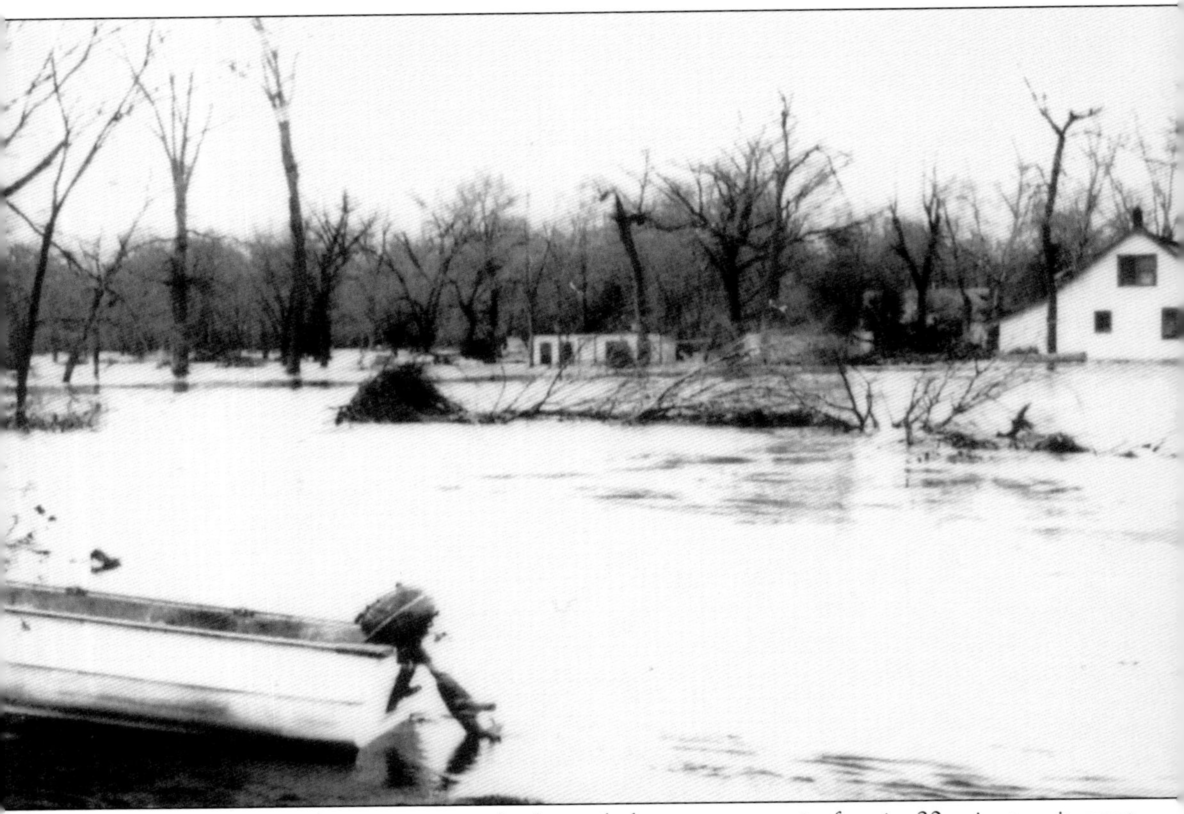

Flooding began when an ice jam broke and the water rose six feet in 20 minutes; it went back down 10 minutes later. The sudden rise and fall of the water level left a pile of ice between the icebreaker and the south shore. The next day the river continued to rise until Highway 101 was flooded for a length of almost a half-mile. About 150 high school boys responded to the call for help. Many of the boys, unable to get to their homes in the country to get boots, simply put on gym shoes and went to work. By shortly after noon, the highway over the river was officially closed to all traffic; the only way to get to Elk River was to cross the bridge in Monticello or Anoka. Several people used boats to navigate the water-filled streets. (Courtesy of Marnette Barthel.)

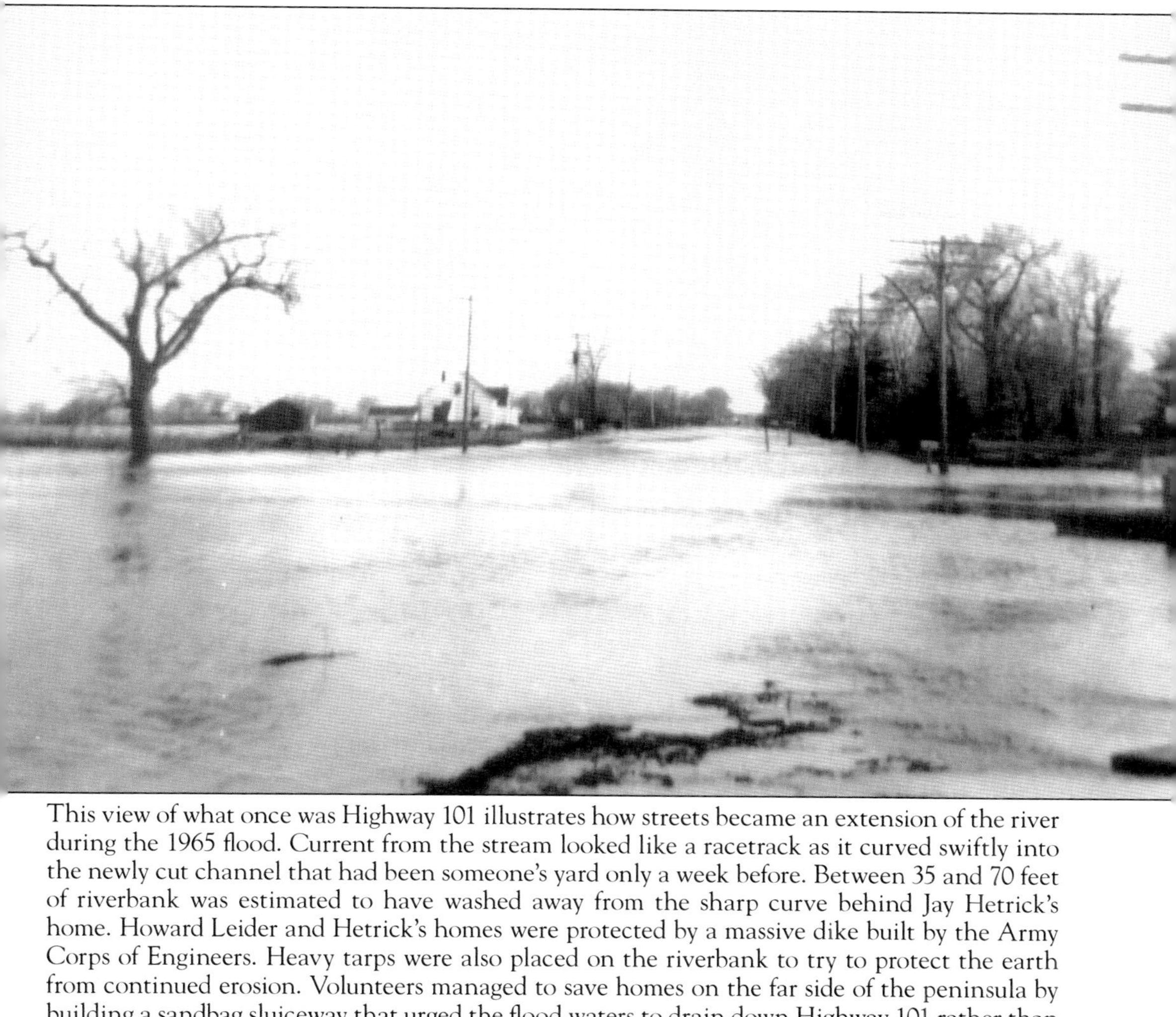

This view of what once was Highway 101 illustrates how streets became an extension of the river during the 1965 flood. Current from the stream looked like a racetrack as it curved swiftly into the newly cut channel that had been someone's yard only a week before. Between 35 and 70 feet of riverbank was estimated to have washed away from the sharp curve behind Jay Hetrick's home. Howard Leider and Hetrick's homes were protected by a massive dike built by the Army Corps of Engineers. Heavy tarps were also placed on the riverbank to try to protect the earth from continued erosion. Volunteers managed to save homes on the far side of the peninsula by building a sandbag sluiceway that urged the flood waters to drain down Highway 101 rather than over the property. (Courtesy of Marnette Barthel.)

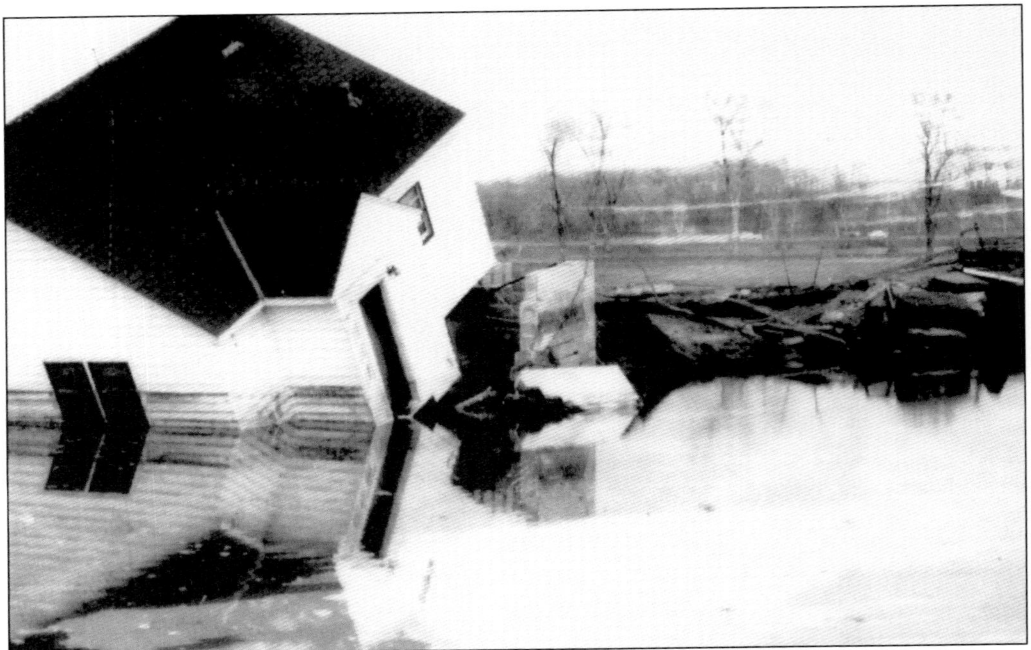

The home of Art Kluge fell into the rushing waters when the channel widened and corroded the home's foundation. Kluge's dog and some chickens were rescued three days after all the residents of the area were evacuated. While the Mississippi was at its crest, the Elk River suddenly rose several feet in two hours and began seeping around the dam. Emergency fire sirens beckoned volunteers to gather at the dam in the middle of the night and work for over three hours building a sandbag dike several hundred feet on each side of the dam. Swirling waters below the dam, which at crest of the Elk and Mississippi Rivers were only six feet beneath the bridge, undermined the south approach, leaving only a three-foot thickness. The county highway department closed the bridge to repair the precarious south approach. (Above, courtesy of Marnette Barthel; below, courtesy of Otsego Heritage Preservation Commission.)

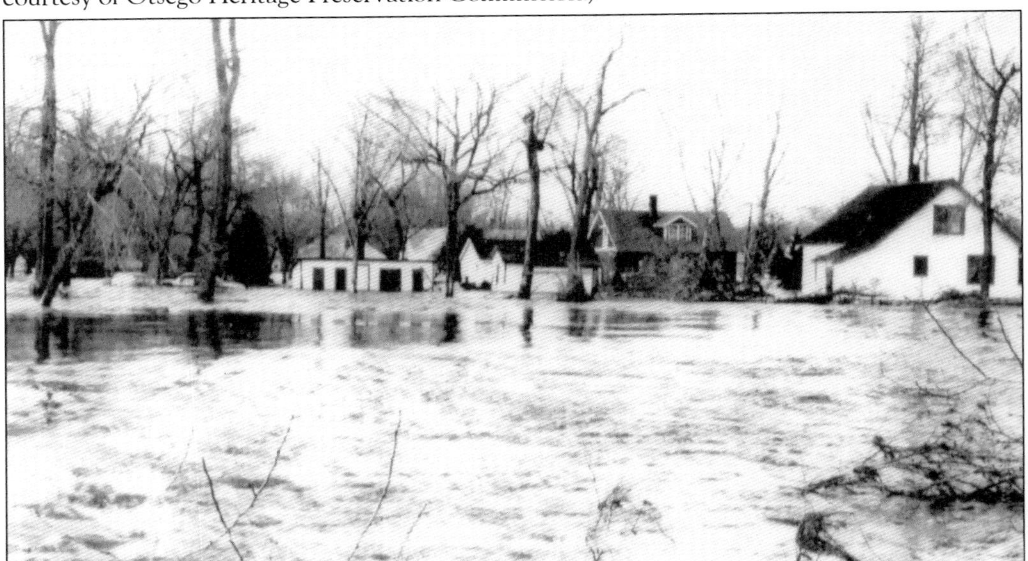

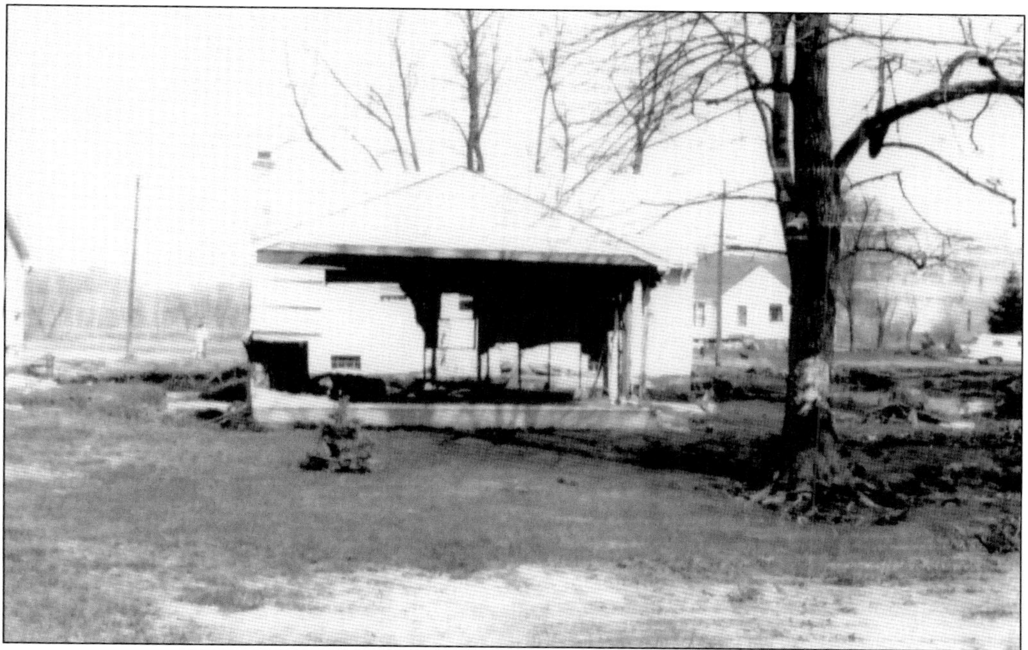

The homes of Annie and Mirand Milless and Irene and Reinhard Ebner, respectively pictured, were badly damaged during the 1965 flood in Otsego. Hundreds of volunteers worked around the clock building and replacing a plywood wall and forming sandbag dikes, but their efforts did not prevent the real estate from eroding away and many homes from becoming ruined. After holding its crest for more than 24 hours, the river began to slowly drop. In five days, the floodwaters were only a little below those reached during the 1952 flood crest. (Courtesy of Marnette Barthel.)

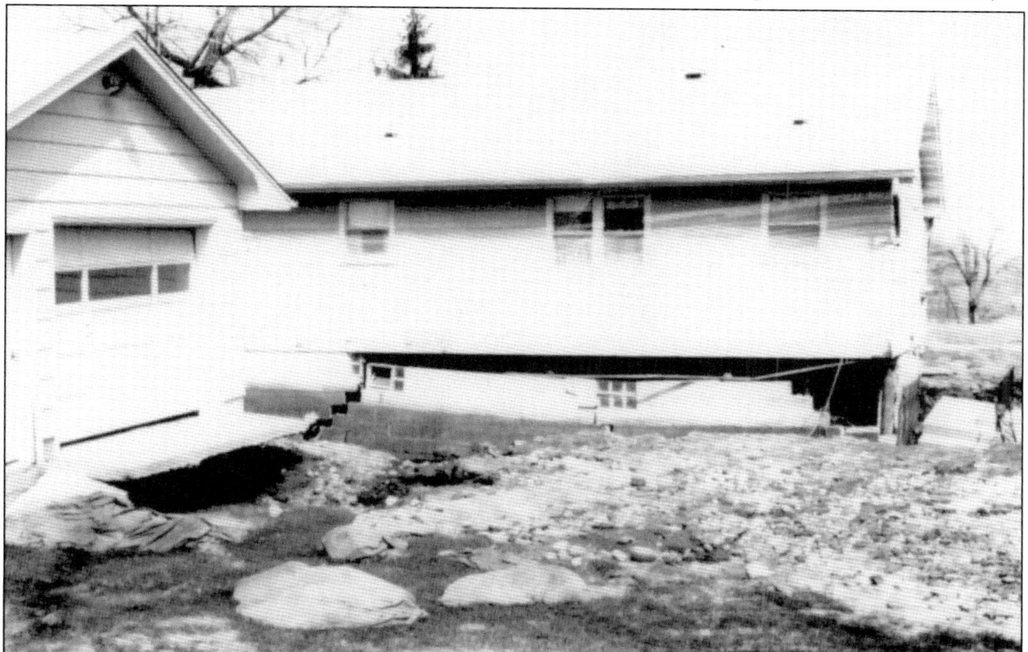

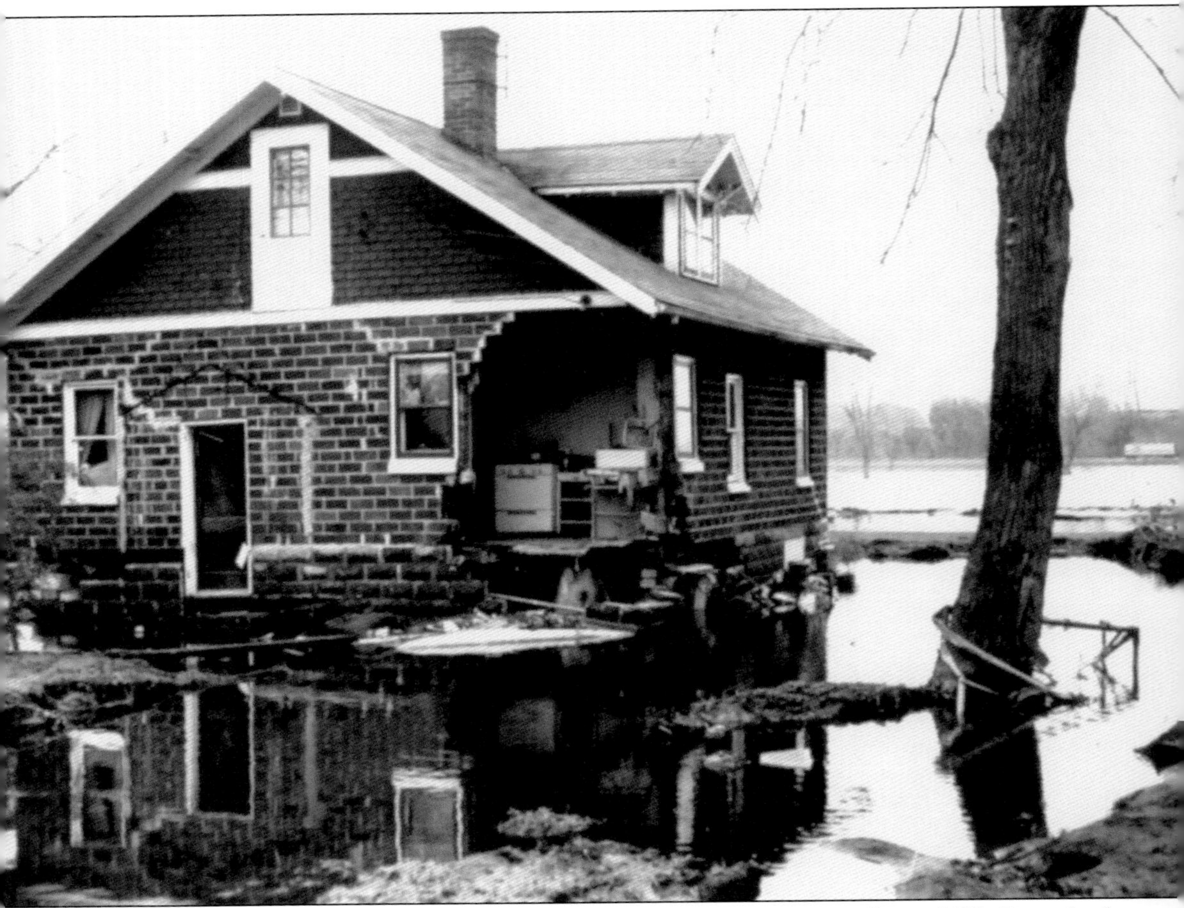

Another flood occurred in 1966 when an ice jam between Monticello and Elk River broke, releasing tons of ice, which traveled downstream. Army engineers and local civil defense officials watched the situation, prepared to spring into action when needed. Heavy equipment was operated continuously for three or four days to build a temporary earthen dike that followed the same plan and route the permanent levee would occupy soon thereafter. Most of the hard work was completed by homeowners, firemen, over 100 high school boys released from school, and other volunteers from the area. The number of volunteers during the 1966 flood was significantly less than in the previous year's disaster. Some speculate the 1966 flood's danger did not seem as imperative. The water was nowhere near as high and few in the community were actually aware of the urgency that existed. (Courtesy of Otsego Heritage Preservation Commission.)

Eight

Family Ties

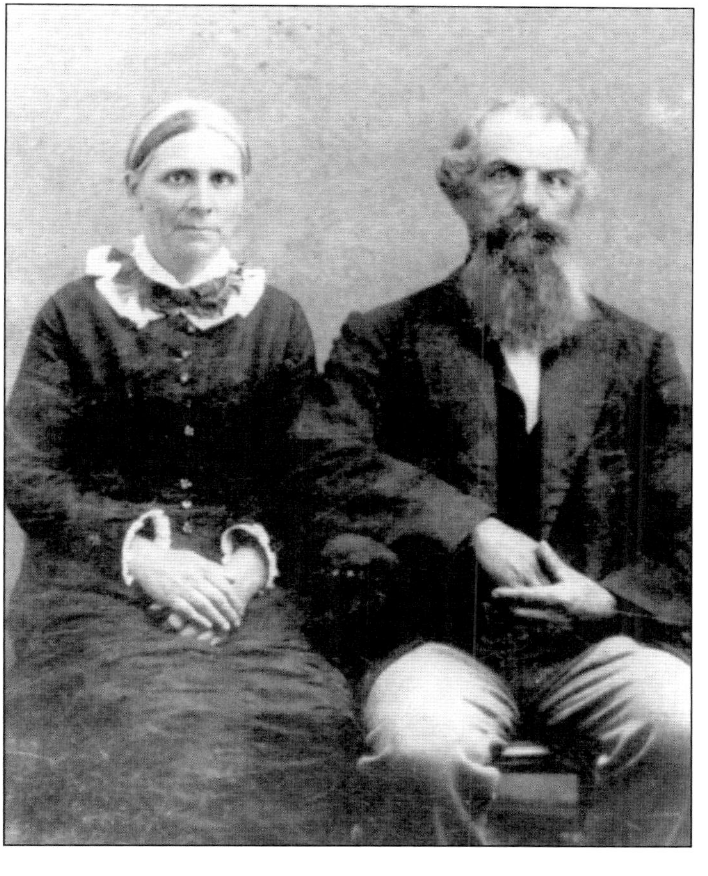

Joseph A. Parker pictured with his wife, Sylvia (McCory Emory) Parker, were the parents of Edson, Elva Annette, Lizzie, and Joseph W. Parker. The family moved to Otsego from Canada in about 1856. Elva Annette married Frank Brown, and Lizzie married Willard Holt. Joseph W. and Myrtle (Smith) Parker are the parents of Alvin, Mildred, and Helen. Helen Parker is Arne Engstrom's mother. Engstrom shared that Joseph A. farmed and some speculated he also had a side business making bottled medicine of some type, based on all the old bottles found around the home when it was torn down in the 1950s. (Courtesy of Arne Engstrom.)

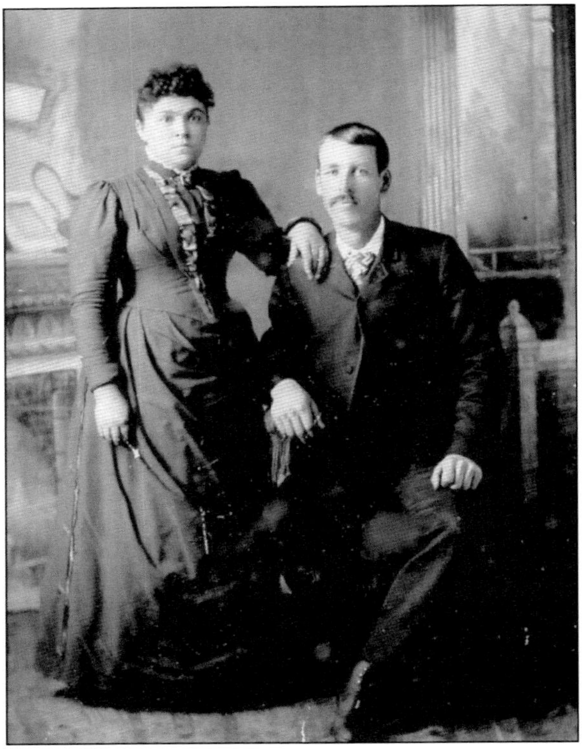

Lizzie Parker married Willand Holt in 1890; this is their wedding picture. They are the parents of Ralph, Clifton, and Erwin. Willard is the author of the *Holt Diary*, which captures the happenings in Otsego over the course of 12 years. Thanks to Holt's journal entries, the community has great understanding of its beginning. Pictured below is Sylvia McCory Emory Parker, Lizzie's mother. (Courtesy of Arne Engstrom.)

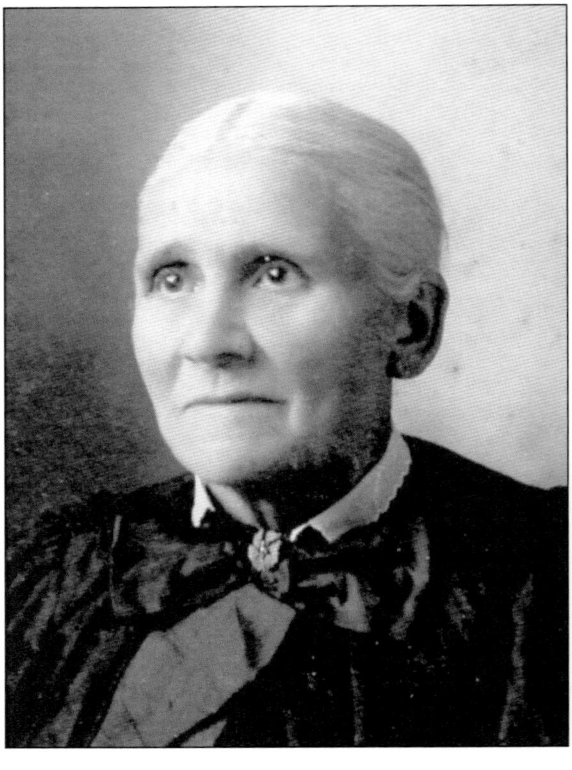

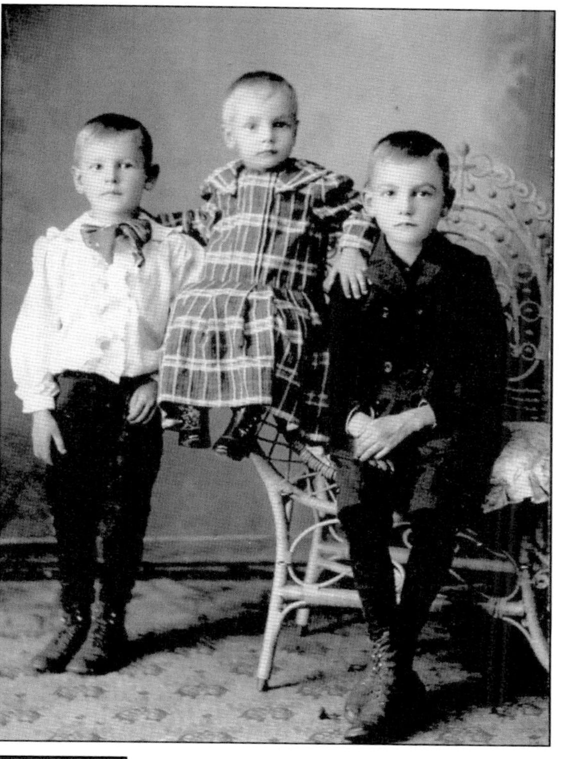

Pictured here on the right in 1904 are, from left to right, Ralph (age 9), Erwin (age 3), and Clifton (age 6). Sadly, Clifton was accidentally shot by Ralph when they were playing in the woods. The incident was witnessed by Willy Bell, who was Alvin and Ralph's lifelong best friend. Bell told Arne Engstrom about the tragic event while chatting at the hardware store one day shortly before his death. Pictured below are Eva and Ralph Holt posing for their wedding photograph. Eva taught school in Otsego. (Courtesy of Arne Engstrom.)

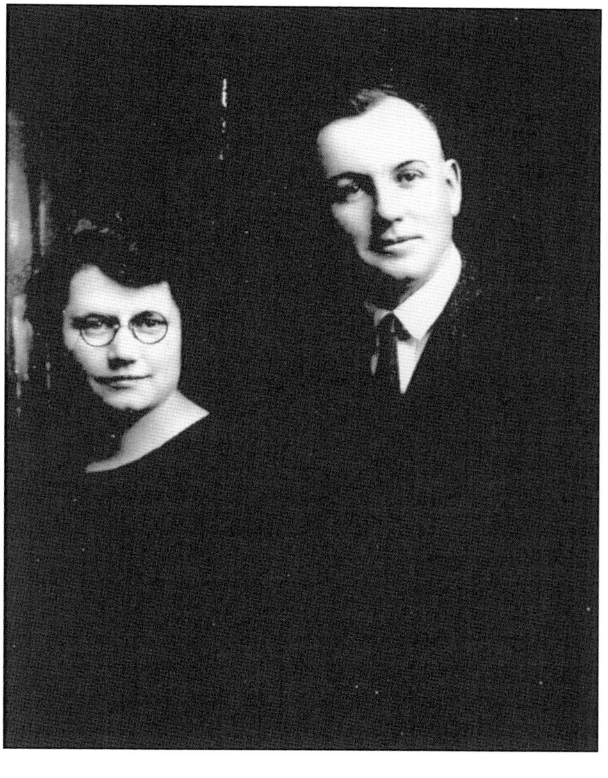

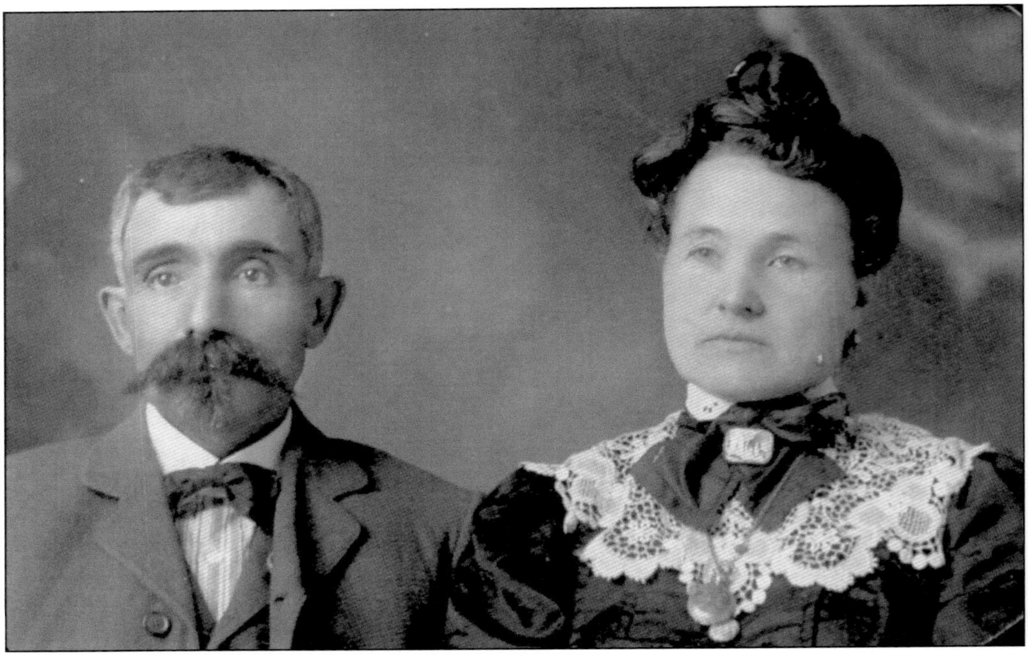

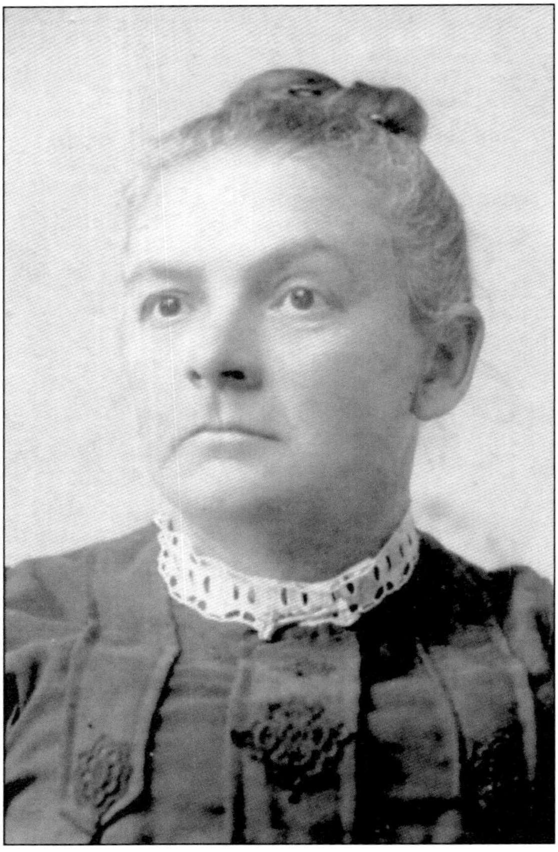

Mr. and Mrs. Edson Parker are pictured above along with Edson's sister Annette (Parker) Brown. Edson and Annette are the children of Joseph A. and Sylvia Parker and Lizzie (Parker) Holt's siblings. (Courtesy of Arne Engstrom.)

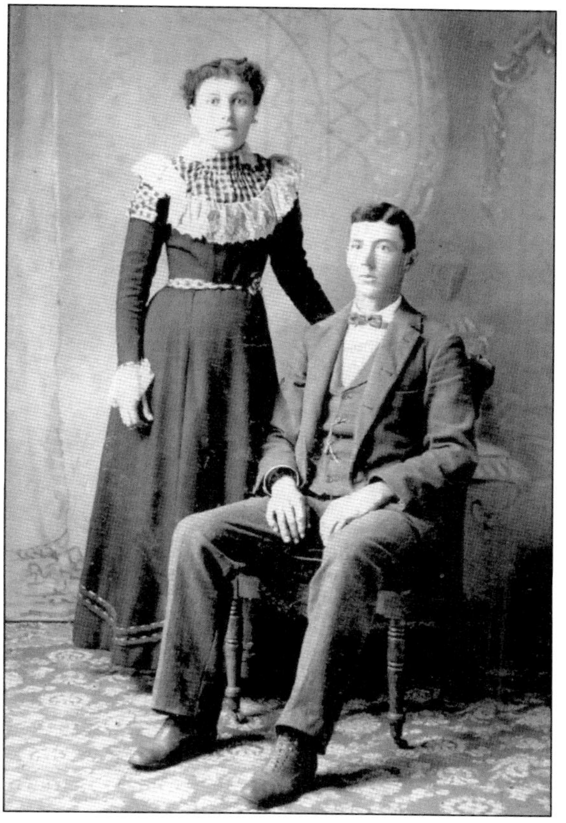

Shown at right is Joseph W. and Myrtle (Smith) Parker's wedding picture, which was taken December 24, 1897. Their children were Alvin, Mildred, and Helen. Alvin married Jeanette Praught. Mildred married Kenneth Stoltz and then Daniel Ludwig. Helen married Arne Engstrom. The Engstroms had two children, Arlene and Arne. Pictured below is the family of Walter and Sadie Smith. They are, from left to right, (first row) Arnold and Leonard; (second row) Marbrie (in Sadie's arms), Sadie, and Walter. Walter is Myrtle's brother. (Courtesy of Arne Engstrom.)

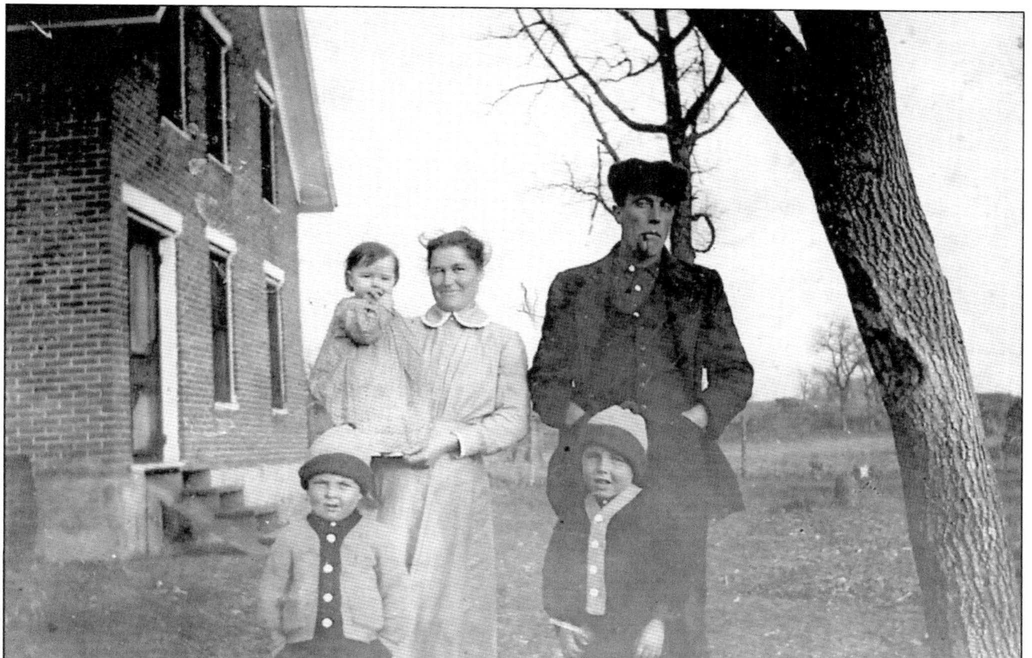

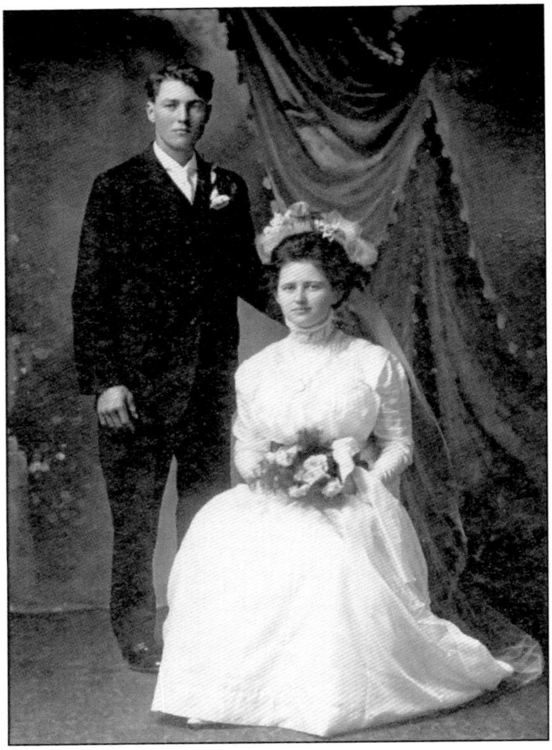

Joseph and Emily Martin were the parents of Annie, Emma, Sophia, Frank, Alfred, Delphine, Laura, Maud, and Emery. Shown at left is a picture of Alfred Martin and Flora Morrisette on their wedding day. The couple was married July 17, 1909, at St. John the Baptist Church in Dayton, Minnesota. The picture below is of Delphine Martin and Frankie Beaudry also shown on their wedding day. During an interview with Adeline (Martin) Weber, she shared that her one-room school had eight grades. Because Adeline was French, she had to teach English to the other French-speaking children when she was only in second grade. Although Weber was supposed to be doing her work, she liked listening to the more advanced lessons, which she feels made her smarter at a younger age. (Courtesy of Adeline [Martin] Weber.)

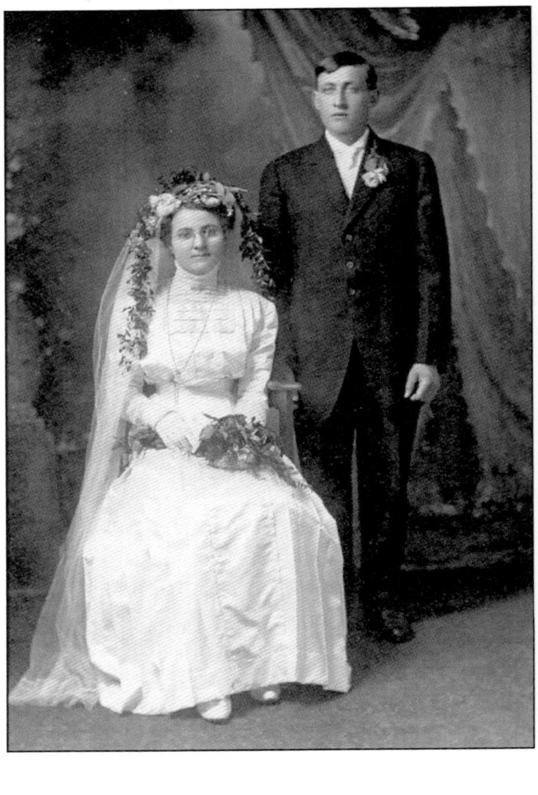

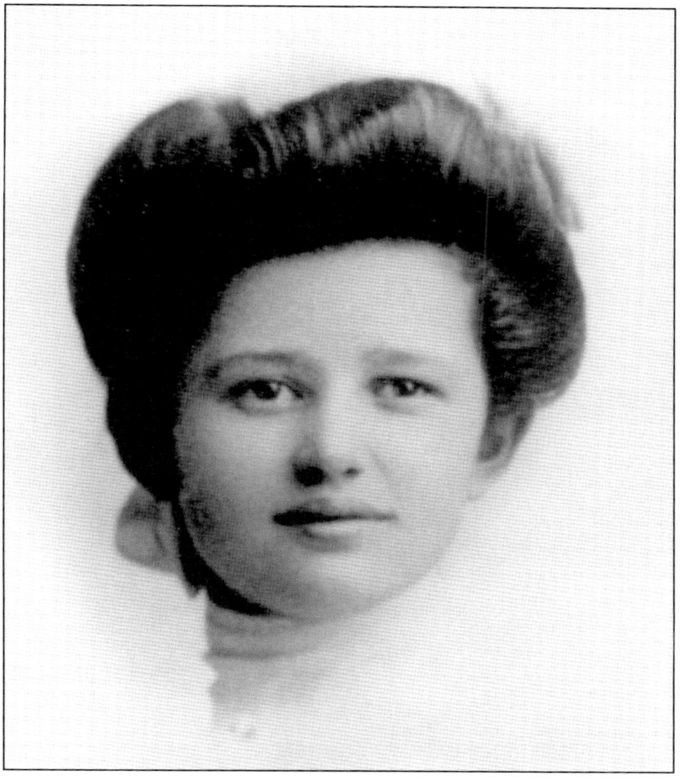

Pictured is Flora (Morrisette) Martin in her younger years and at the age of 90. Adeline Weber shared that her grandparents came down the St. Louis Seaway from Canada using a Native American guide. Grandpa Morrisette was looking for good farmland. (Courtesy of Adeline [Martin] Weber.)

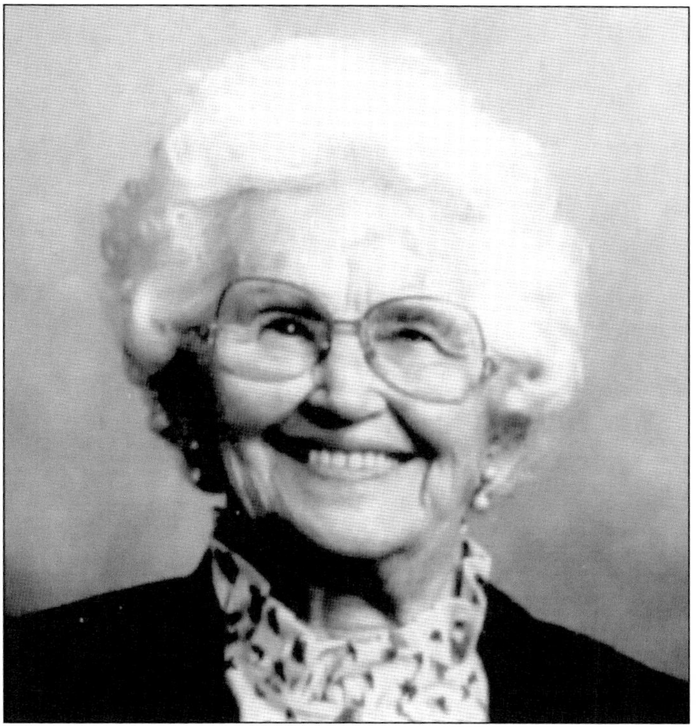

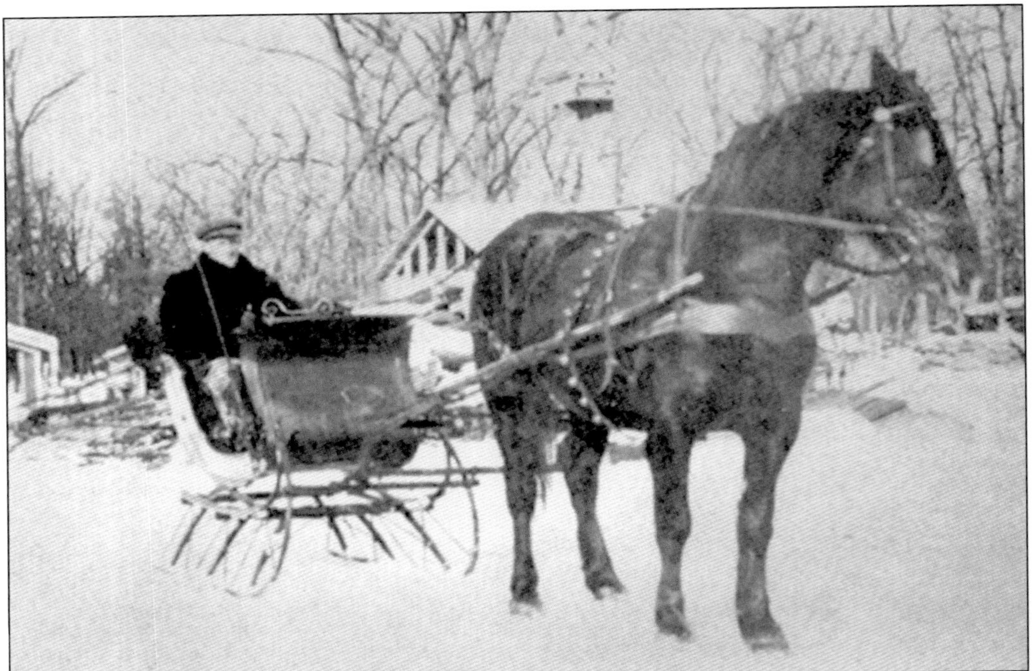

This 1911 picture above shows Sumner Davis in a cutter. Sumner, son of Joseph and Emeline (Spencer) Davis, was born in Otsego on December 5, 1871. Sumner never married. He lived with his brother Orion's family until he passed away on April 1935. Pictured below are, from left to right, Myrtle (Williams) Davis, Claude Davis, Emeline (Spencer) Davis, Grace Davis, Joseph Davis, and Arthur Davis. Joseph Davis came to Otsego in 1866. Joseph and Emeline had 11 children—5 girls and 6 boys. (Above, courtesy of Andrew Davis Jr.; below, courtesy of Wright County Historical Society.)

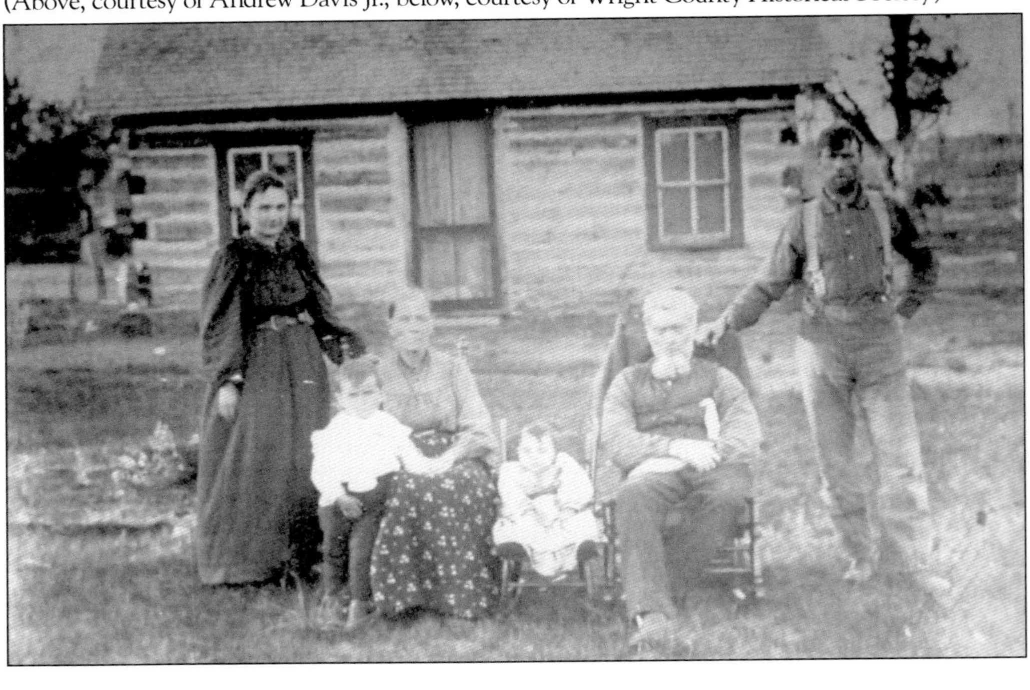

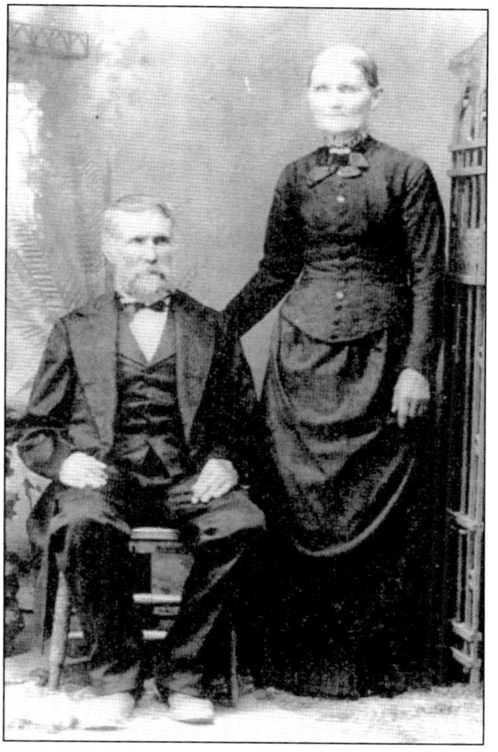

Harvey Hicks Sr. and his wife, Sally, are pictured on the right. The Hicks and Borthwich families came to Otsego from Nova Scotia. Harvey died June 29, 1896 and Sally died April 26, 1894. Pictured below is Eliza (Hicks) Stickney, daughter of the Hicks. (Courtesy of Otsego Historic Preservation Commission.)

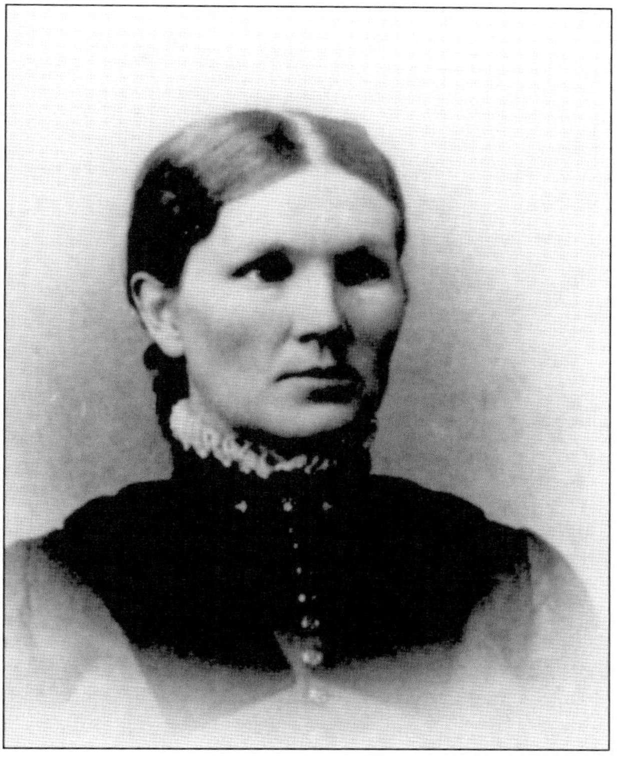

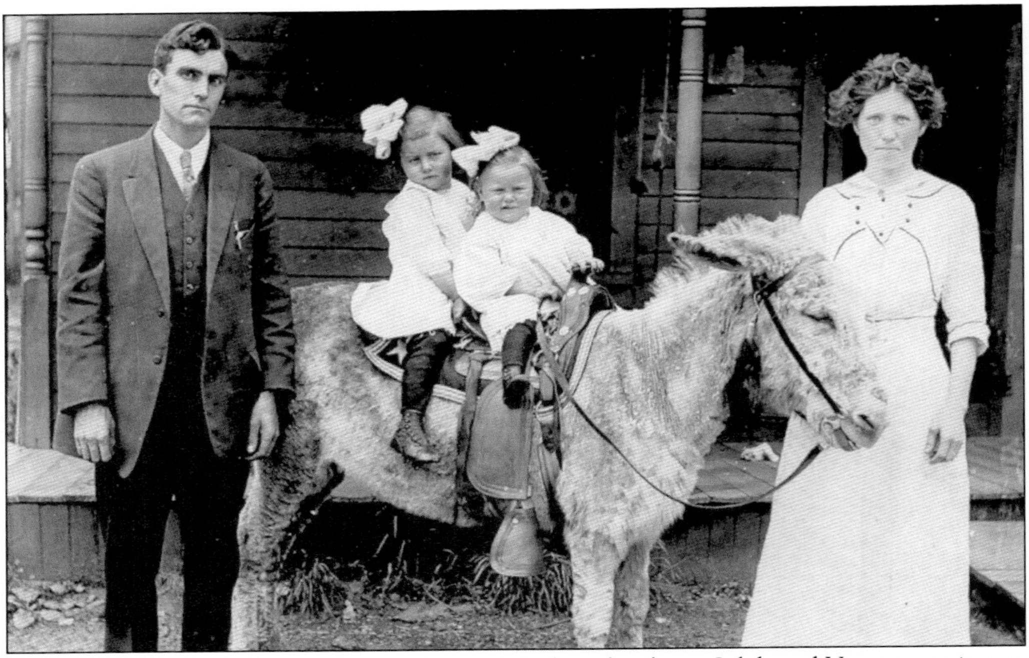

Clinton and Freda Smith are pictured above with their daughters, Lilah and Vernice, posing on a donkey in about 1915. Also shown below is a picture of John and Ellen Hamlet taken in about 1910. Hamlet owned a hotel in Elk River that was located above the bank of Elk River. John is the grandson of Joseph and Charlotte (Snow) Hamlet. (Above, courtesy of Arne Engstrom; below, courtesy of Wright County Historical Society.)

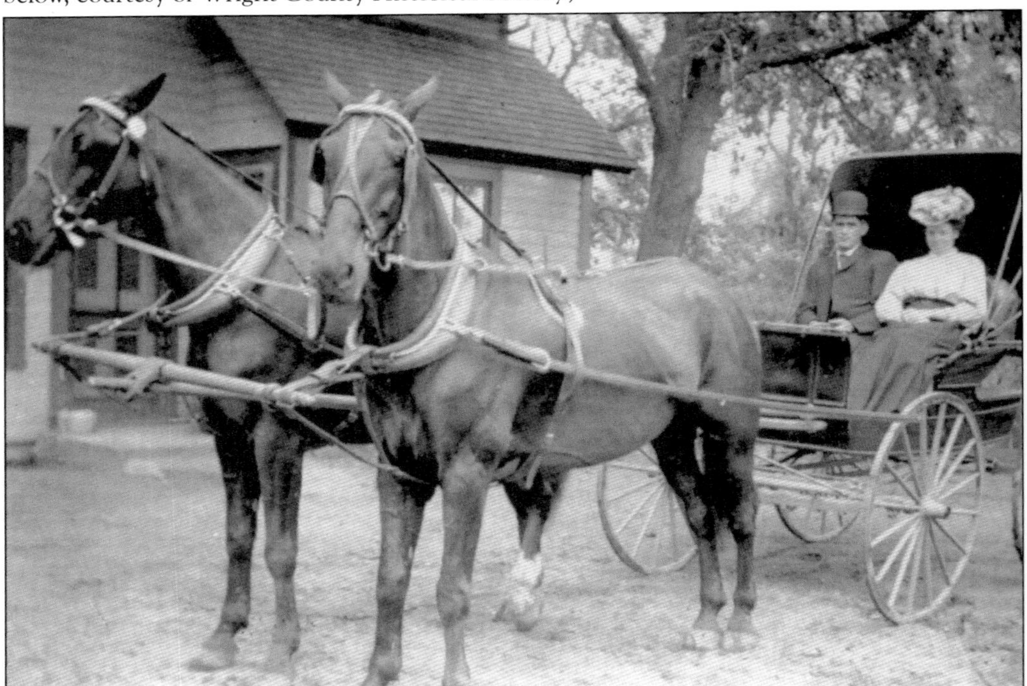

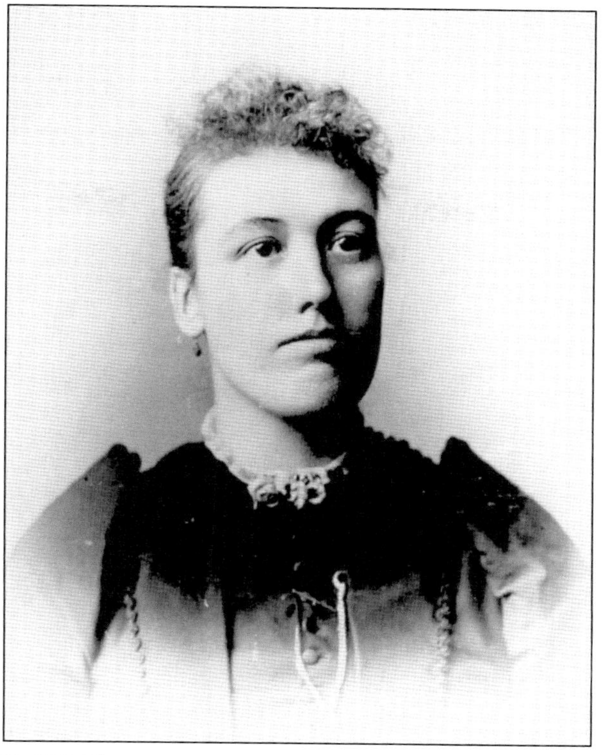

Pictured here are Nancy Ingersoll, born 1864, and George Crocker Ingersoll, who was born 1866. Nancy and George are the children of David and Eunice (Hillman) Ingersoll; Julia (Ingersoll) Holt is their sister. Nancy married Ed Chambers. The Ingersoll family is known in the area for the Ingersoll Brick Factory, located on the farm site. Clay from the bank of the river provided the substances needed to create bricks, which were shipped as far down the river as Anoka. (Courtesy of Otsego Heritage Preservation Commission.)

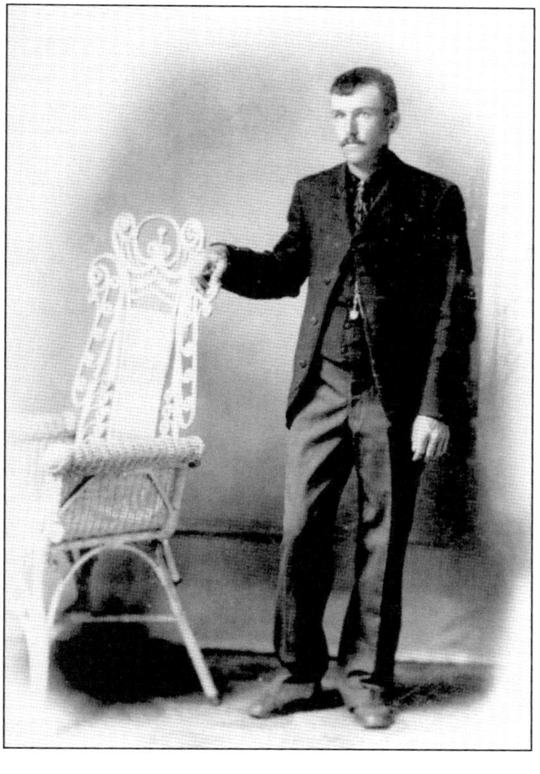

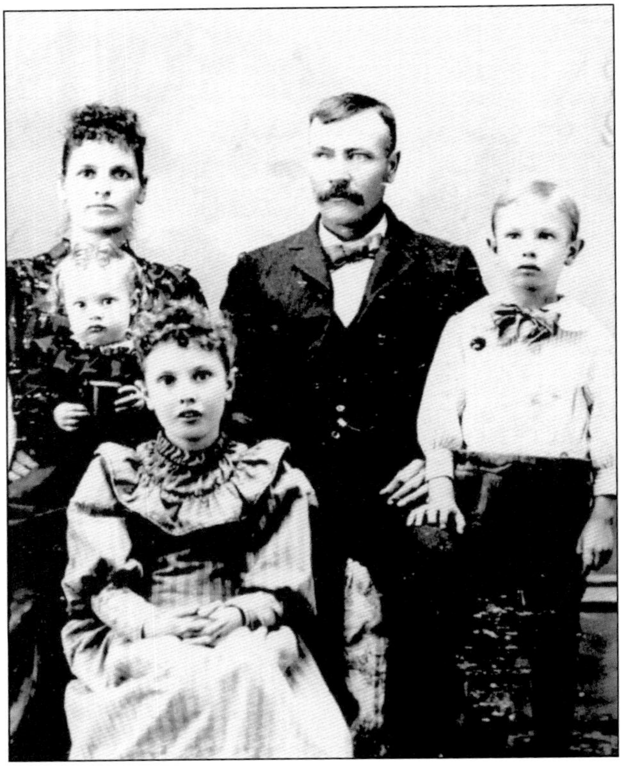

Will Mosman and Alice (Holt) Mosman are pictured on the left with their children. Also shown below is a photograph taken in 1887 after Mathilde Collette's funeral. Dennis Collette is in the chair on the left and the parish priest is in the chair on the right. Collette's sons are Phillip, Octave, Ovide, Theodule, Arcadius, Frederic, Alfred, Joseph, and William. Missing from the picture are Collette's three daughters, Sophranie, Emma, and Obeline. (Courtesy of Otsego Heritage Preservation Commission.)

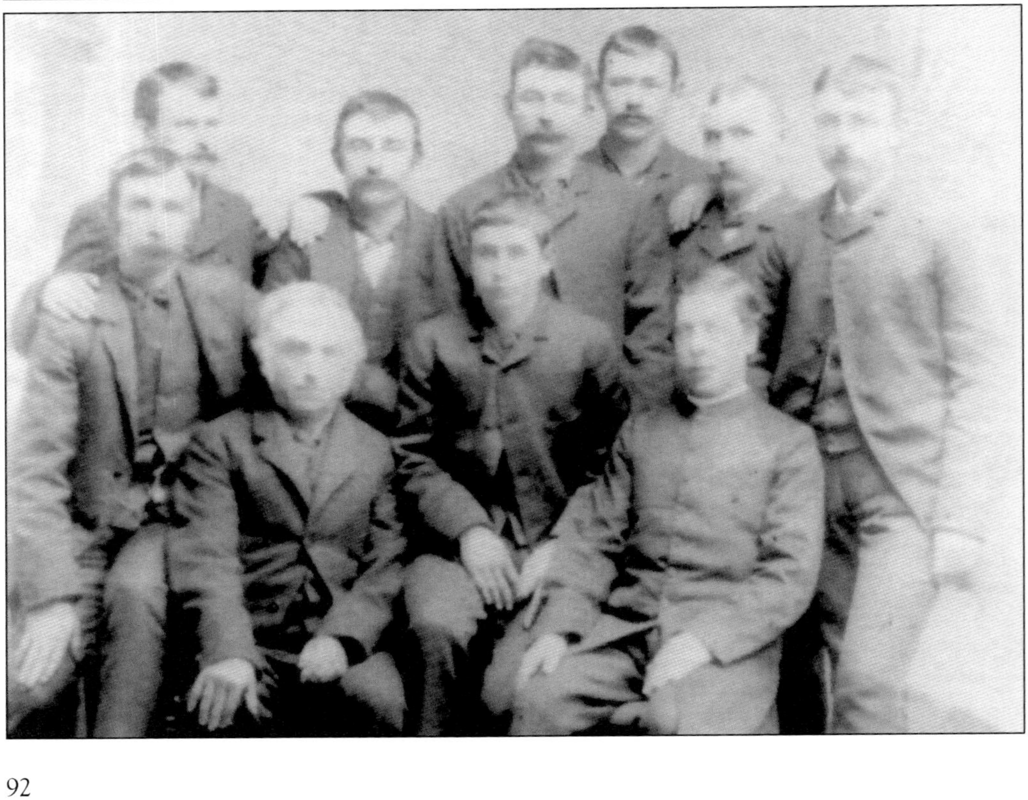

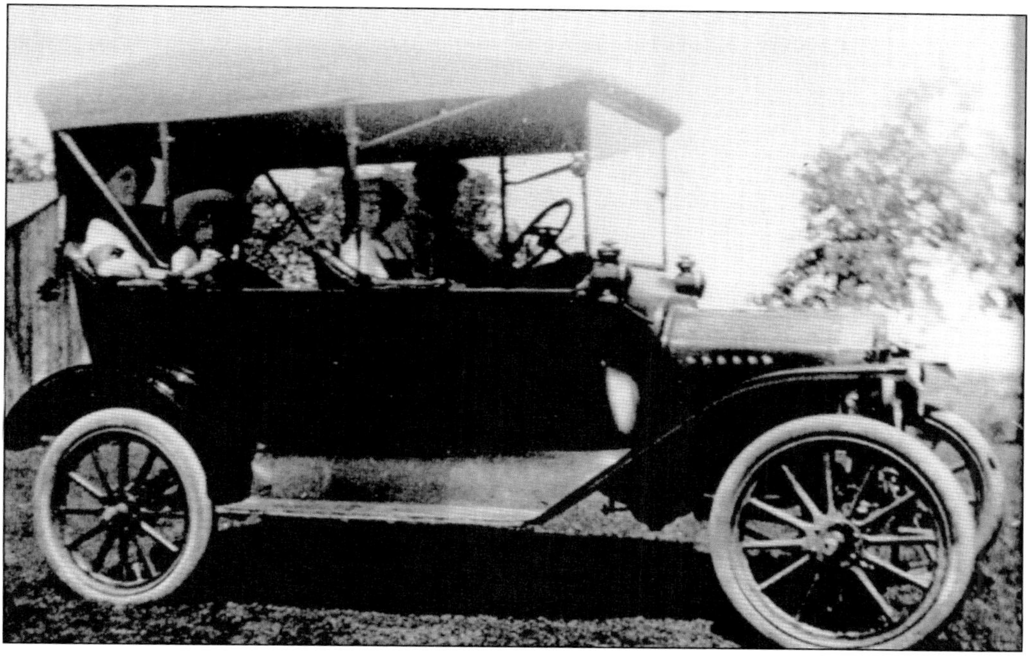

Pictured above in the car are Guy and Dorothy "Dot" (Holt) LaPlant with their children. Gus Holt is also shown here on the right. (Courtesy of Otsego Heritage Preservation Commission.)

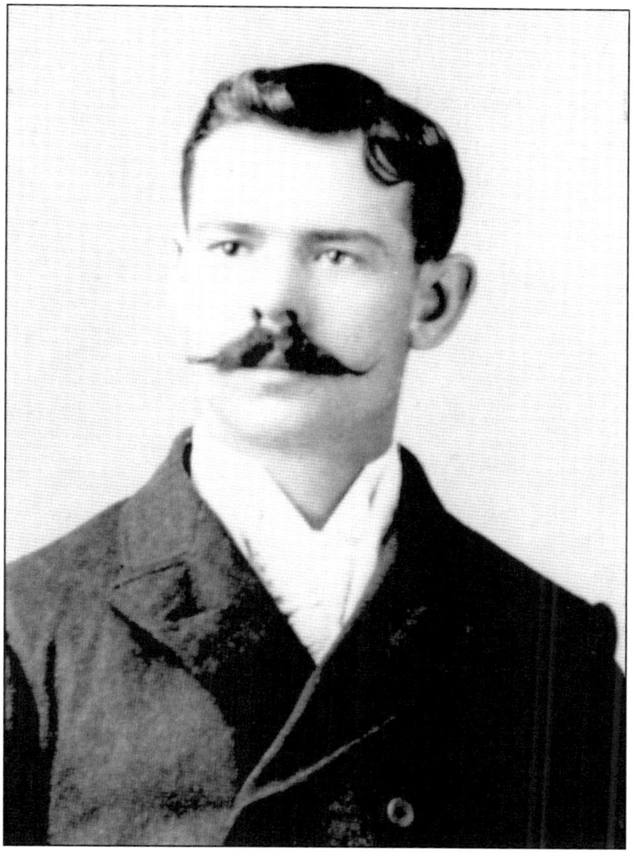

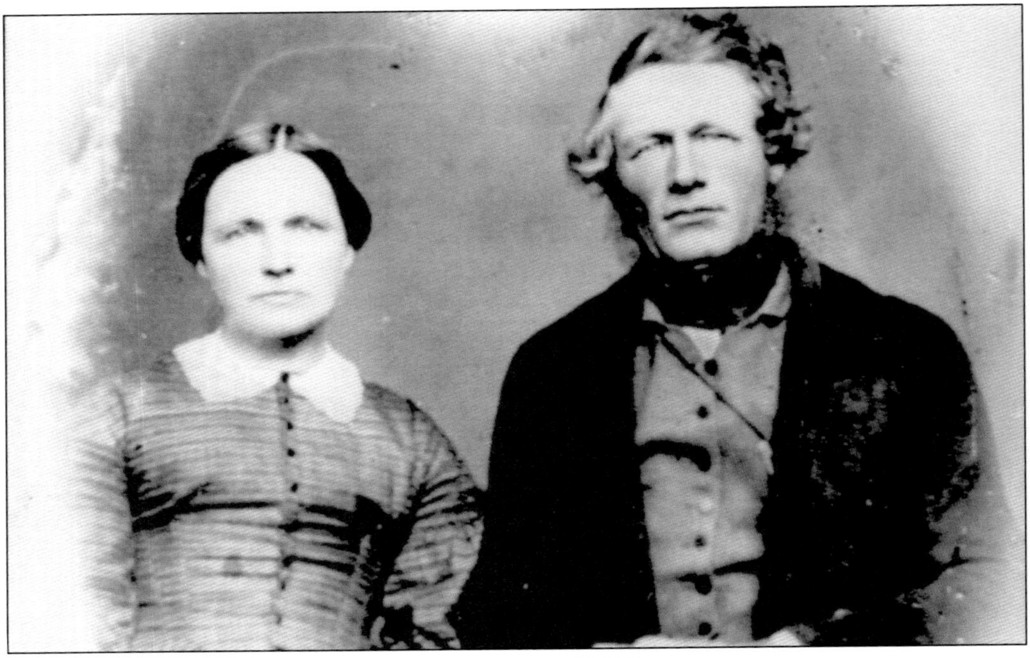

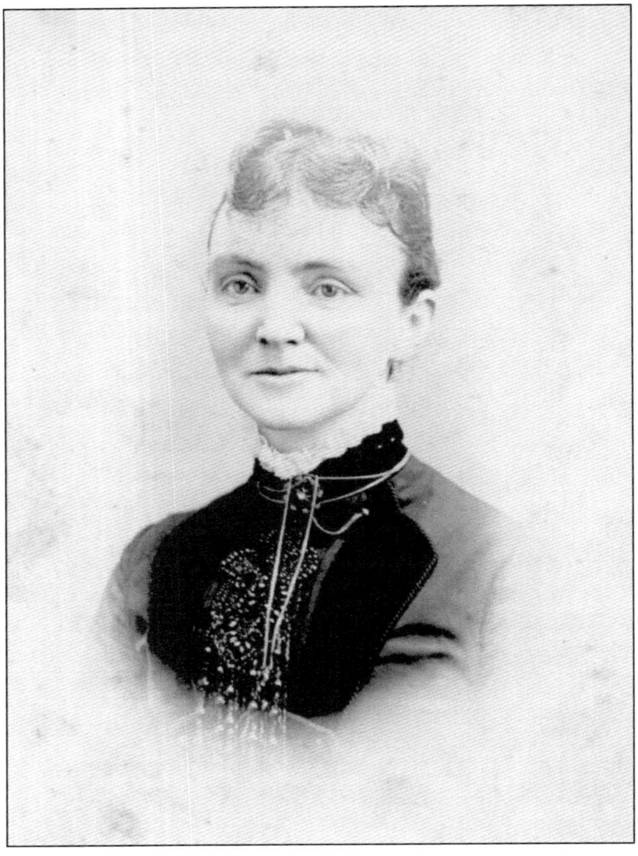

Pictured above are Ambrose and Narcissa (Merrill) Bryant. Flora Jane (Bryant) Cooley was their daughter. Flora was the mother of Daisy Ada (Cooley) Orton, who was the mother of Lorayne (Orton) Smith. Pictured at left is Ellen W. Cooley, Burton S. Cooley's sister. (Courtesy of Otsego Heritage Preservation Commission.)

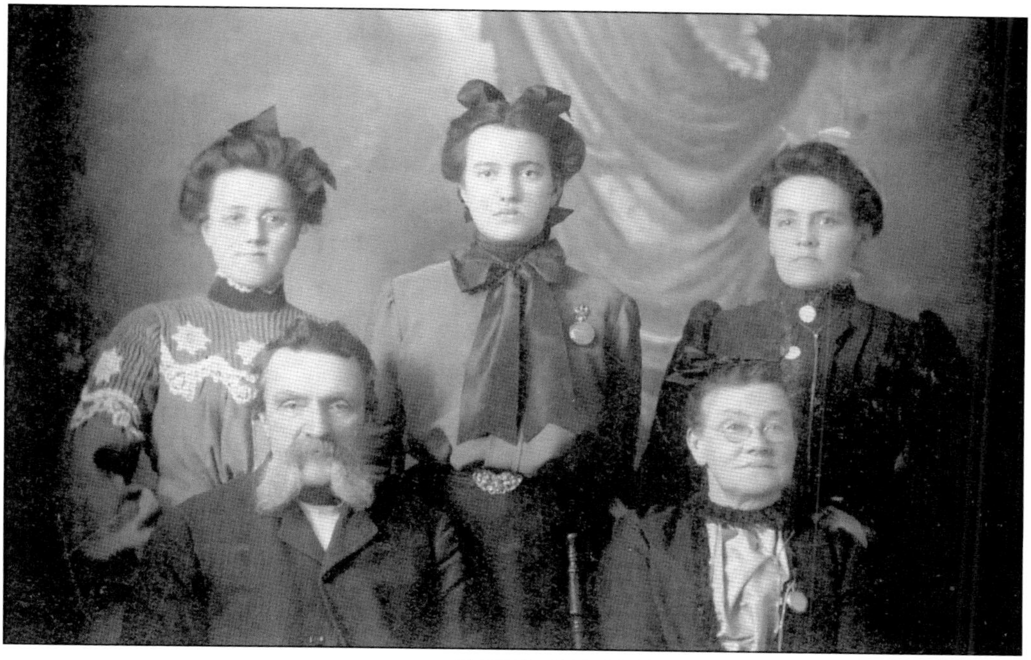

In the photograph above, seated are Burton Sidney Cooley and Florinda "Flora" Jane Bryant, the parents to three daughters, who are shown from left to right: Myrtice Ellen, Daisy Ada, and Eva (known as "old crabby Aunt Cooley"). Robert Cooley was their son. Notes on the back of the picture indicate that Myrtice married Herb Orton and upon her death, Daisy then married Herb and helped raise the children. Eva was married to Will Pepin. This picture was taken in 1904, before Burton moved to Arkansas, where he died in 1925. Also shown at right is a picture of Myrtice taken at her graduation in 1907. (Courtesy of Otsego Heritage Preservation Commission.)

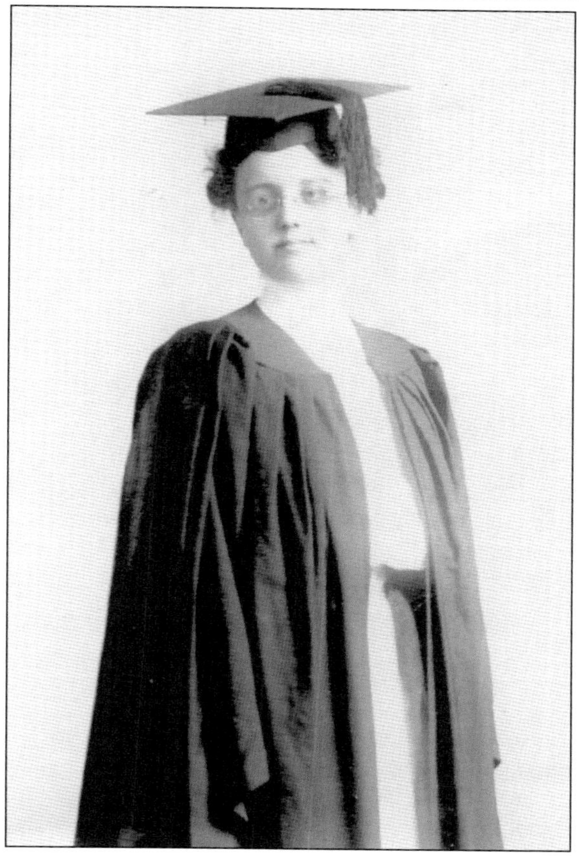

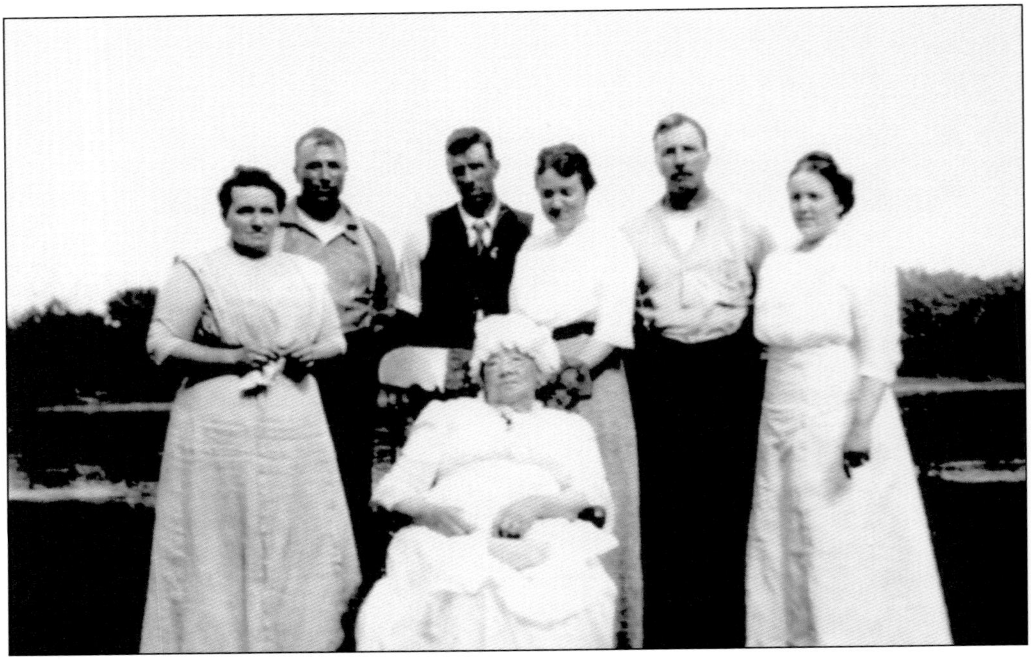

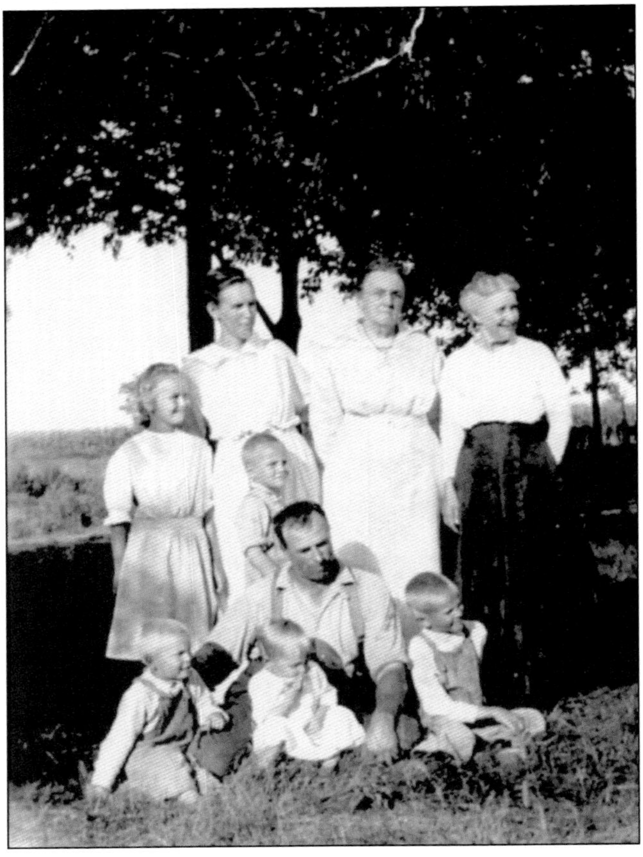

This image above was taken in 1915. Flora (Bryant) Cooley is seated with her children, who are, from left to right, Eva (Cooley) Pepin, Herbert Cooley, Sidney Cooley, Daisy Cooley, Bret Cooley, and Myrtice (Cooley) Orton. Flora's husband, Burton, was a Civil War veteran. The other picture, taken in 1918, is of more Cooley family members. They are, from left to right, (first row) Herbert Eugene Cooley, Margaret Clara Cooley, and Gordon West Cooley; (second row) Arthur Borthwich Cooley and Herbert West Cooley; (third row) Doris Muriel Cooley, Lucy Lydia (Borthwich) Cooley, Ada Marie (Cooley) Snow, and Mrs. Amzi Thorpe. (Courtesy of Otsego Heritage Preservation Commission.)

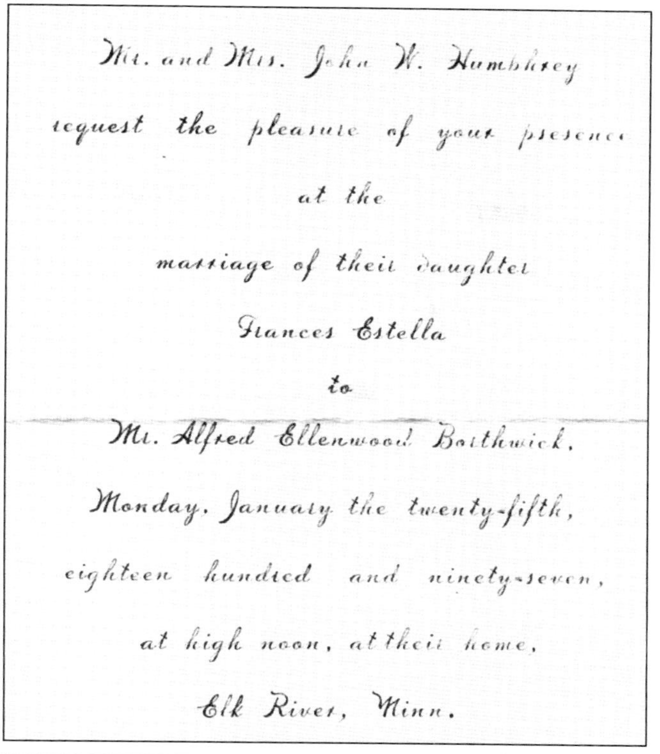
Mr. and Mrs. John W. Humphrey
request the pleasure of your presence
at the
marriage of their daughter
Frances Estella
to
Mr. Alfred Ellenwood Borthwick,
Monday, January the twenty-fifth,
eighteen hundred and ninety-seven,
at high noon, at their home,
Elk River, Minn.

Shown here is the wedding invitation and wedding picture for Frances Estella Humphrey and Alfred Ellenwood Borthwick's nuptials. They were married on January 25, 1897. (Courtesy of Otsego Heritage Preservation Commission.)

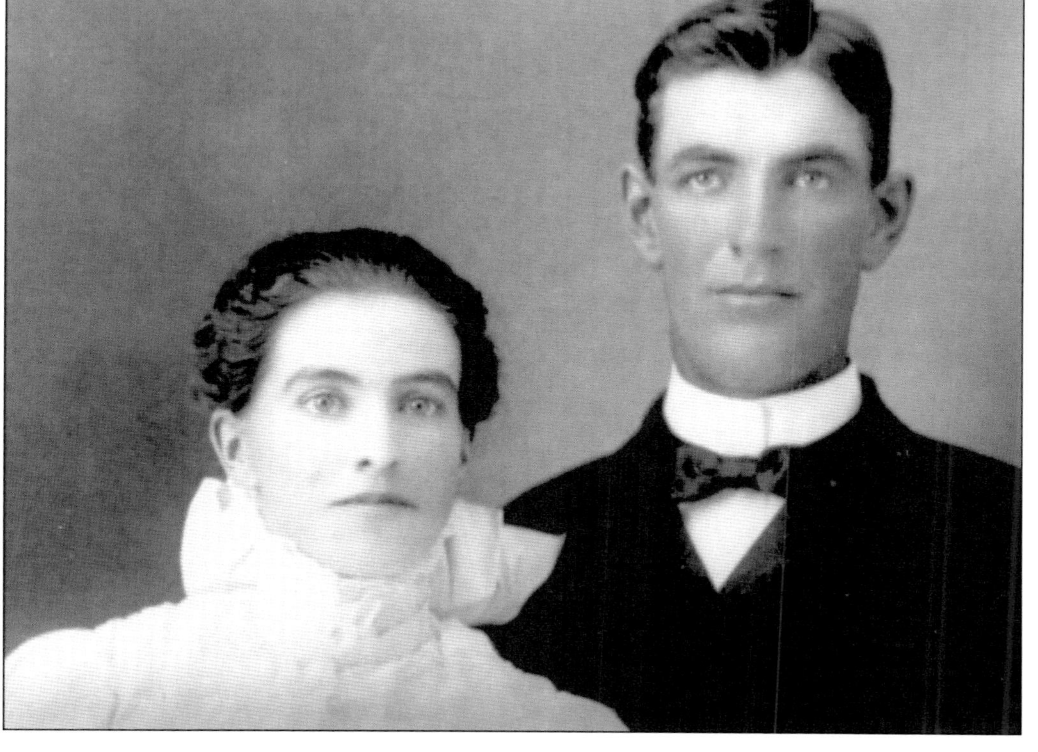

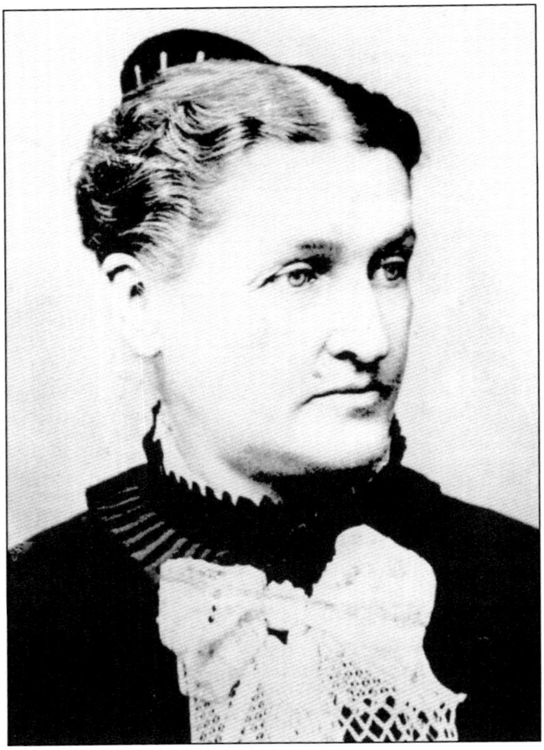

Emily (Lewis) Regester and Aaron B. Regester are pictured here. (Courtesy of Otsego Heritage Preservation Commission.)

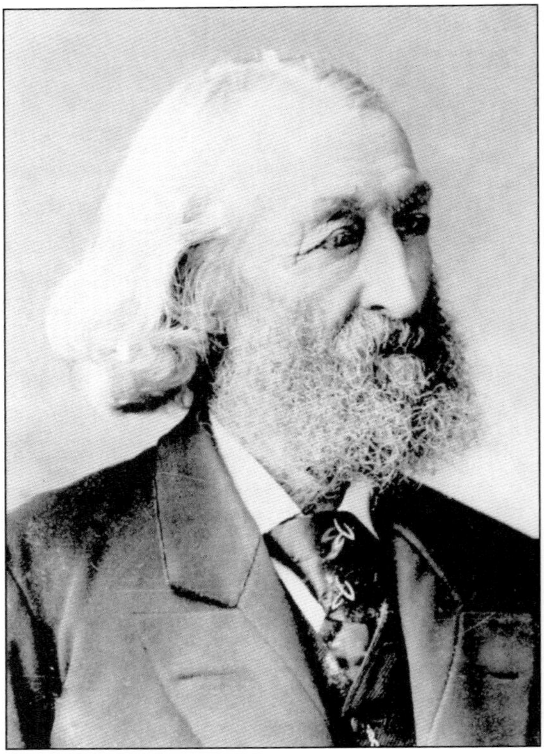

Pictured here are Estella (Humphrey) Borthwick and her brother Dr. Harry Baker Humphrey. Humphrey came with his parents to Otsego in 1882, where they settled on a farm about one and a half miles south of Elk River and three miles north of Dayton. At the age of 18, he started high school in Elk River. Humphrey built his own boats to row across the Mississippi River to get to class; in the winter, he ice skated when possible. Humphrey enrolled at the University of Minnesota in 1895 and went on to become a world-renowned scientist. Humphrey was the uncle to both Vice Pres. Hubert H. Humphrey and Dr. Harry Borthwich. (Courtesy of Otsego Heritage Preservation Commission.)

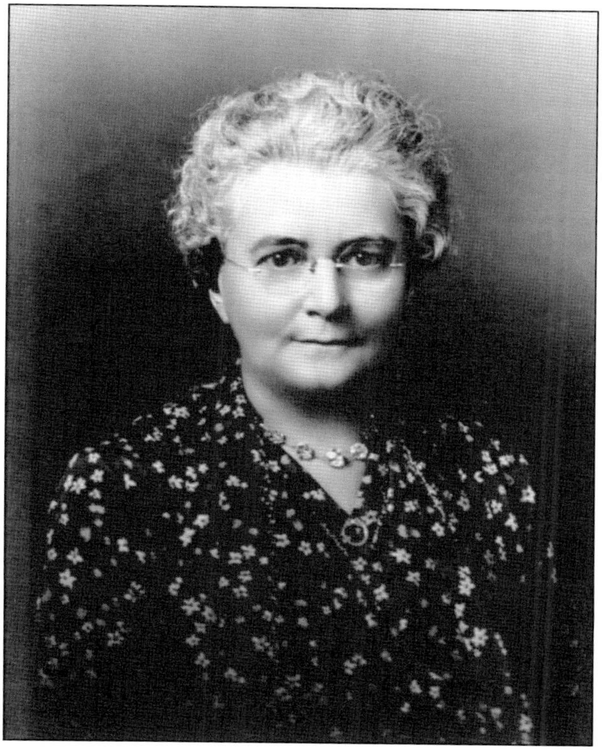

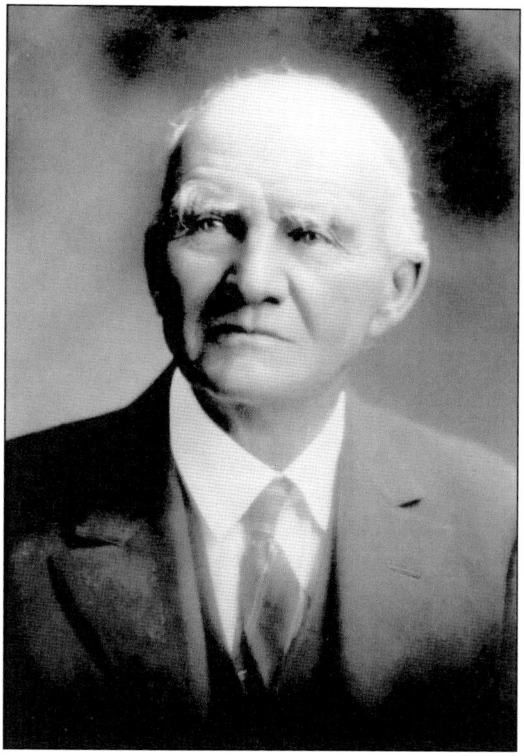

HUBERT H. HUMPHREY
MINNESOTA

United States Senate

WASHINGTON, D.C. 20510

June 18, 1973

Dr. and Mrs. Harry A. Borthwick
13700 Creekside Drive
Silver Spring, Maryland 20904

Dear Harry and Myrtes:

I am sure it has been a long time since you received a photograph of Muriel and myself. We just thought you might like to have the enclosed which was taken recently.

Sincerely,

Hubert

This letter from Hubert H. Humphrey was sent to Harry and Myrtes Borthwick along with this picture of Hubert H. Humphrey and his wife, Muriel. (Courtesy of Otsego Heritage Preservation Commission.)

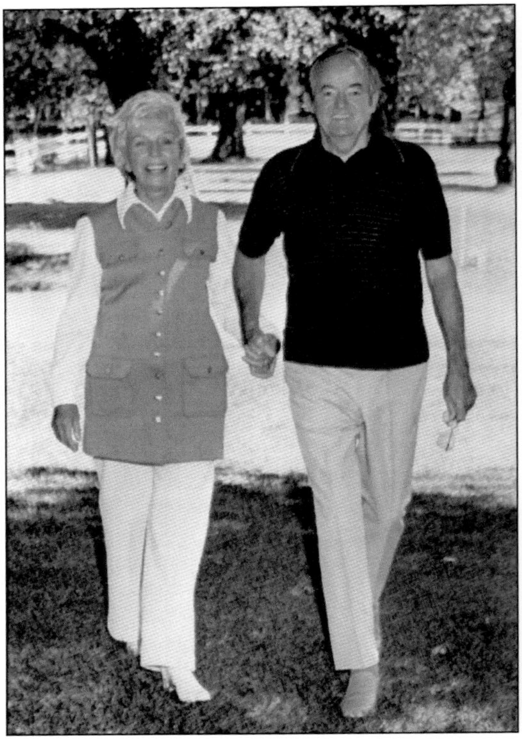

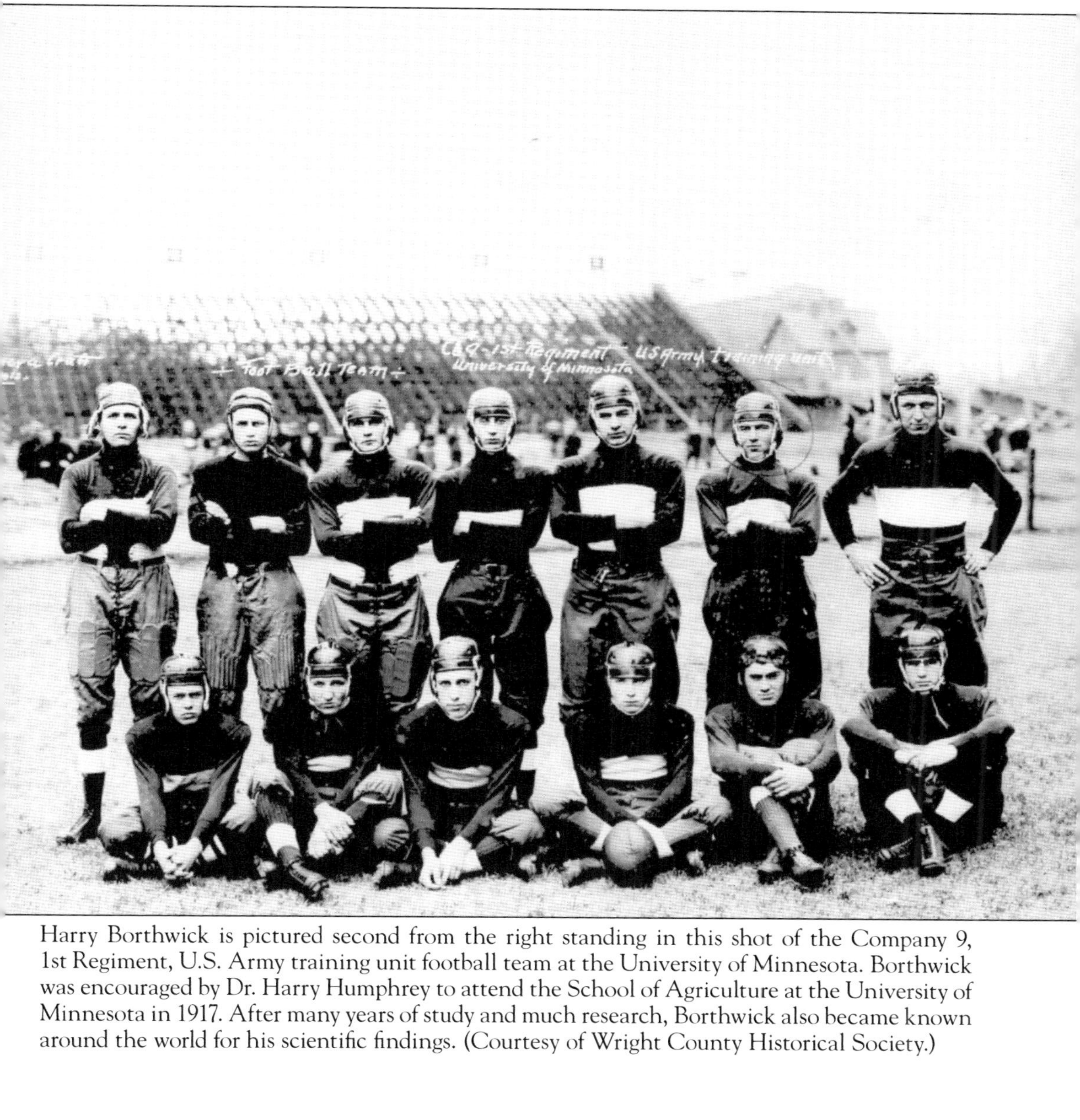

Harry Borthwick is pictured second from the right standing in this shot of the Company 9, 1st Regiment, U.S. Army training unit football team at the University of Minnesota. Borthwick was encouraged by Dr. Harry Humphrey to attend the School of Agriculture at the University of Minnesota in 1917. After many years of study and much research, Borthwick also became known around the world for his scientific findings. (Courtesy of Wright County Historical Society.)

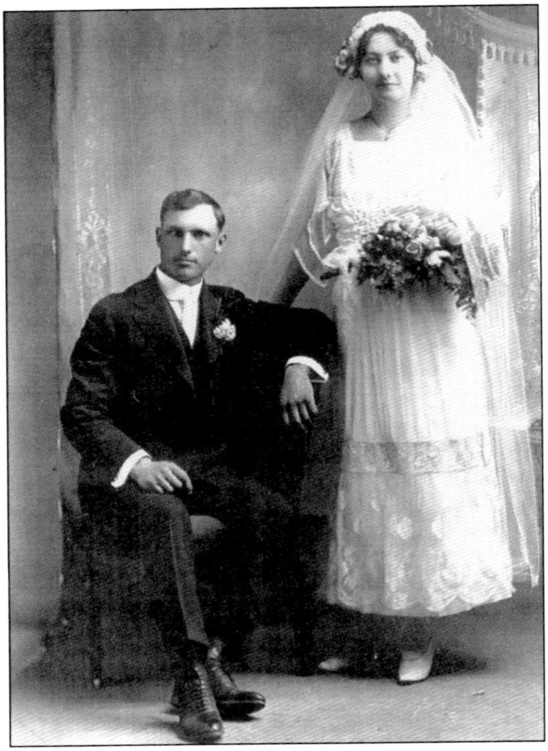

Ellen and Joe DeMars are captured at left posing on their wedding day. The other wedding picture is of Edward and Rose (Gonyea) Carron, Raymond Carron's parents, taken in the early 1900s. (Left. courtesy of Otsego Historic Preservation Commission; below, courtesy of Diane DeMars.)

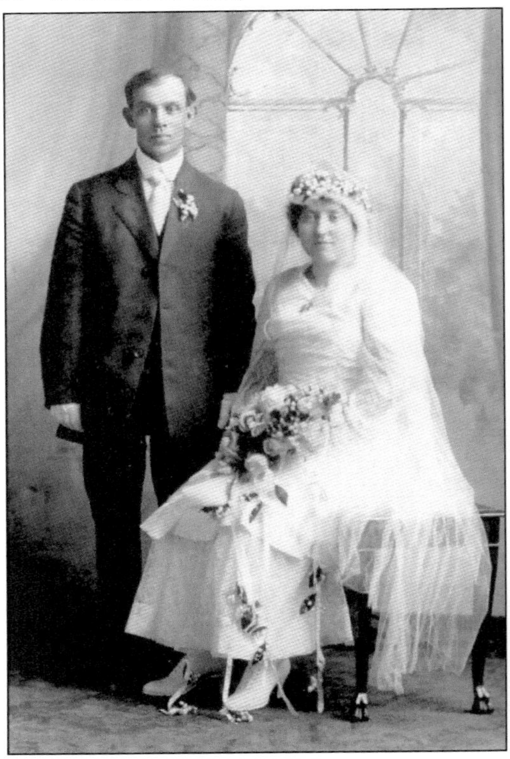

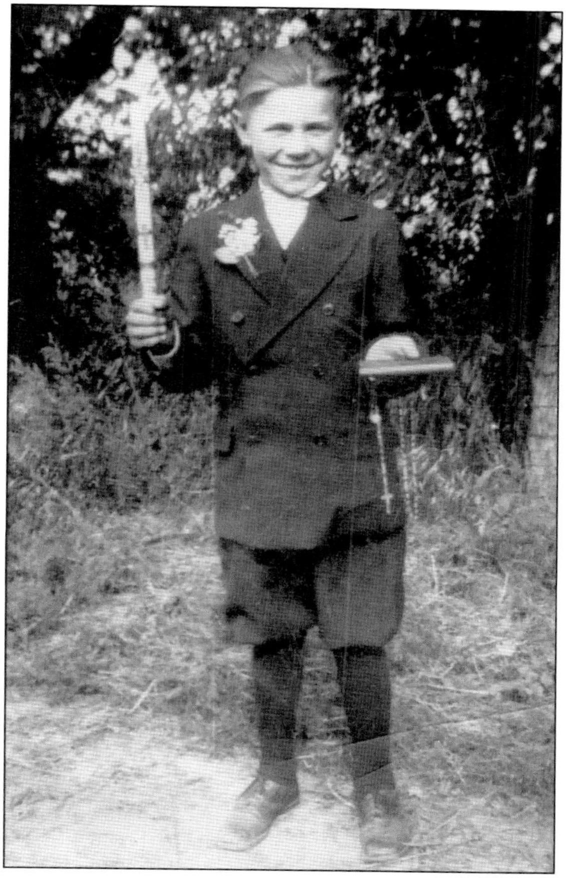

Raymond, seen at right, took his first communion on the Carron farm in Otsego. His parents were Edward and Rose (Gonyea). Raymond was married to Jeanette Marie Paisley on June 27, 1942. That same year, he purchased the original homestead from his uncle and aunt, Mitchell and Victoria (Carron) Tebo. In addition to farming, Carron owned and operated the Carron Bus Service for the Elk River and Monticello school districts. Shown below is Raymond with several vehicles he restored. (Courtesy of Diane DeMars.)

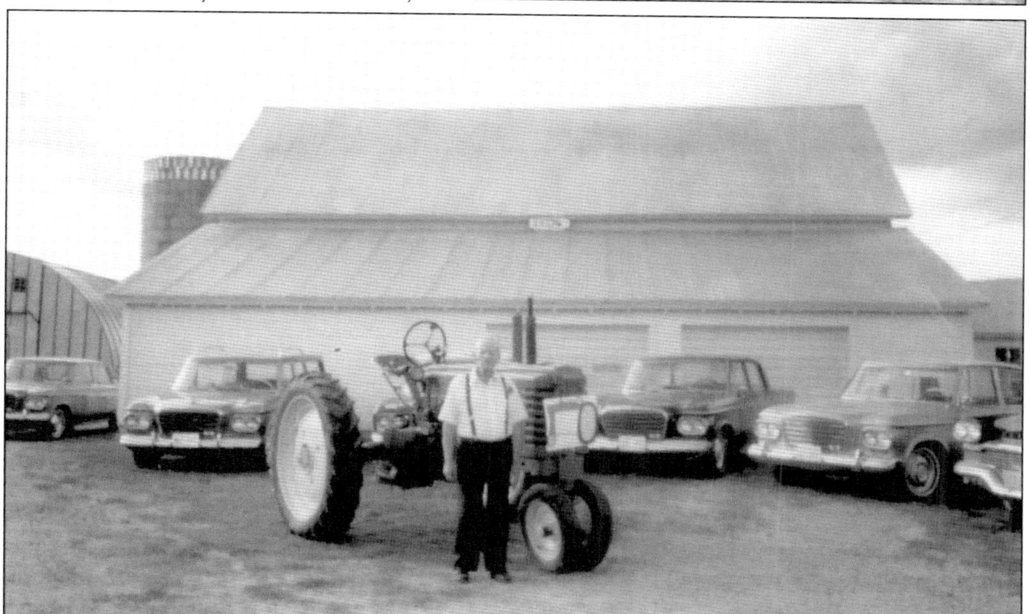

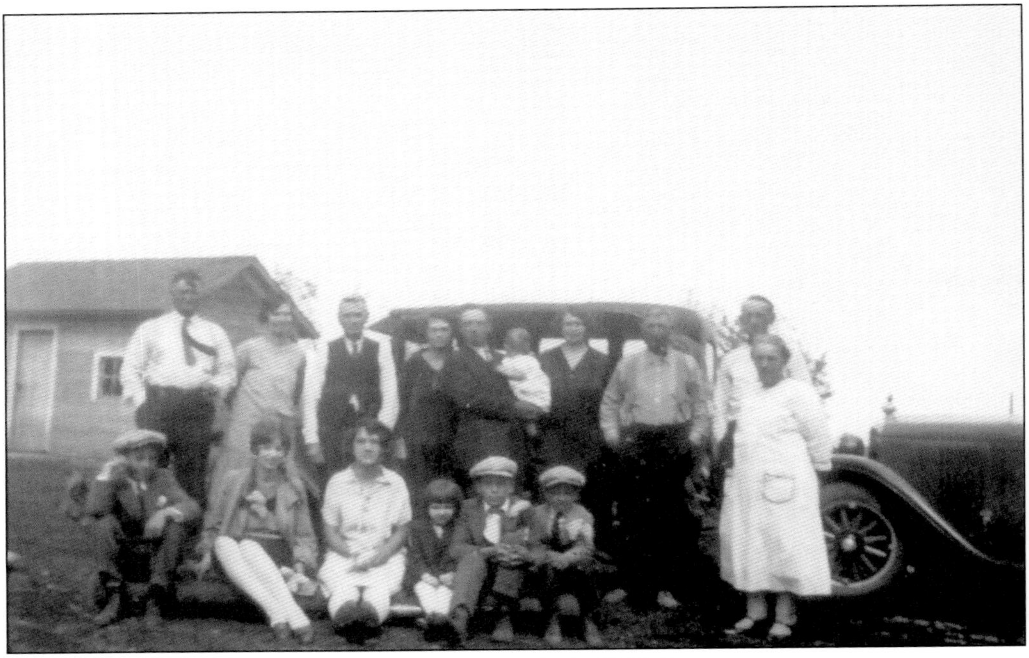

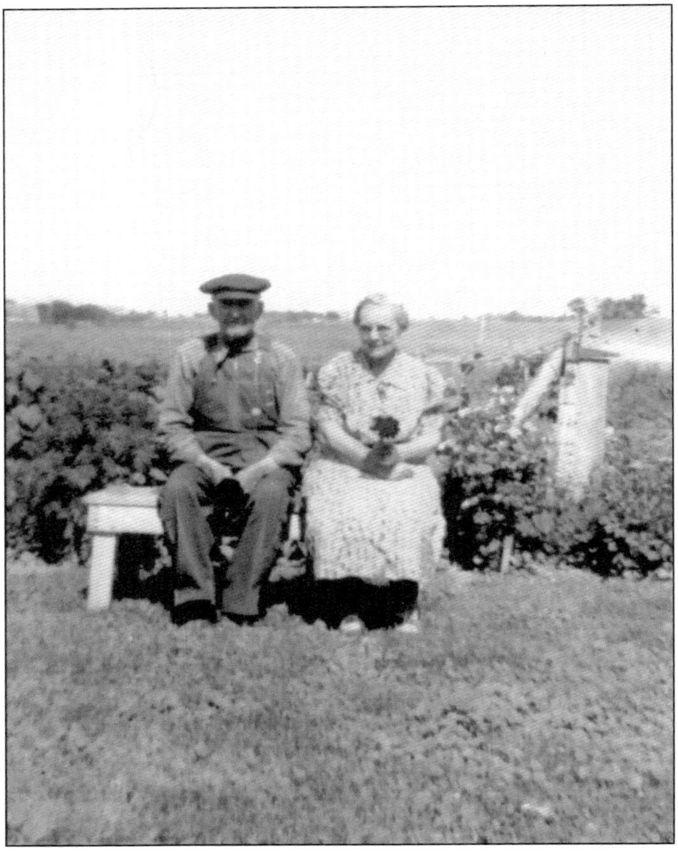

Mitchell and Victoria (Carron) Tebo celebrated their 50th wedding anniversary with family and friends. The Tebos did not have any children, but they were dearly loved by the community. On the left, Mitchell and Victoria (Carron) Tebo are shown sitting on a bench. (Courtesy of Diane DeMars.)

Pictured at right are, from left to right, Mitchell, Frank, and Fred Fournier. Lloyd Cyr shared the following story as told by his grandmother Caroline. Caroline DeMars married Mitchell Fournier in 1881. The Fourniers had two daughters, Ida and Theresa. In 1885, the family moved to Pembina, North Dakota by oxcart following the Red River Trail. While in Pembina, Theresa died. Shortly thereafter, another daughter, Minnie, was born. Mitchell died when Minnie was only six months old. Caroline moved back to Dayton with her children and later married Joe Corrow. The wedding picture of Caroline and Joe is shown below. Like many families, the spelling of their last name was captured in many different ways, such as Corrow, Caron, and Carron. (Courtesy of Lloyd and Marie Anne Cyr.)

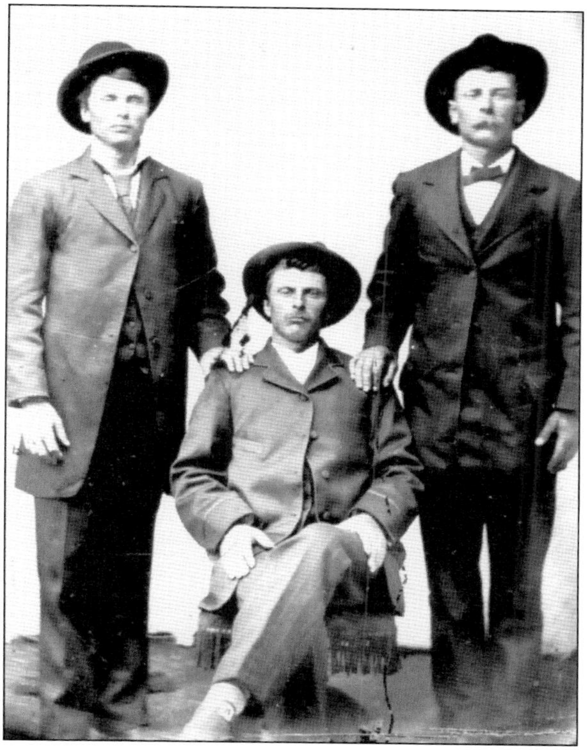

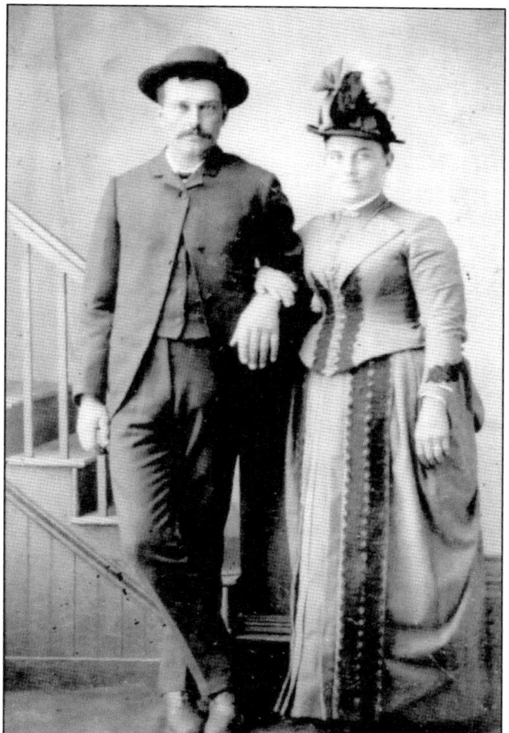

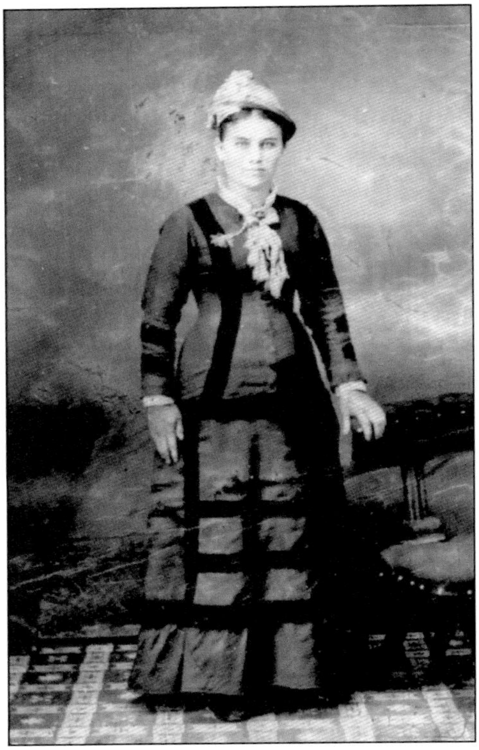

This picture of Caroline (DeMars) Corrow was taken in 1890. The family picture below was taken in 1892. Seen in this family picture are, from left to right, Richard Corrow seated on Joe Corrow's lap; Albert Corrow standing in front of Ida Fournier; Caroline (DeMars Fournier) Corrow; and Minnie Fournier. Yet to be born are Fred and Georgiana Corrow. (Courtesy of Lloyd and Marie Anne Cyr.)

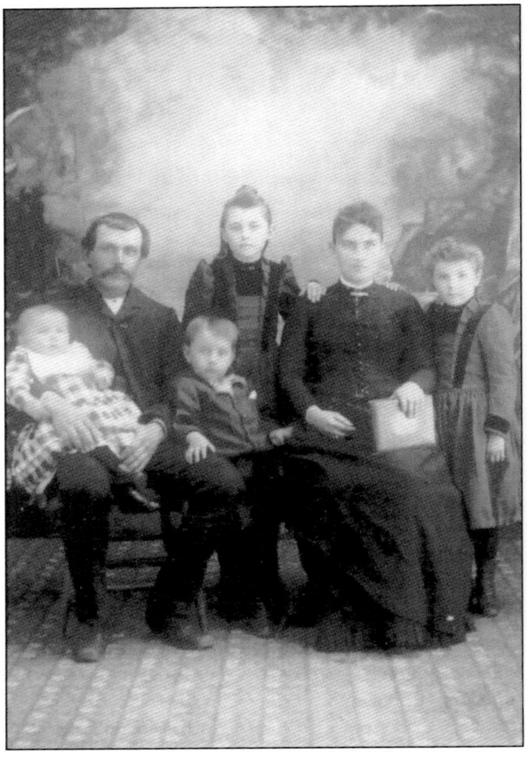

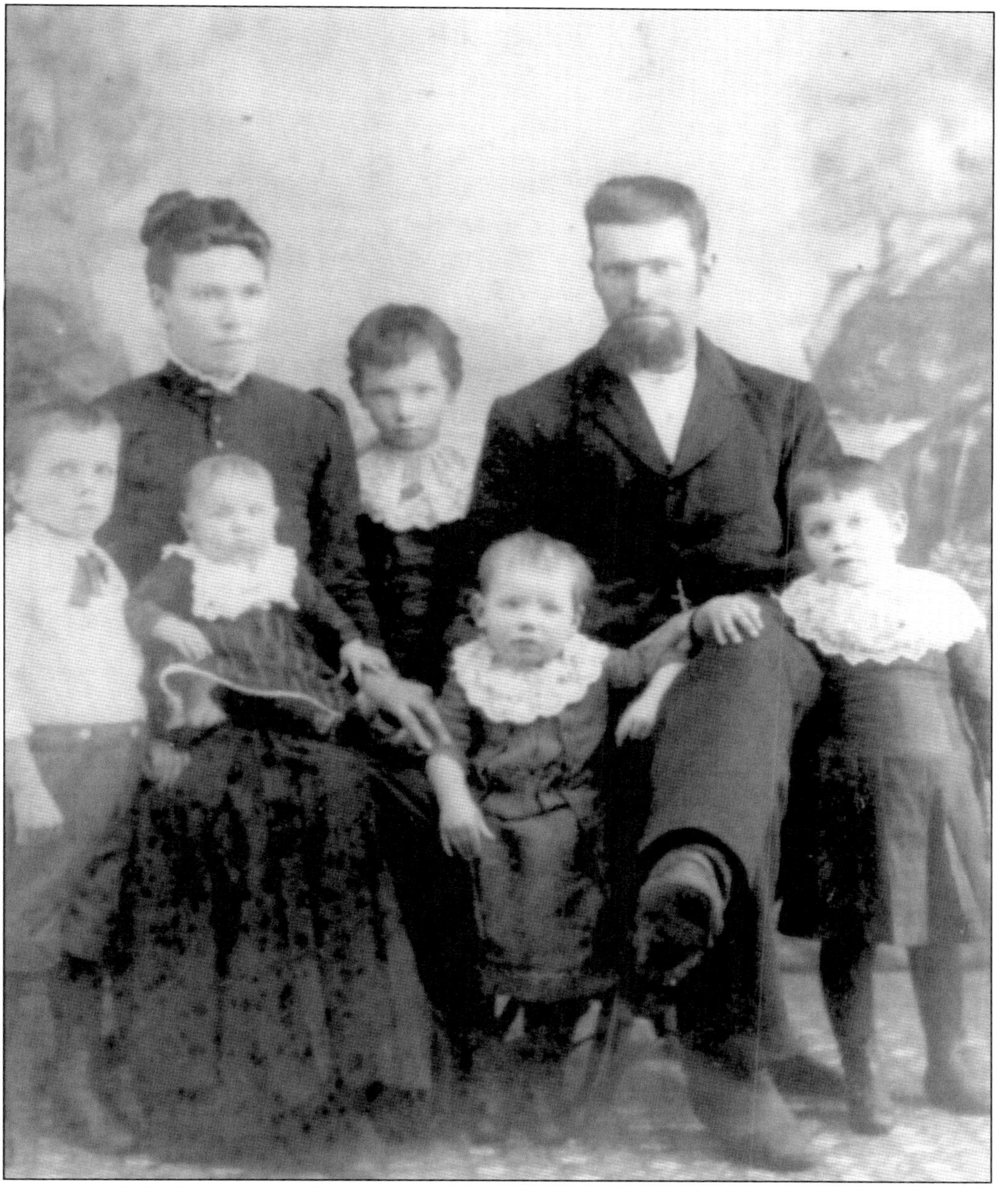

Taken in 1890, this image includes the parents George and Mary Elizabeth (Ebner) Lahn with their children, who are shown from left to right, Richard, Gertrude, Clara, Ida, and Nora. This is one of only two pictures taken that included George Lahn. He passed when he was only 41 years old from a condition known as Bright's disease, an inflammation of the kidneys. Mary Elizabeth was left to care for nine children. Keeping with tradition, after a full year of mourning, Clara was allowed to marry. In 1908, five Ebner children joined the Lahn family for two years after their mother died of cancer. The children were offspring of William and Margaret (Becker) Ebner; Mary Elizabeth's brother's children. Margaret died of cancer only six weeks after giving birth to a daughter, Ruby. Mary Elizabeth raised Ruby while the other children were cared for by their father after the initial stay in the Lahn home. (Courtesy of Wenda [Lahn] Duerr.)

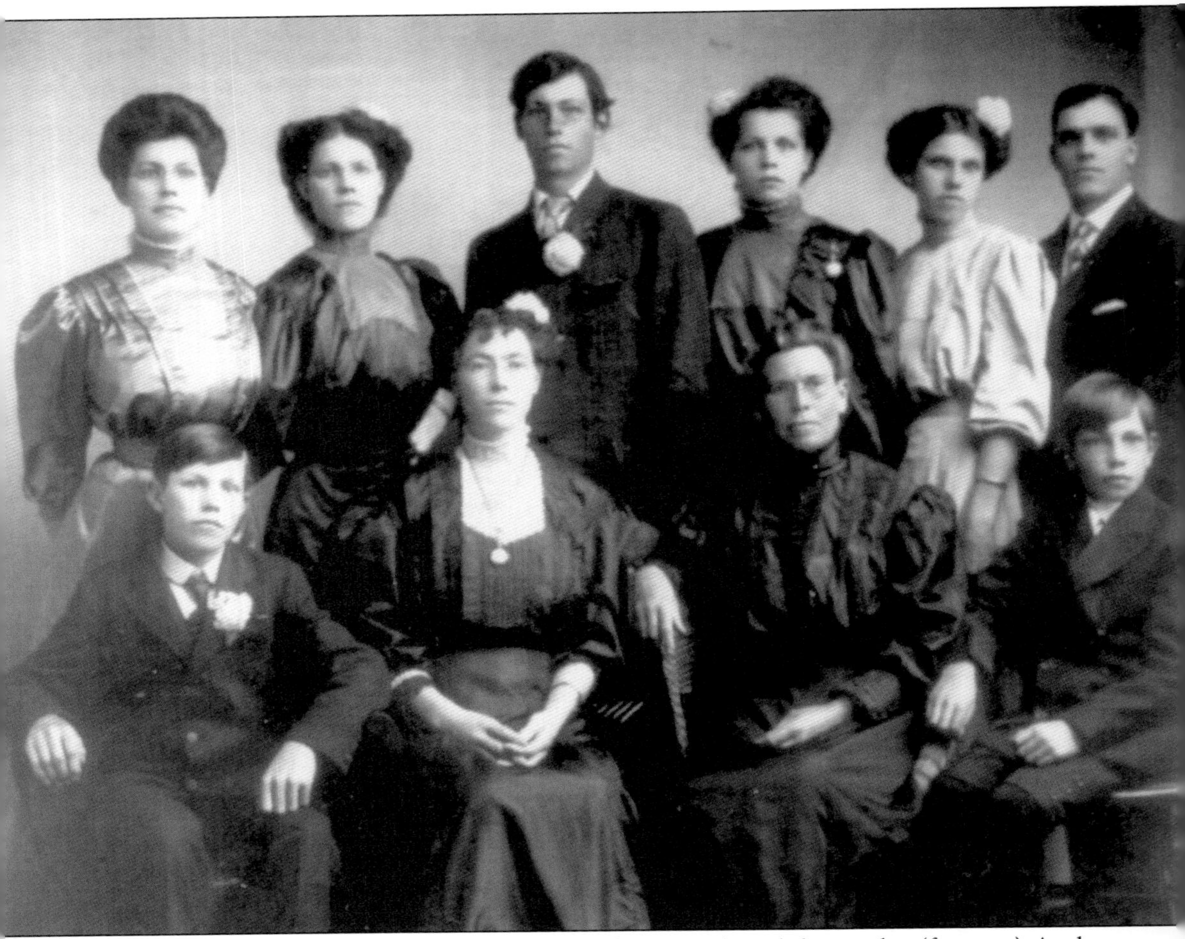

This picture was taken in August 1910. Seen here are, from left to right, (first row) Anthony, Clara, Mary Elizabeth, and Ralph (Wenda [Lahn] Duerr's father); (second row) Nora, Ida, Albert, Gertrude, Theresa, and Richard. The family shopped in Anoka, which was a one-hour buggy ride with a light buggy and fast horse or a two-and-a-half-hour ride with a loaded buggy and two horses. Going to Minneapolis took five-and-a-half to six hours; it would be an overnight adventure for those who went. This is the first picture on record of Ralph. Because one of the children could not pronounce "grandma," Mary Elizabeth was referred to as "Goshie" by the entire family. (Courtesy of Wenda [Lahn] Duerr.)

Posing are Margaret and Joseph Vasseur. Joseph was born Levasseur, but changed the spelling to Vassar until his later years when he settled on Vasseur. Joseph was a brick maker. He used the clay found on his farm to create the blocks rather than a compound found on the riverbank. Vassar and Company's annual production was about 250,000 bricks, selling for $7 to $8 per 1,000. In 1881, the brick company sold 300,000 for $8 per 1,000 in small lots at the kiln or large lots, which were loaded at the Itasca Station. The Vasseur bricks were cream and yellow in color and have been used in many buildings in the area; the most well known is the St. Michael Catholic Church. The picture of children playing below was taken in the early 1920s on the Vasseur farm. (Courtesy of Joan Vasseur.)

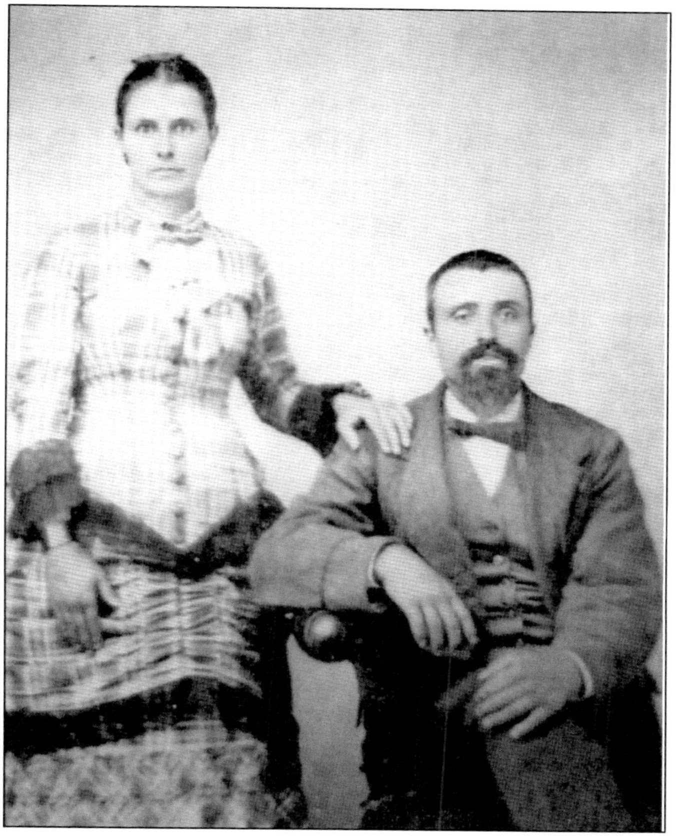

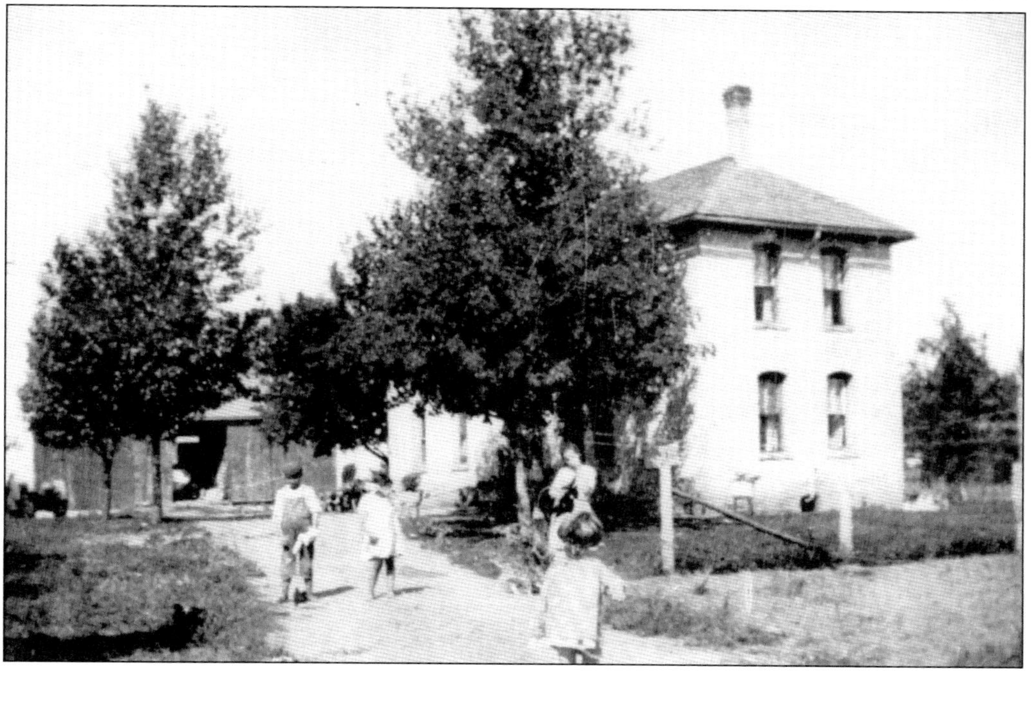

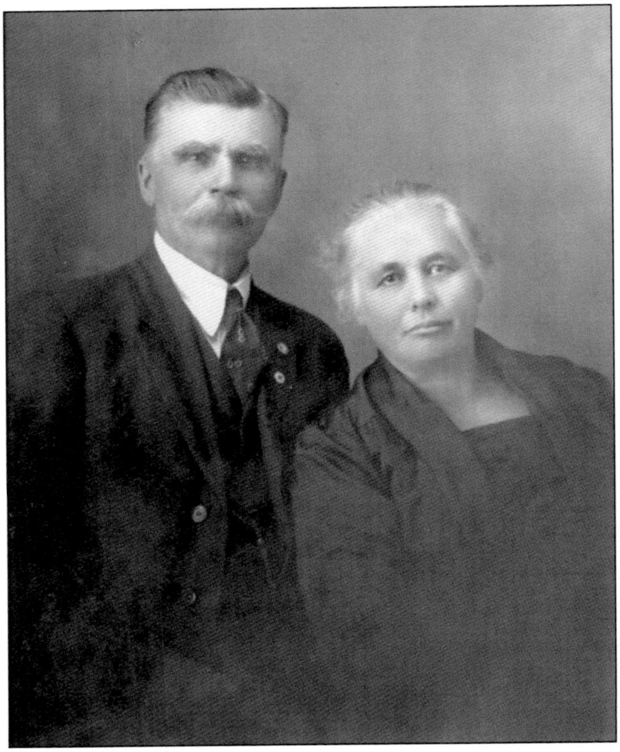

Pictured on the left are Ferdinand and Zerilla (Bourgeois) Lefebvre. Zerilla is also a member of the five-generation image seen below. In this image are, from left to right, (first row) Pierre Rouillard, patriarch born 1819; Robert Lefebvre, great-great-grandson born 1904; and Rose (Rouillard) Bourgeois, daughter born 1841; (second row) Zerilla (Bourgeois) Lefebvre, granddaughter born 1860, and Johnnie Lefebvre, great-grandson born 1878; standing front center. (Left, courtesy of Patty and Richard Lefebvre; below, courtesy of Mary Anne McNeil.)

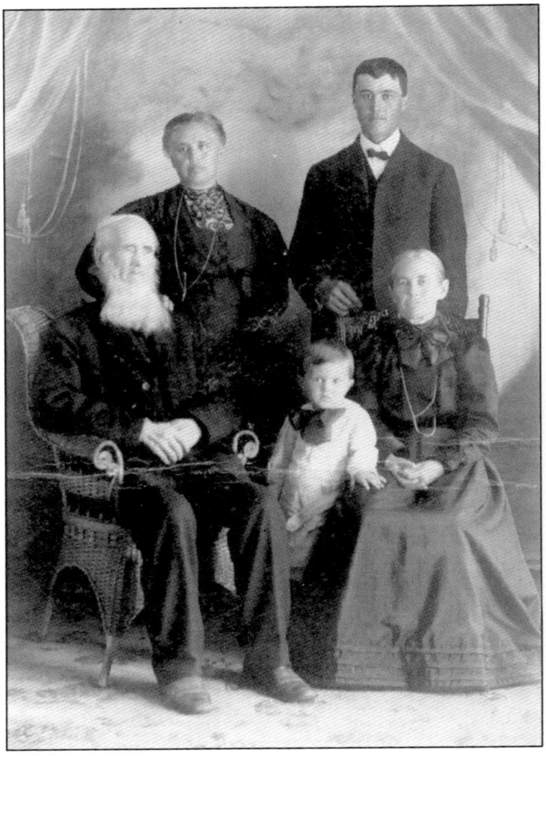

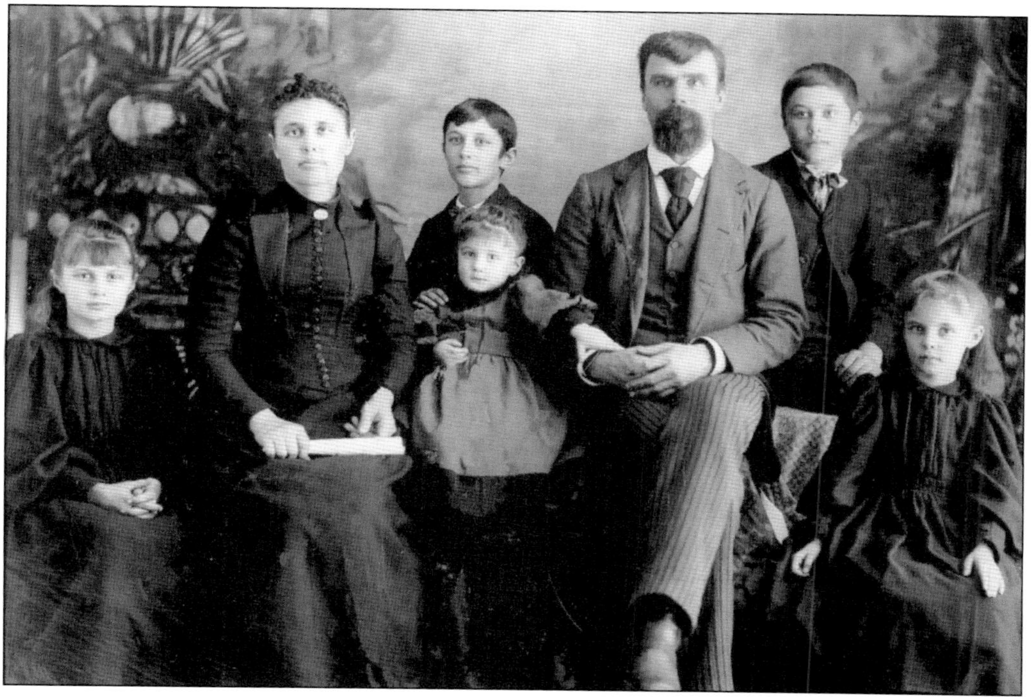

Married in 1878, Ferdinand and Zerilla (Bourgeois) Lefebvre are pictured above with their children. Eventually the family included Johnnie, Joe, Noel, Camille, Aurora, Eugena, Josephine Rose, Lucille, and Odel. A daughter died when she was only one year of age. Zerilla's parents, Gene and Rose Bourgeois, gave them a 160-acre farm where the round barn is located. Bourgeois helped all five of the son-in-laws get started in farming. Lefebvre's son Johnnie married Emma. They are pictured at right on their wedding day. (Above, courtesy of Wanda Lefebvre; right, courtesy of Gordy Lefebvre.)

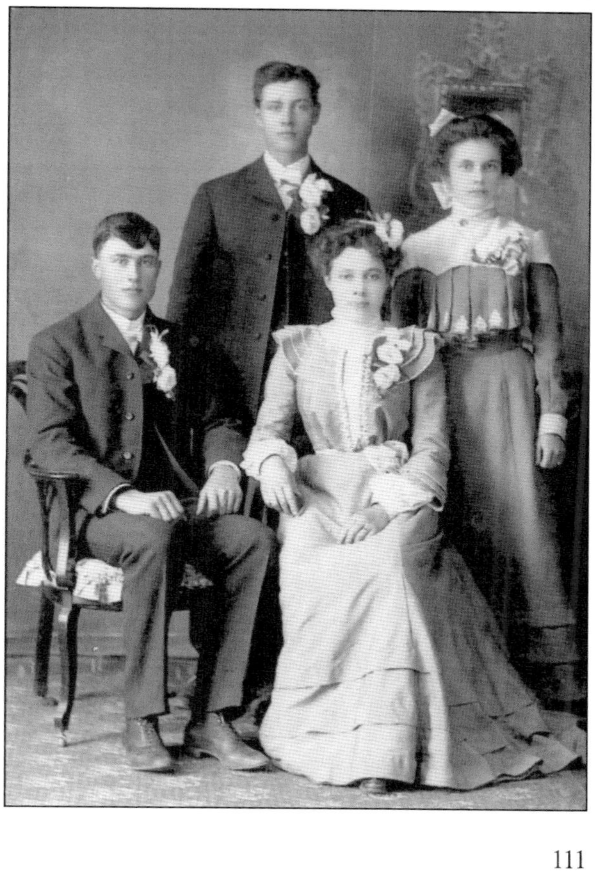

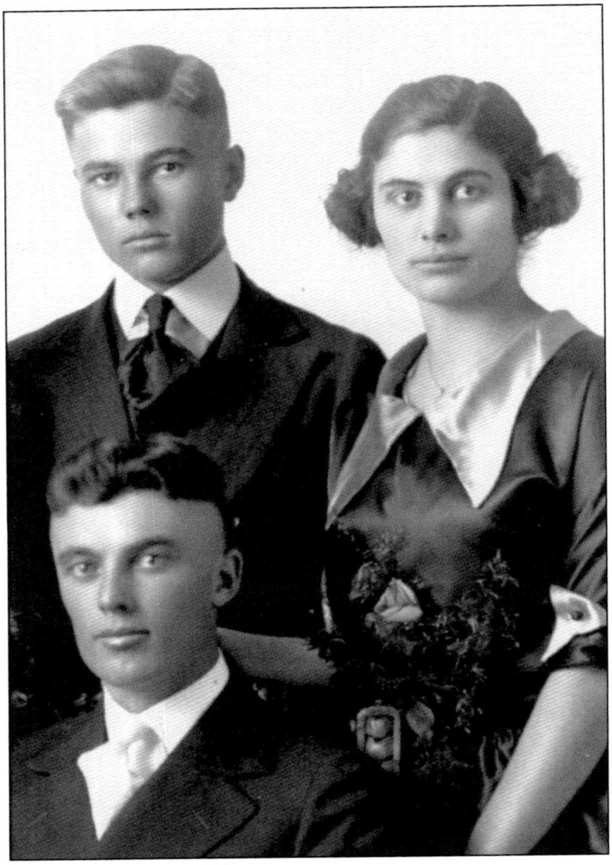

Ferdinand and Zerilla's children Noel, Camille, and Lucy Lefebvre are pictured at left. Brothers Johnnie, Joe, and Noel decided to farm. Camille attended the University of Minnesota and Harvard where he studied botany. Camille later worked for the Department of Agriculture in Washington, D.C. Noel married Mary Holland and raised six children. Noel's sons, Leon, Eddie and Eugene ran the trucking company Noel started. It is known as Lefebvre Companies and is currently operated by Leon's sons. Johnnie, Ferdinand's oldest son, married Emma Martin in 1903 and farmed in Otsego. They had six children as well. At the age of 34, Johnnie was stricken with appendicitis. The doctor operated; however, the appendix had ruptured and infection spread throughout his body. He died that night. Johnnie's sons are pictured below from left to right, Robert, Elmer, Lu, and Wilfred Lefebvre. (Letf, courtesy of Patty and Richard Lefebvre; below, courtesy of Mary Anne McNeil.)

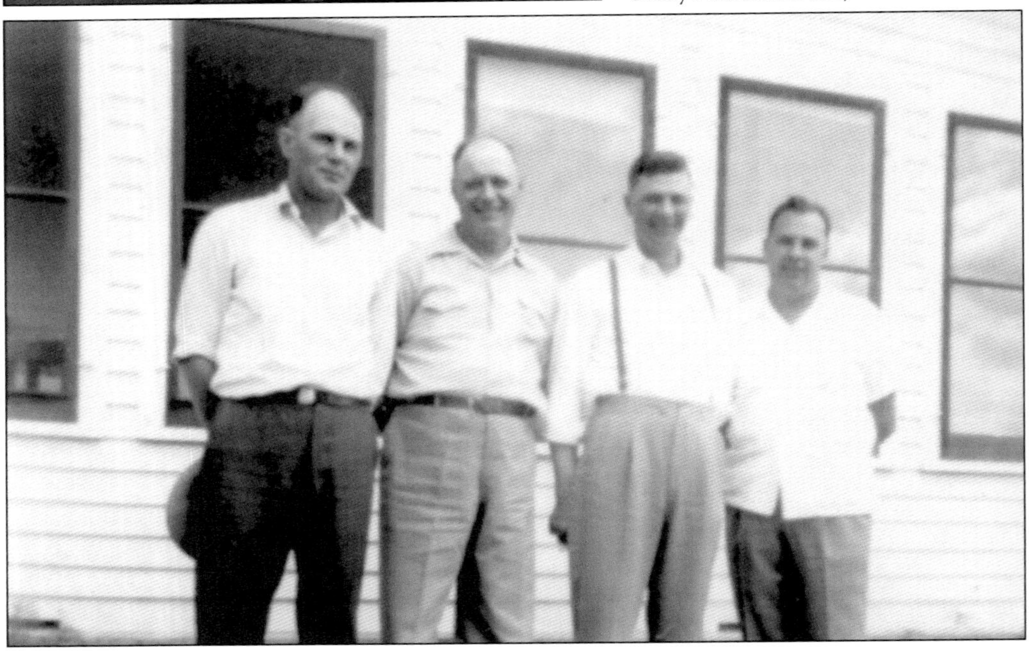

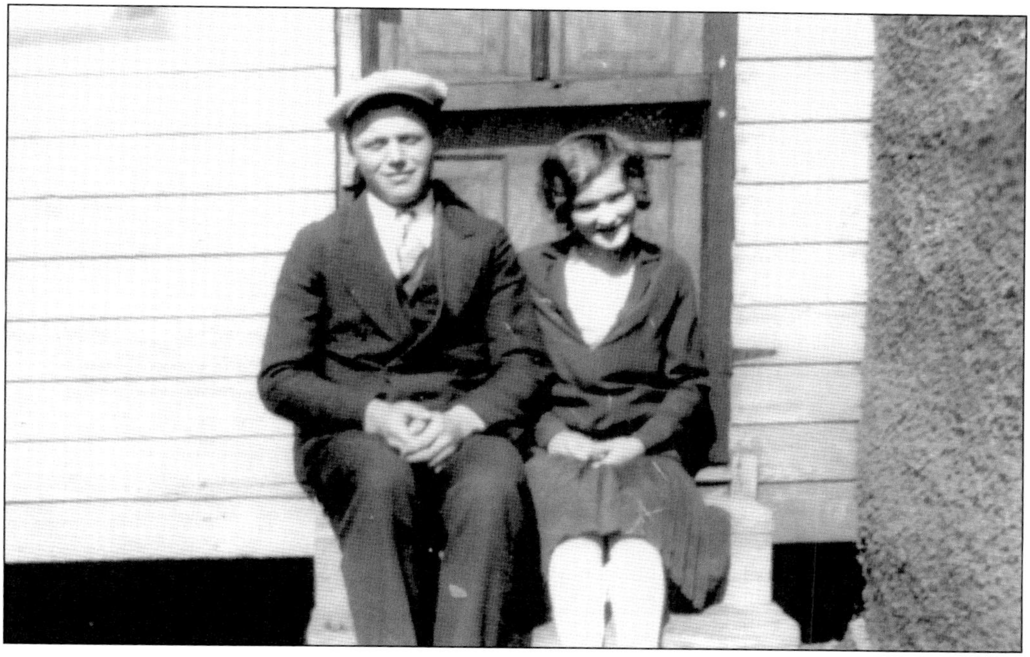

Seated on the front steps above are Richard Lefebvre's parents, Elmer and Grace. In the other picture, Richard is in the arms of his father, Elmer, who is standing next to Grace. This picture was taken September 1935. (Courtesy of Patty and Richard Lefebvre.)

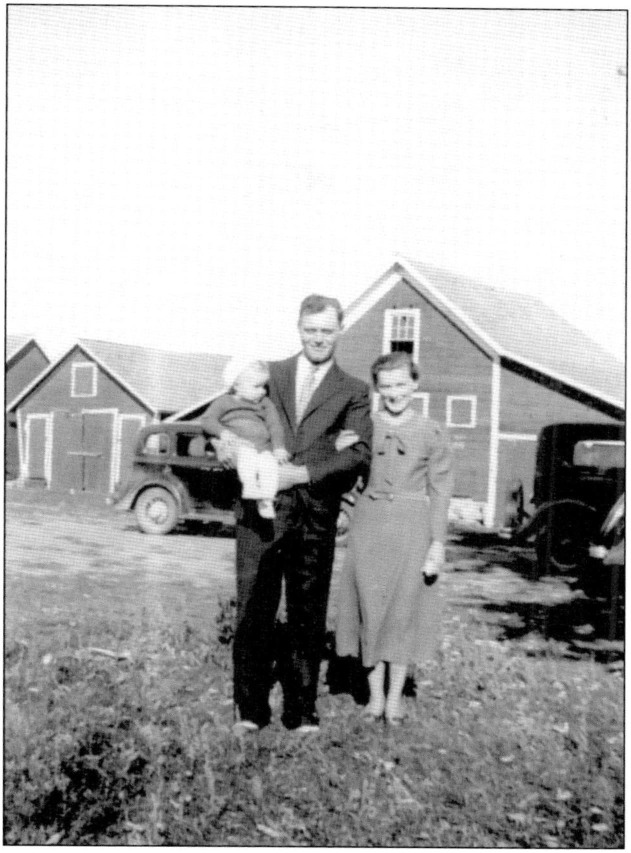

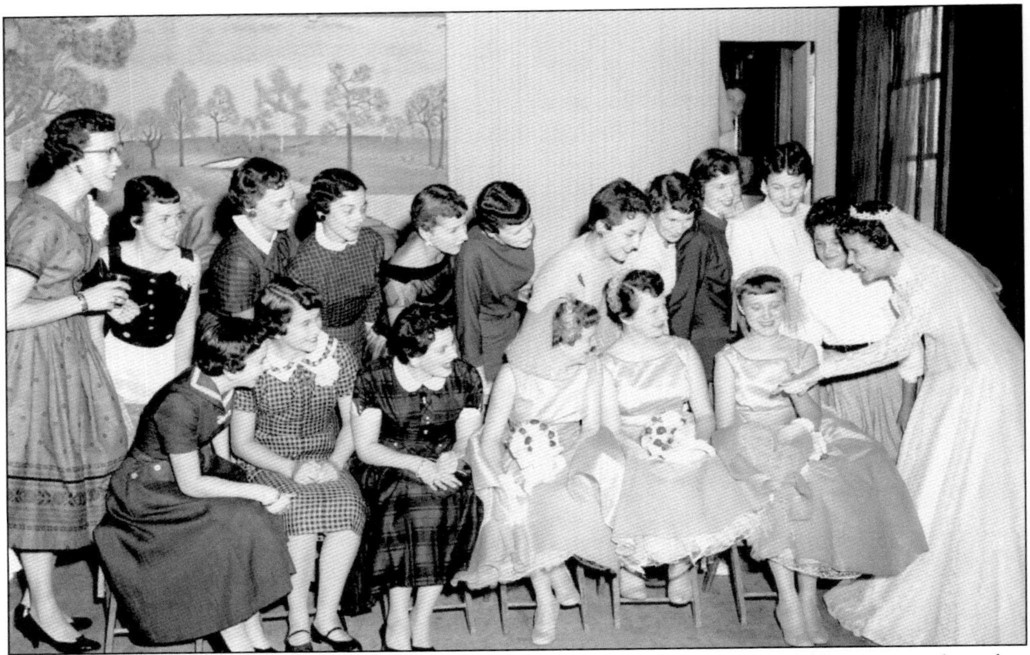

An article from the *Elk River* newspaper dated August 18, 1956, mentioned 90 guests gathered at the Crow Tavern Saturday for Patty Thibodeau's wedding shower. The reason 90 people attended the shower was due to an old tradition of putting an announcement at the post office and allowing anyone that put $1 in the collection box attend the shower. The money was collected and a gift was purchased. Patty shared that not everyone was invited to the wedding, so this was the town social to show support for the couple. Patty (Thibodeau) Lefebvre is pictured above showing her ring to her friends and bridesmaids. Also captured, below, is a shot of Patty keeping her new husband, Richard, in line at the party after the wedding. Everyone had a lot of fun. (Courtesy of Patty and Richard Lefebvre.)

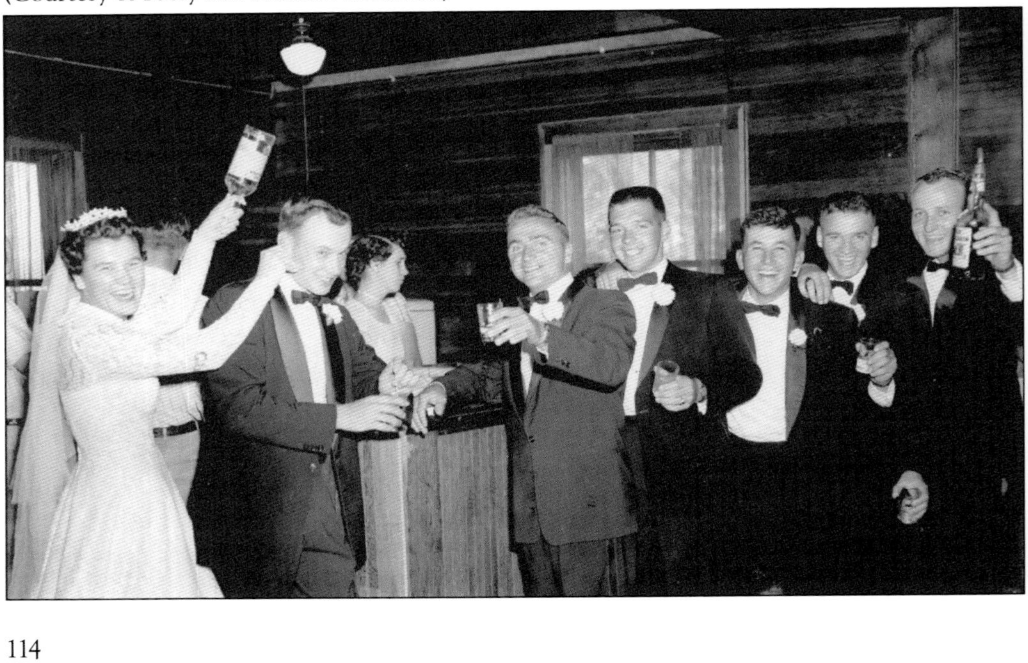

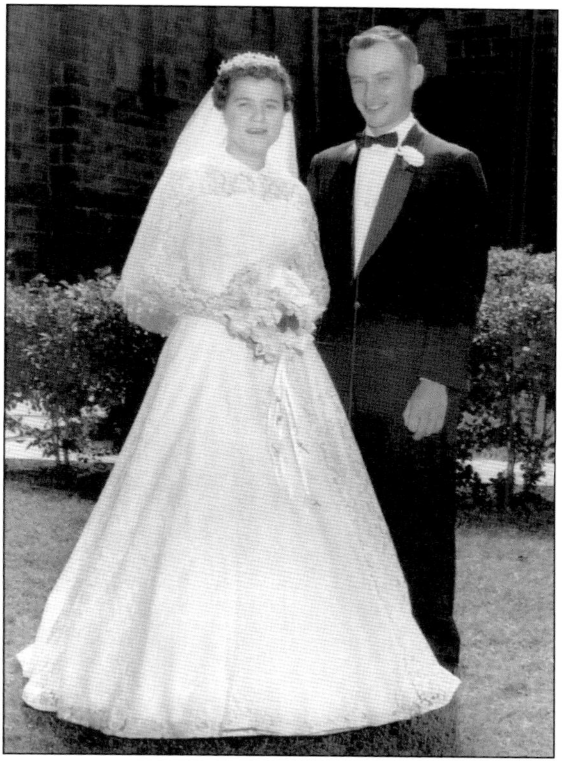

Pictured are Richard and Patty on their wedding day and 50 years later at their anniversary party with their children's families. (Courtesy of Patty and Richard Lefebvre.)

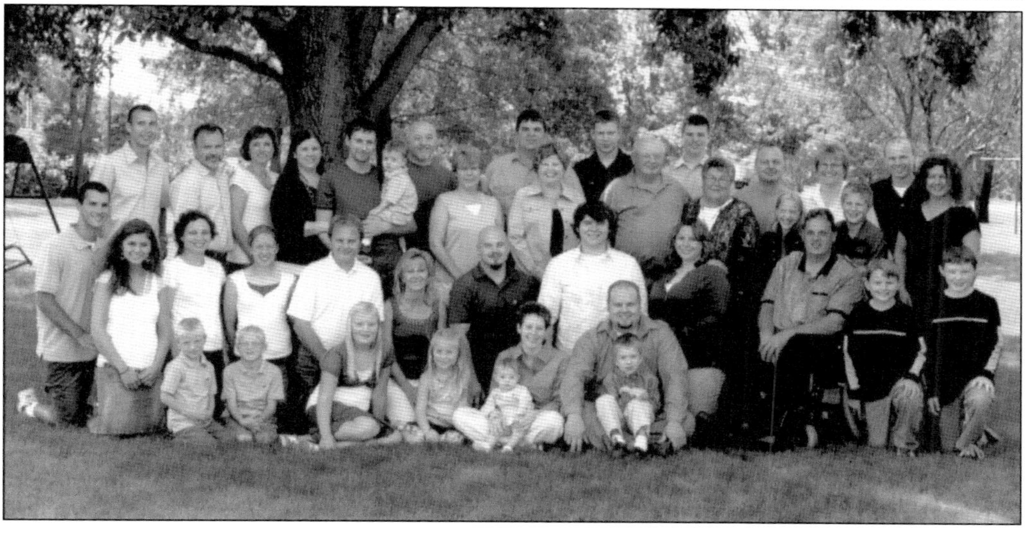

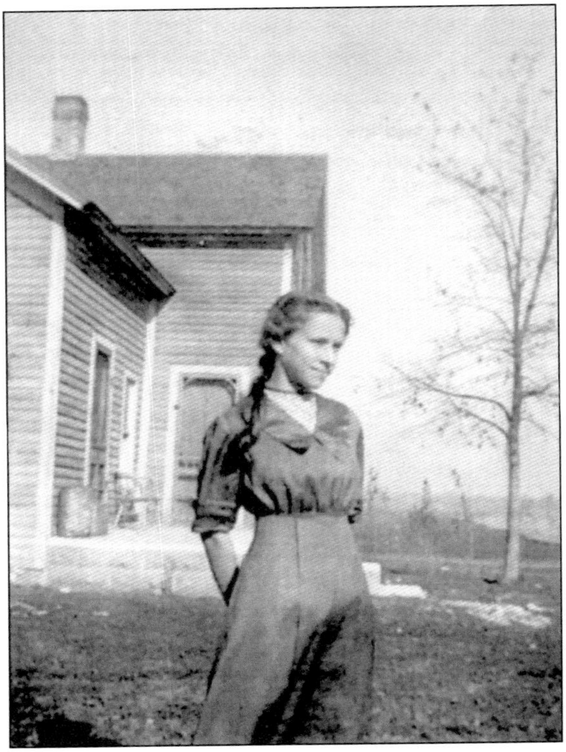

This picture at left, taken in 1915, is of Frances Spencer. Pictured below are Lewis and Climena (Spencer) McDonald on what is believed to be their wedding day. (Left, courtesy of Otsego Heritage Preservation Commission; below, courtesy of Wright County Historical Society.)

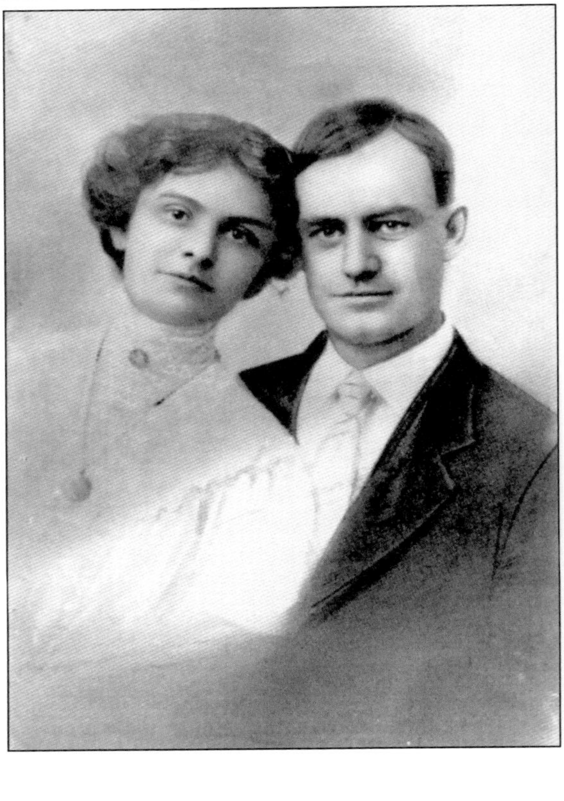

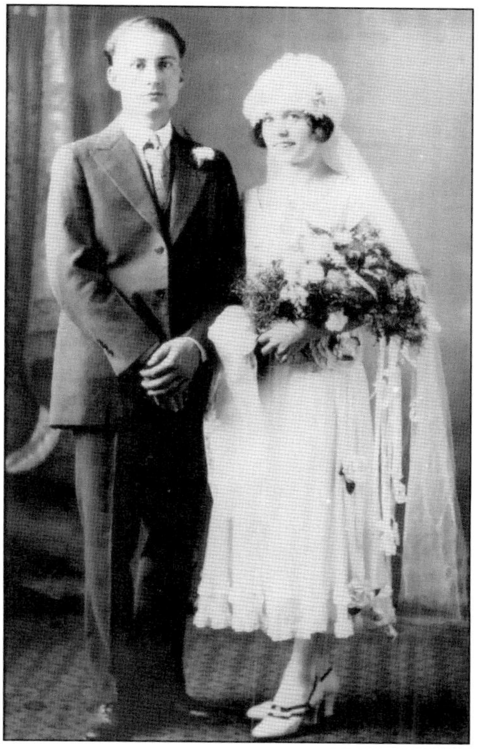

Both of these pictures were taken of Harold and Buddice (Spencer) Collins on their wedding day. Seated below is Buddice (Spencer) Collins and standing is, from left to right, Harold Collins, Pat Kilmartin, and Anne Melin. (Courtesy of Pamella Collins.)

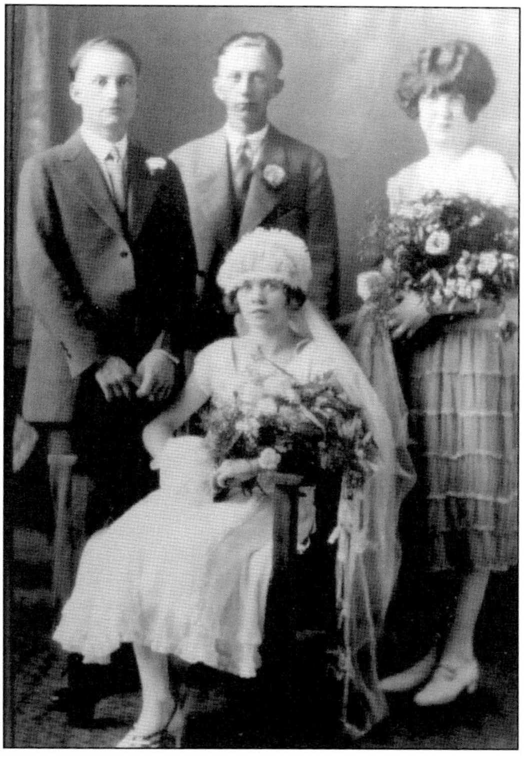

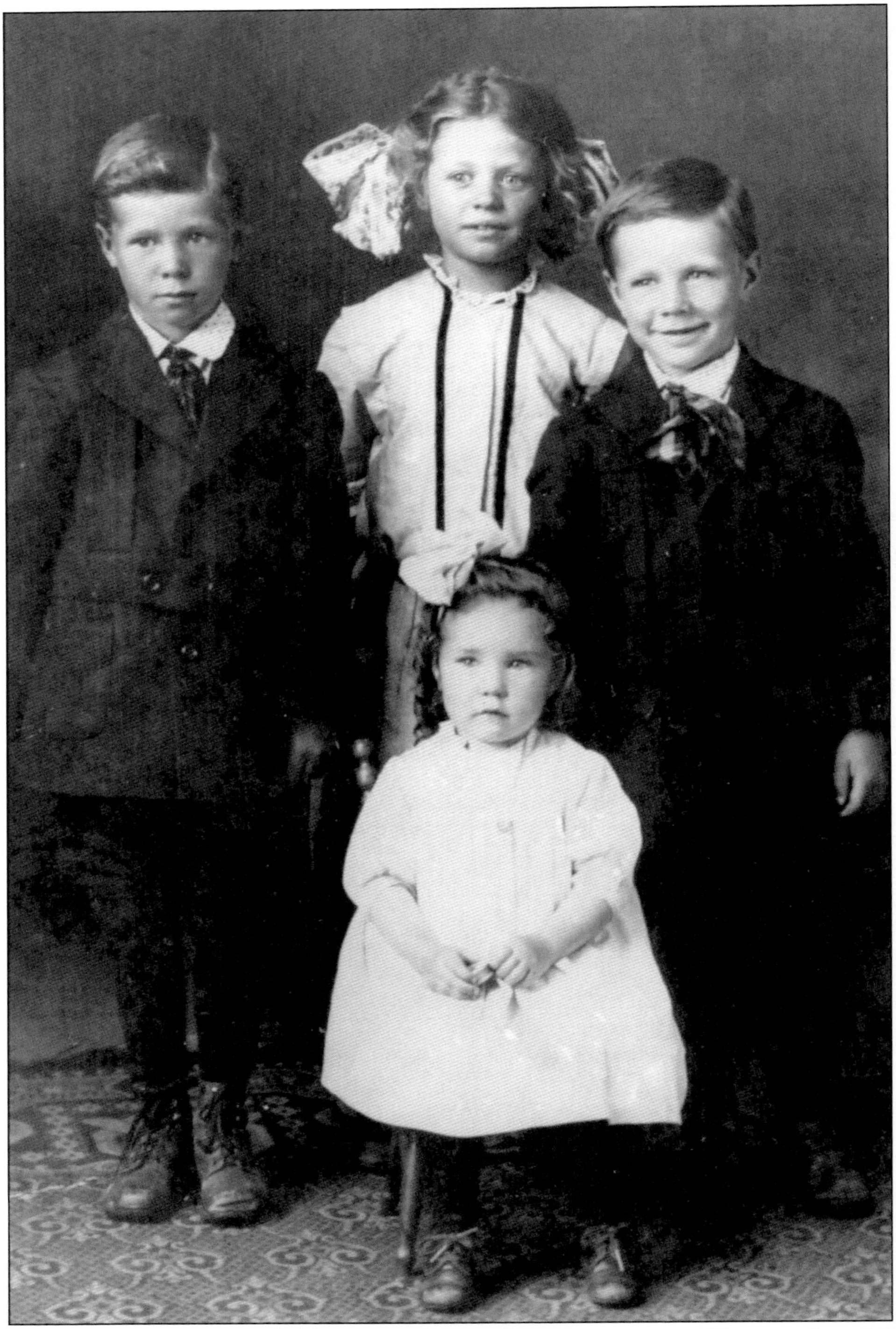

This picture of the Spencer children was taken in their younger years. They are, from left to right, Charles, Buddice, Kenneth, and standing in front is Florinda. Not pictured are their siblings Arletta and Glen. (Courtesy of Pamella Collins.)

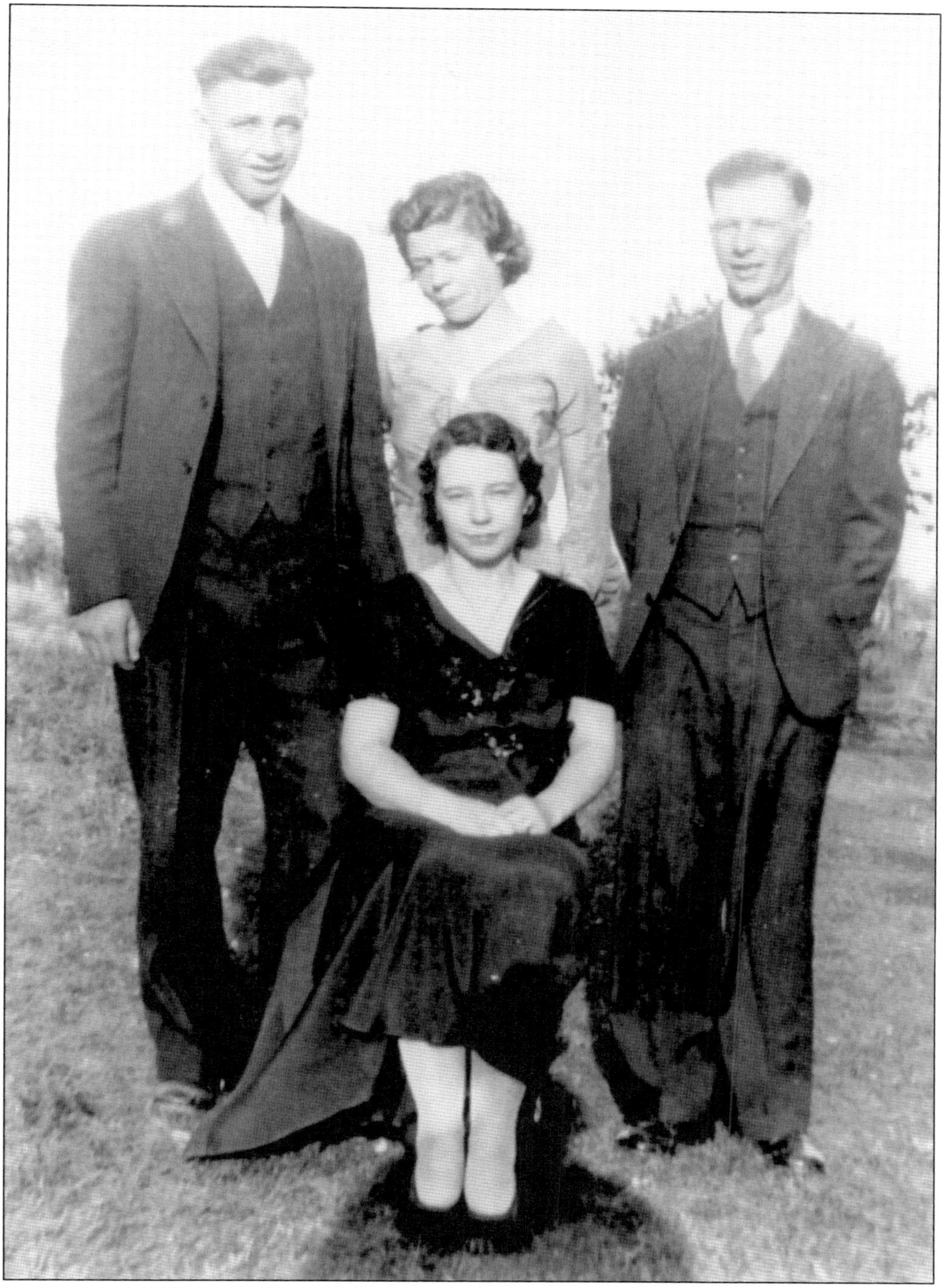

The Spencer children as young adults are seen here, pictured left to right: Kenneth, Buddice, Charles, and seated is Arletta. Not pictured are their siblings Florinda and Glen. Kenneth, the oldest child, was hurt during a logging accident and developed an infection that could not be treated because penicillin had not been invented yet. Kenneth had been married less than a year when he passed. (Courtesy of Pamella Collins.)

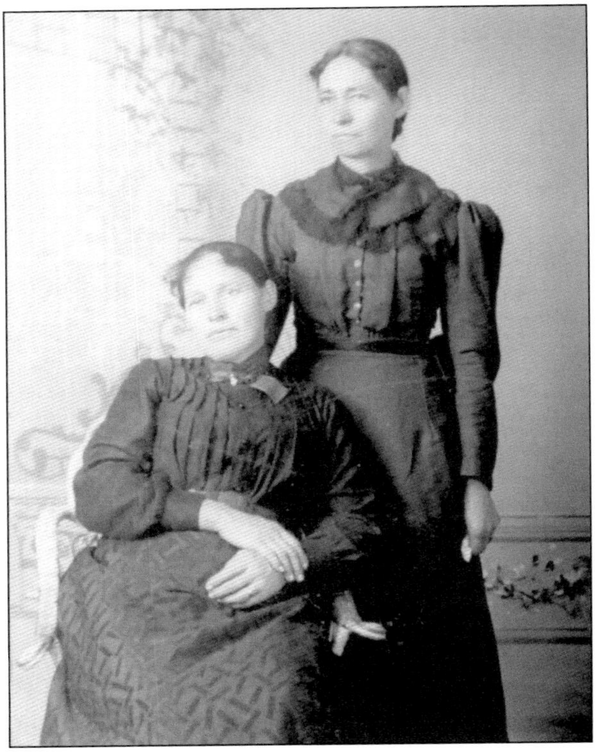

Pictured at left are the Roy sisters, Sarah Jane (Roy) Davis (left) and Ellen Mary (Roy) Osgood. Pictured below is Richard Ricker. (Courtesy of Otsego Heritage Preservation Commission.)

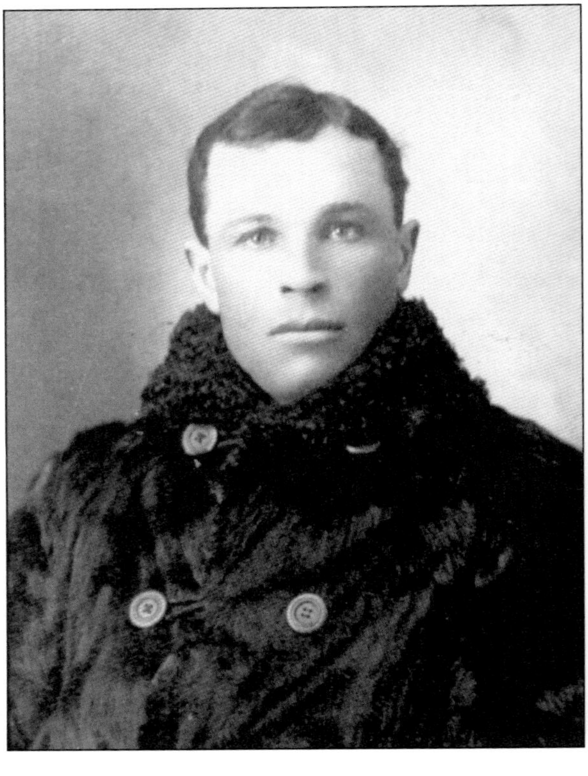

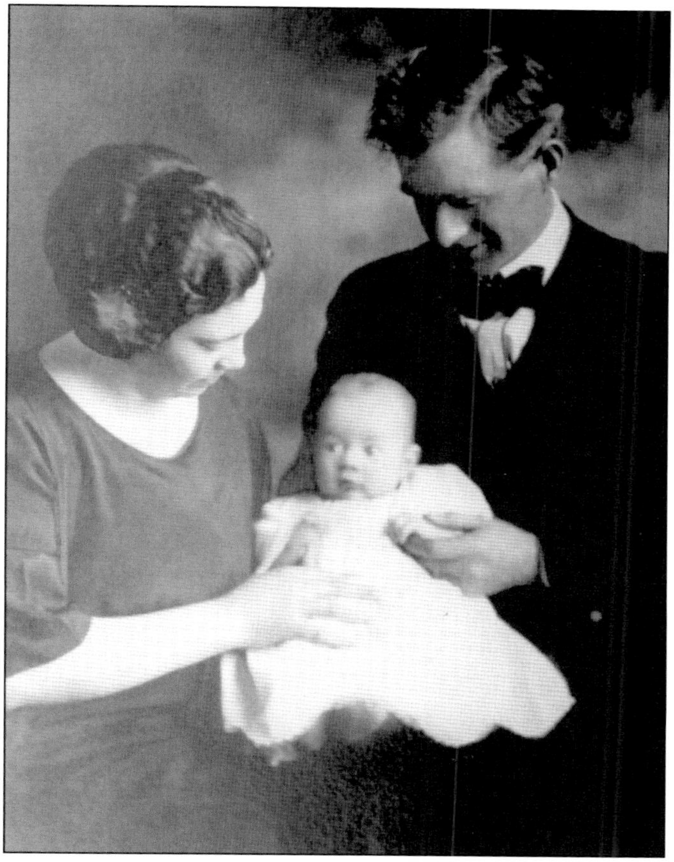

Mr. and Mrs. Con Flaherty are pictured at right with their child Morgan. Also shown below is Lauretta (Hagel) Hallberg with her mother, Evelyn Hagel, sitting on the side porch of the Pouliot's farm. (Right, courtesy of Norman Schwanbeck; below, courtesy of Elma [Hagel] Pouliot.)

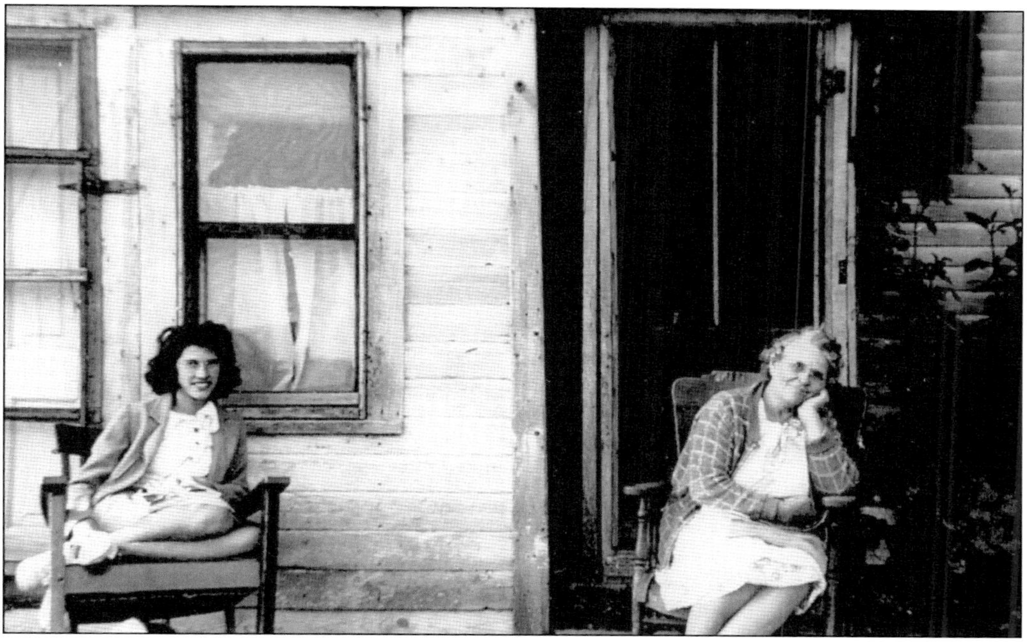

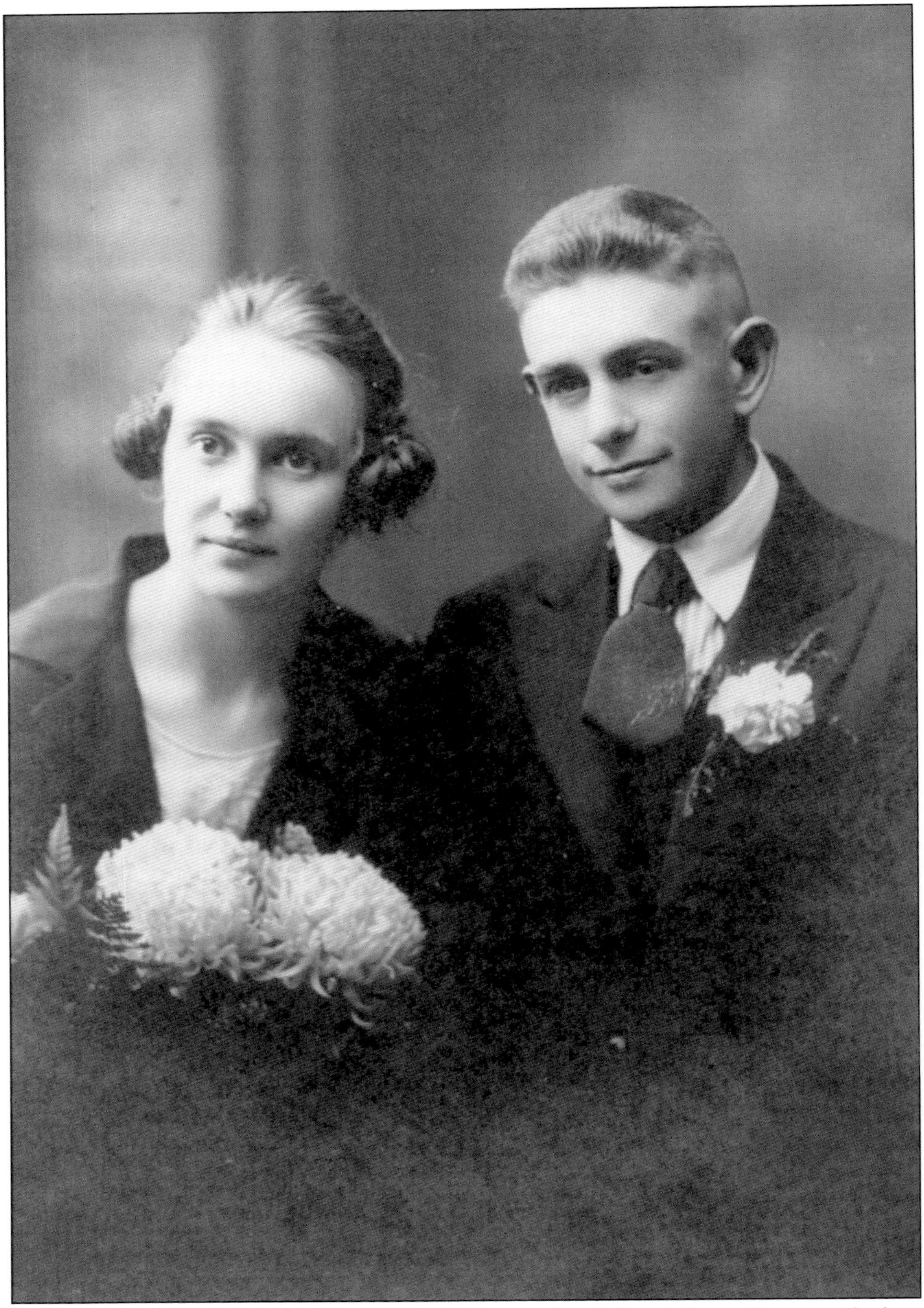

Richard Hauan was born September 12, 1900. Hauan played the violin and was a gifted tenor. Hauan married Eva Pauline Hagen on December 22, 1920. The Hauans moved around a lot because the times were very bad for farmers. The family finally moved to Otsego in 1939. In 1940, the Joyer family became the Hauan's neighbors. The Joyers had 11 children. Pictured are Richard and Eva Pauline (Hagen) Hauan. (Courtesy of Merle and Mary Ann [Hauan] Eden.)

ELLIS ISLAND
1892–1992

TM © 1987 SL/EIF, INC

The Statue of Liberty-Ellis Island Foundation, Inc.

proudly presents this

Official Certificate of Registration

in

THE AMERICAN IMMIGRANT WALL OF HONOR

to officially certify that

INGEBRIGT IVERSON HAUAN

who came to America from

NORWAY

is among those courageous men and women who came to this country in search of personal freedom, economic opportunity and a future of hope for their families.

Iacocca
:atue of Liberty-Ellis Island
ation, Inc.

LIBERT
1886·198
® © 1982 SL/EIF, INC

This is the official certificate of registration for Ingebrigt Iverson Hauan who came to the United States from Norway through Ellis Island. Ingebrigt was born in Norway where he learned the trades of baker and shoemaker. Hauan came to America and married Anna in 1887. Anna had twin daughters from a previous marriage; her first husband, Christopher Beck, was in an accident, leaving the six-month-old children in the care of their mother. The Hauan children were Gena (Beck), Julia (Beck), Marie, Ole, Alfred, Herman, Stella, and Richard. (Courtesy of Merle and Mary Ann [Hauan] Eden.)

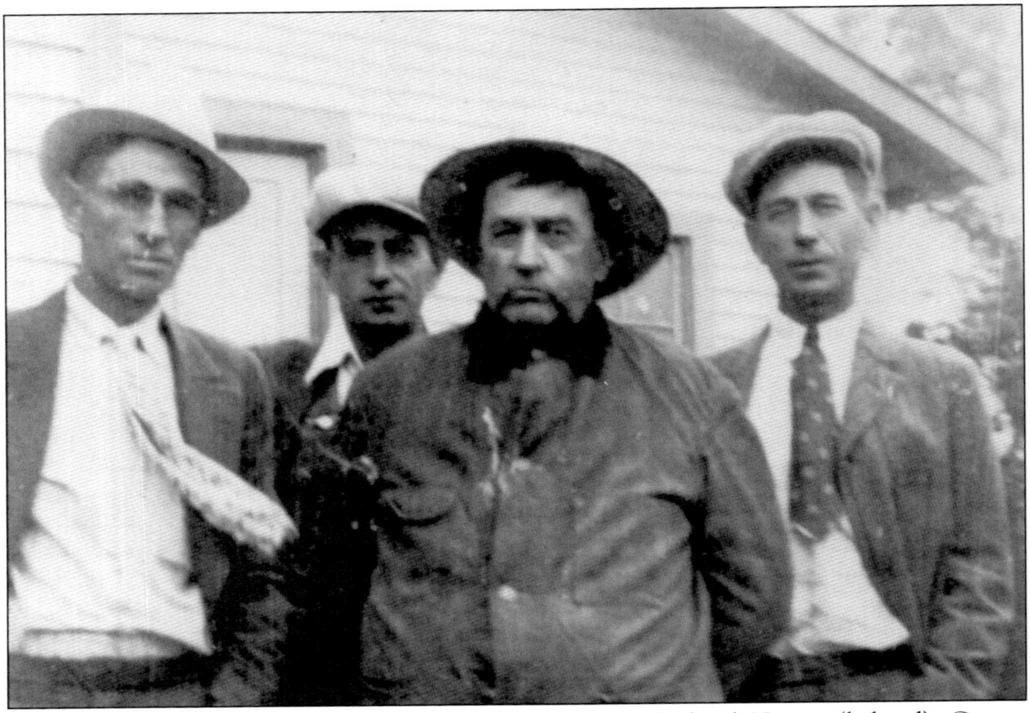

Pictured above are, from left to right, Herman Hauan, Richard Hauan (behind), George Jorgenson, and Alfred Hauan. Ole Hauan is taking the picture in about 1941. Below are, from left to right, Ingeborg (Akvik), Kjell, Paul, and Hans Hauan. (Courtesy of Merle and Mary Ann [Hauan] Eden.)

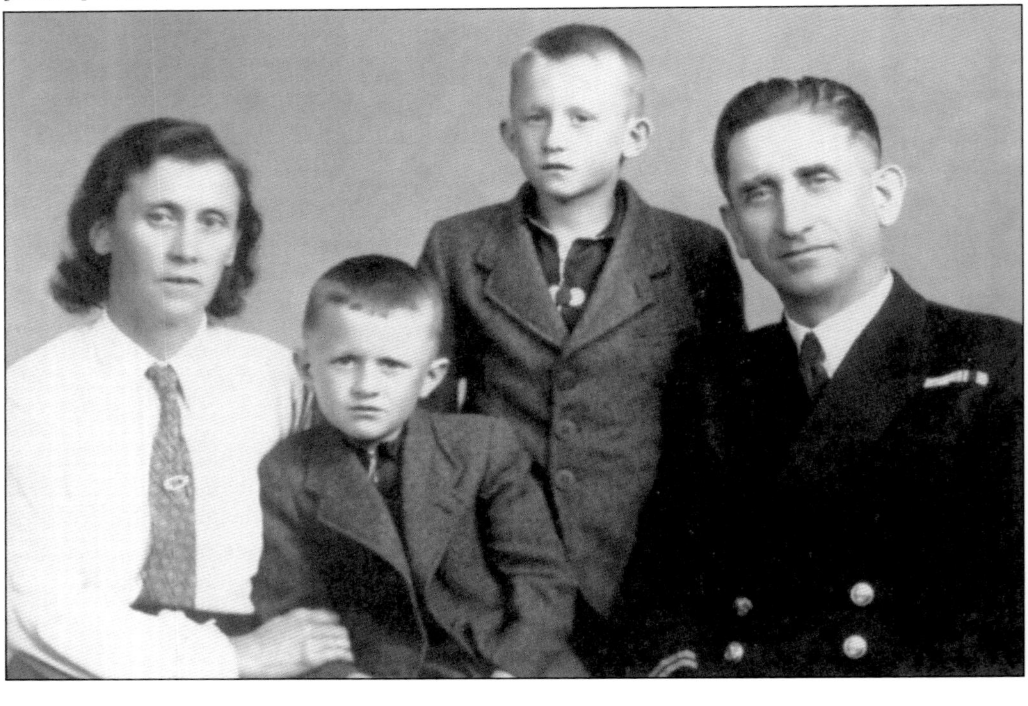

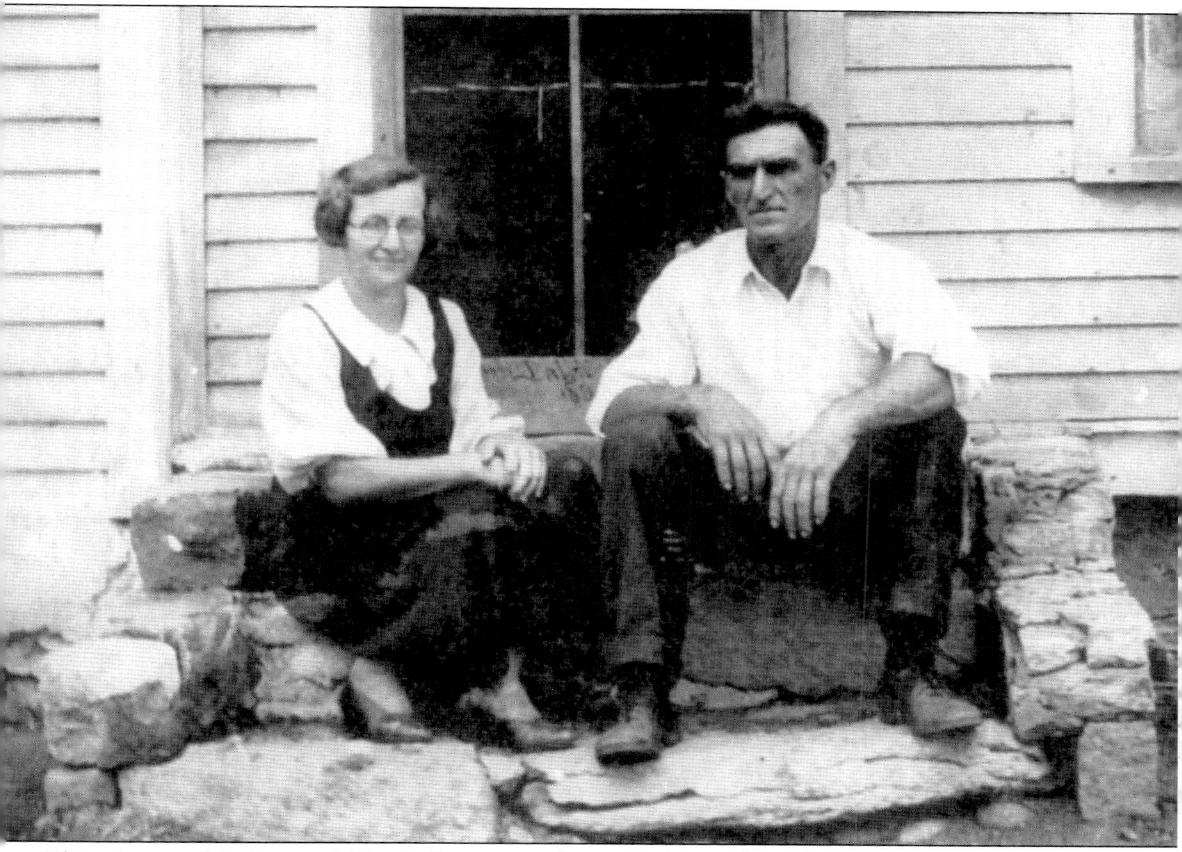

This picture of Arthur and Maude Joyer was taken in 1933. Arthur's father was George Joyer. As a young child, George Joyer left Ireland and set sail with his parents for Canada. Both of George's parents died from the plague during the journey. George was adopted by a French family. When he was old enough, George moved to Otsego and married Justine Chouinard. (Courtesy of Michelle [Christian] Matchie.)

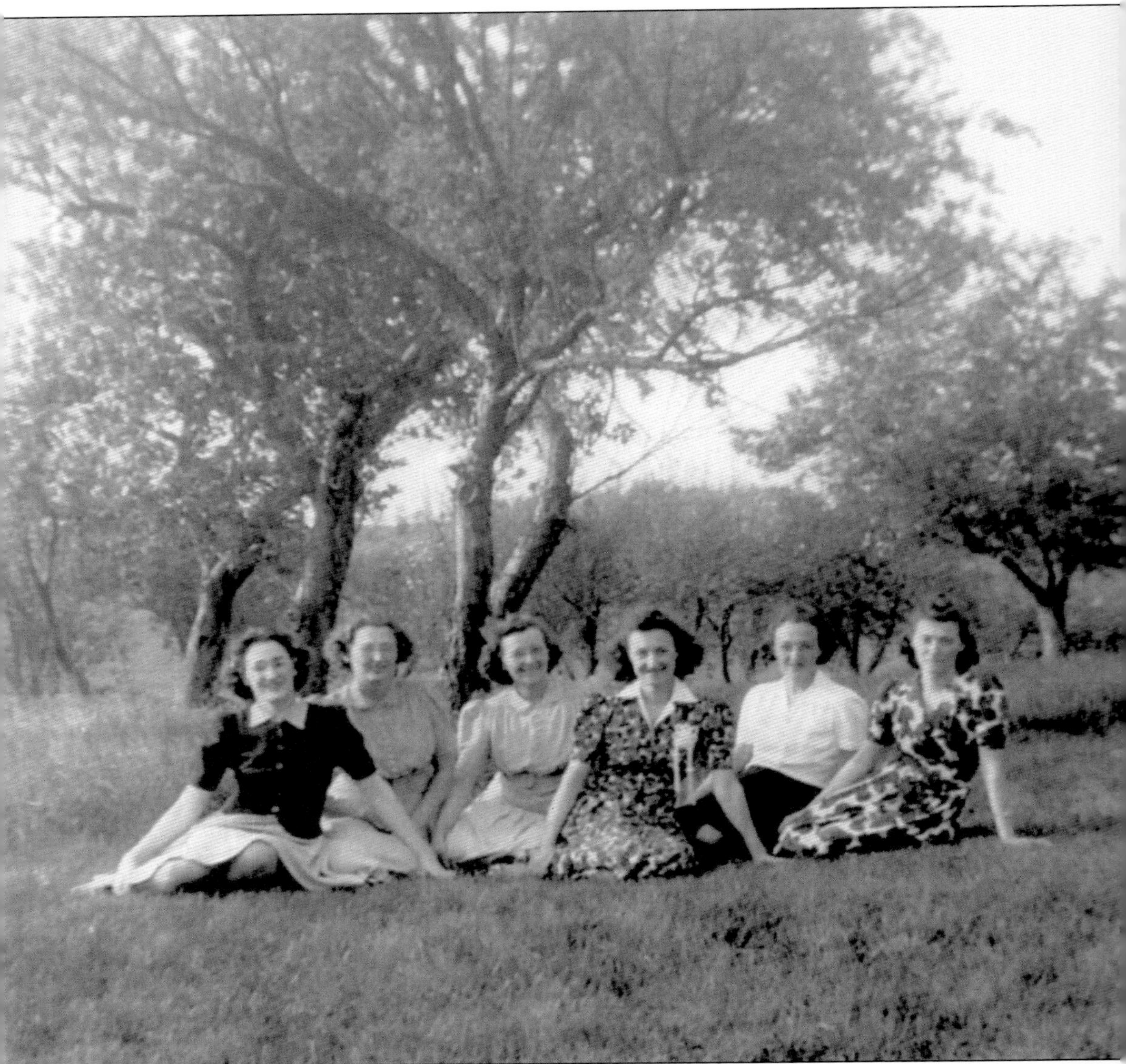

Seated on the grass enjoying a summer day in 1941 are Maude Joyer and her daughters. Pictured are, Marion, Ella, Maude, Doris, Verna, and Clarice Joyer. Ella was Chuck, Dave, and Michelle Christian's mother. (Courtesy of Michelle [Christian] Matchie.)

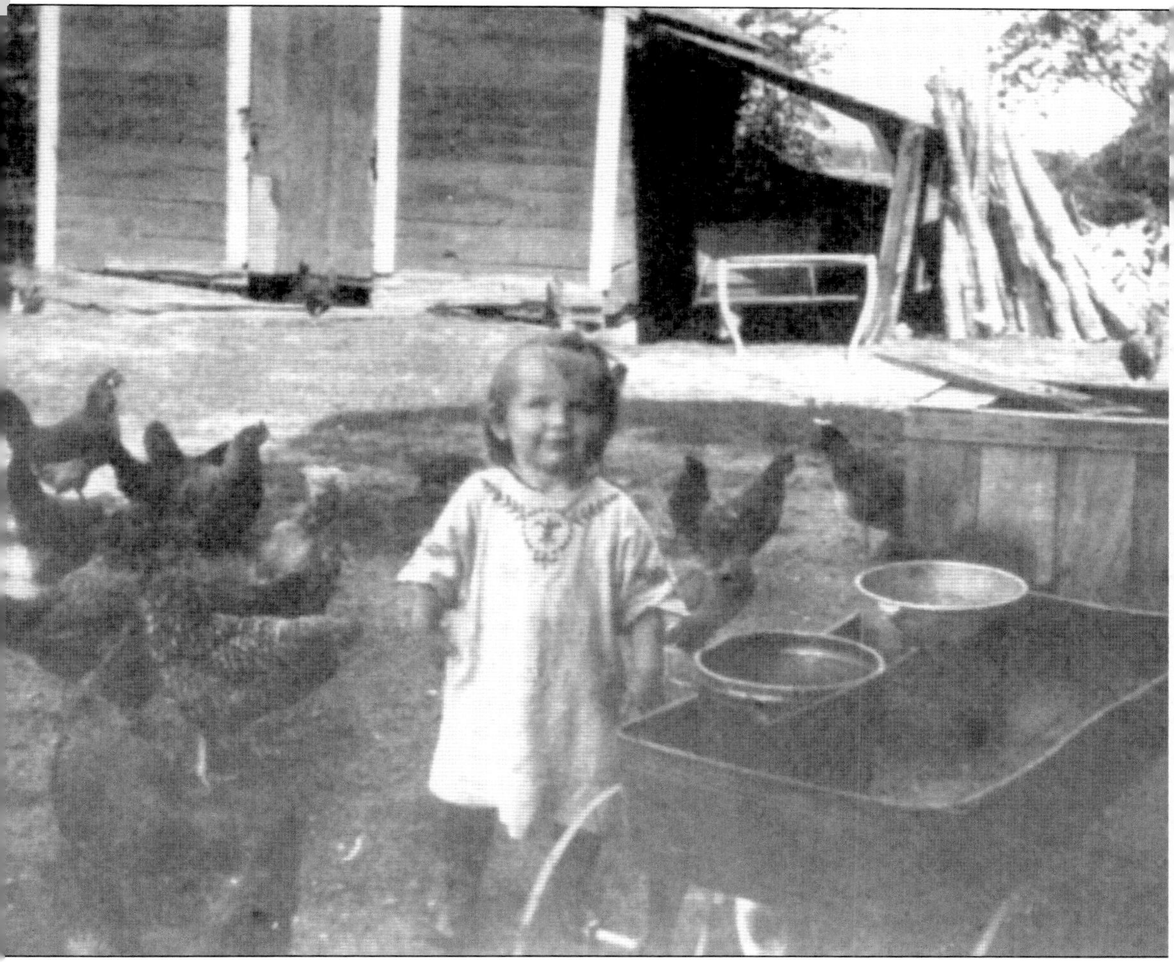

David Ingersoll built a log cabin on land near the river. Later he built a brick home made from the clay found on the riverbank. Ingersoll established a brick factory, which supplied bricks for many homes. The Ingersoll farm was sold to Will and Guy Ridler in 1901. Guy married Verna Ingersoll, David's granddaughter. In 1902, Joseph Kiichli purchased the farm. When his son Edward and Minnie Dorothea (Miller) were married in 1905, Joseph said, "If you two will go out there and farm for ten years, the place will be yours." Edward and Minnie accomplished this task and became the owners of the Ingersoll farm. Pictured playing with the chickens at the Ingersoll farm is Edith (Kiichli) Kluge. (Courtesy of Arne Engstrom.)